Evangelicals and the Bishops' Pastoral Letter

edited by DEAN C. CURRY

CHRISTIAN COLLEGE COALITION

GRAND RAPIDS, MICHIGAN
WILLIAM B. EERDMANS PUBLISHING COMPANY

First edition published 1984 by William B. Eerdmans Publishing Companv.
255 Jefferson Ave., S.E., Grand Rapids, Michigan 49503

Library of Congress Cataloging in Publication Data

Main entry under title:
Evangelicals and the bishops' pastoral letter.
    Includes bibliographical references.
    1. Catholic Church.   National Conference of Catholic Bishops.
Challenge of peace — Addresses, essays, lectures.
    2. Atomic warfare — Religious aspects — Christianity — Addresses,
essays, lectures.   3. Peace — Religious aspects — Christianity — Ad-
dresses, essays, lectures.   4. Catholic Church — United States — Pas-
toral letters and charges — Addresses, essays, lectures.
    5. Catholic Church — Doctrines — Addresses, essays, lectures.   6.
    Evangelicalism — United States — Addresses, essays, lectures.
    I. Curry, Dean C., 1952-   .
BX1795.A85C39   1984 Suppl.   3   261.8'73   84-4005
ISBN 0-8028-1985-0

Contents

Foreword

ARCHBISHOP JOHN J. O'CONNOR*

The little village of Panmunjom stands in the no-man's-land between North and South Korea. It is the site of the negotiations over the exchange of prisoners from the Korean conflict. By Panmunjom is a bridge called *The Bridge of No Return*. Once released from prison camps, those who crossed that bridge were forbidden ever to return to their native land.

In looking at *The Bridge of No Return*, one feels the deep sadness of knowing how we human beings cut ourselves off from one another, how ready we are to seal our own fate for the rest of time, to close out all hope of reconciliation, to offer one another only a one-way street that leads only to a *Bridge of No Return*.

Because of their passionate conviction that for Almighty God there is no such thing as a bridge of no return, the Roman Catholic Bishops of the United States committed themselves in November of 1980 to an extensive study of bridge building—the building of a bridge to peace with justice. With Pope John Paul II they believe deeply that *"Peace is possible."* This is the belief that drove them through more than two years of often agonizing effort. This was their starting point and their goal:

A member of the five-man committee of bishops that drafted "The Challenge of Peace," Archbishop O'Connor is currently Archbishop of New York. Prior to assuming his present position, Archbishop O'Connor had been vicar general of the Military Vicariate of the Roman Catholic Church in the United States and Bishop of Scranton.

that God never abandons us, never cuts us off. With God there is no bridge of no return.

Were the thrust of the Bishops' Pastoral Letter, "The Challenge of Peace: God's Promise and Our Response," to be summarized in one sentence, it might well be, precisely: *Peace Is Possible*. One cannot understand what the bishops have attempted, or the primary purpose of this document, without understanding that belief.

It is true, of course, that we cannot hope to achieve enduring peace unless we control those weapons of war that can almost literally destroy the world. The bishops therefore considered it absolutely imperative to talk about *war* in a pastoral letter that confronts us with the challenge to *peace*. Unfortunately, however, publicity surrounding the pastoral letter has focused almost exclusively on what has been said about war, and has paid far less attention to what the letter says about peace—what it is and how to achieve it. Yet each pope of the nuclear age—Pope Pius XII, John XXIII, Paul VI, and John Paul II—makes clear that *peace is not merely the absence of war*, as the bishops point out. The letter is very emphatic.

> The Catholic tradition has always understood the meaning of peace in positive terms. Peace is both a gift of God and a human work. It must be constructed on the basis of central human values: truth, justice, freedom, and love. The Second Vatican Council stated the Church's traditional concept of peace:
>
>> "Peace is not merely the absence of war. Nor can it be reduced solely to the maintenance of a balance of power between enemies. Nor is it brought about by dictatorship. Instead, it is rightly and appropriately called 'an enterprise of justice' (Is. 32:7).
>>
>> Peace results from that harmony built into human society by its divine founder and actualized by men as they thirst after ever greater justice."

As an indispensable prerequisite to the building of peace with justice, the pastoral calls, *not* for unilateral disarmament by the United States (as some critics believe), but, with Pope John Paul II, for *multi*lateral disarmament, with each nation maintaining appropriate defenses against the possibility of unjust aggression while moving toward disarmament, but truly and sincerely *moving*. It calls for negotiations, based on realism. It calls for serious consideration of a global body realistically fashioned to help end war and maintain peace with justice. It calls for prayer and for disciplinary practices. And it calls, above all, for reverence for all human life. About this, the pastoral letter is crystal clear.

It is a significant virtue of *Evangelicals and the Bishops' Pastoral Letter* that chapter after chapter seems to recognize the *élan vital* of the bishops' effort: *that peace is possible*. Not every commentary on the pastoral reflects the same recognition. During the letter's lengthy incubation, for example, when draft after draft was being widely publicized, attention seemed riveted on such issues as the inclusion or exclusion of an episcopal judgment on the MX missile, the latest word on a nuclear freeze, the respective degrees of naiveté or reality expressed in reference to the Soviet Union, the degree of accord or discord between the bishops and the White House, and whatever other easily discerned proposals or hypotheses loaned themselves to ready dramatization. Not a few of the analyses proliferating since the final version of the pastoral was approved and published have continued to focus on the same kinds of things. The result is a growing body of literature that comes very close to missing altogether what the bishops were really up to in undertaking the pastoral letter in the first place, and in tenaciously seeing it through.

Evangelicals and the Bishops' Pastoral Letter is not guilty of this critical oversight. It takes quite seriously the bishops' contention that peace is possible, and recognizes it, implicitly or explicitly, as the driving force behind and within the pastoral letter. Eschewing the "cute" and avoiding both preoccupation with "who struck whom" in the debates among bishops during the formulation of the letter, and the temptation to impute motives to its formulators, or to provide "fascinating glimpses" and "exposés," the evangelical writers included in this work have done their homework on the text of the letter itself, and have provided a refreshingly serious and objective analysis. They seem to have been able to do this not only because of their own considerable expertise, but because they have responded to the plea expressed by the pastoral letter itself. They have evidently *read* the letter with meticulous care, "in all its complexity"; they have attempted to evaluate it in its *entirety*—not selectively; they have honored its repeated distinctions among "levels of authority": universally binding moral principles; formal, official Catholic Church teaching binding Catholics in conscience; prudential moral judgments made by the bishops, deserving of serious study and respect, but not binding in conscience.

Because they recognize the vision of the bishops in primarily wanting to convince the world that peace is neither a lost cause, nor spewed forth, Maoist fashion, from the barrel of a gun, but that it must be prayed for, worked for, negotiated for, and even, but as a last resort, fought for, most of the evangelical writers included here attempt to evaluate the pastoral letter from the very perspective of whether or not it seems to advance or to impede the possibility of peace that it proclaims. And they consistently recognize, as well, what many commentaries have missed—that the bishops never separate peace from *justice*. It is only peace with justice that is considered true peace. In other words, this collection of essays evaluates the pastoral on its own terms—a fair approach, indeed. It is an approach made even fairer in the current instance because the writers clearly work from the text of the letter rather than from media reports or their own prejudgments. "What does the letter actually say?" they seem to ask, and for the most part their answers are remarkably accurate. (Some will discern interpretations to which each contributor to the bishops' pastoral would take strong exception. The "misinterpretations," if they might be called such, are judgment calls, in which even very significant differences of opinion and viewpoint are to be expected.)

It is refreshing, too, that the collection of writings addresses, respectively, each section of the pastoral letter, giving appropriate weight to each, with special importance attributed to sections that the bishops themselves consider highly important, but that, again, have frequently gone unnoticed. Chapters such as "Biblical Perspectives on War and Peace" and "Promoting Peace in a Nuclear Age" are illustrative.

The introductory essay of this collection avers that "there have been too few examples of [evangelical] attempts to seriously examine from a balanced perspective the full range of biblical, strategic, and moral issues that relate to war and peace in our modern world." If this allegation is valid, the current collection is a major step toward recovering lost ground. As "an effort on the part of several American Evangelicals to weigh into the current national debate in a significant way," it is exceptionally successful. The Introduction suggests further, "Evangelicals in particular . . . should welcome the efforts of the American Catholic bishops" in addressing the issues of war and peace "with an incisiveness and sensitivity unknown in the evangelical debate over this issue." It might well be added that the American Catholic bishops are quite likely, in turn, to welcome the incisiveness and sensitivity of the essays in this collection, including those essays that reject certain of the pastoral letter's proposals and hypotheses. Such criticism will almost certainly be welcomed because of its objectivity, even when it takes very strong issue with some of the pastoral's basic propositions, or disagrees with the thinking of the bishops at large, and of the committee of bishops that formulated the letter. In a number of instances, the criticism raises questions that the pastoral letter does not, in truth, fully answer, or, in some cases, attempt to answer. In other instances, it demands a more rigorous application of syllogistic reasoning than may always appear to be evident in the pastoral letter, or in any committee-formulated document whose survivability depends on a majority vote!

For virtually every challenge to the pastoral, however, one or another of the evangelical writers offers a sympathetic insight, an expression of appreciation, an argument in support of the document's general thrust. Particularly encouraging to a Catholic reader, perhaps, is the discovery of strong evangelical support for certain positions cherished by Catholics, such as the inherent right to life shared by every human being, from conception to death, and the unconditional rejection of abortion. Of further encouragement is the collection's recognition of the bishops' sincere determination to ground the pastoral letter in the Sacred Scriptures, and to try to maintain that grounding throughout the letter's entire argumentation, even when a particular argument is more immediately based on human logic, natural law, political and military realities, tradition, or papal and conciliar proclamations. Such insight characterizes, for example, the chapter entitled "Biblical Justice and Peace: Toward an Evangelical–Roman Catholic Rapprochement," and that entitled "Biblical Peace and the Kingdom of God." This is not at all to suggest that the writers of such chapters necessarily agree with the way in which the bishops have used the Sacred Scriptures, or with the scriptural interpretations given in the pastoral letter (they do seem generally to credit Old Testament usage, but to fault that of the New Testament, as much for texts omitted, as for those allegedly interpreted too glibly). Rather, it is to recognize what seems to be their sense of optimism over what they perceive as the direction in which Catholic apologetics is moving today, and their own desire to be encouraging.

Professor David Martin (President of the International Conference of the Sociology of Religion) avers, perhaps with tongue in cheek: "It is not unknown for evangelicals to get warmer as the overall climate gets colder" (*Daedalus*, Winter 1982). Whatever Professor Martin's view of such, there is enough warmth toward the bishops' efforts in this evangelical collection to suggest that the current temperature of the Cold War, the very real fear of a nightmarish hot war, and a sobering recognition of the urgent need for what Pope John Paul II calls a "moral about-face" may be nudging both Evangelicals and Catholics to reexamine one another's tenets, shorn of the stereotyping that has possibly worked a much graver disservice to both than has been recognized. This is not to encourage exploitation of a facile affinity between extreme right-wing conservative Catholicism and a politicized form of radical Evangelicalism, both reducible to just another brand of moral secularism or civil religion. It is to suggest quite the contrary—that both the pastoral letter and this collection of commentaries on the letter express a conviction attributed by Professor Martin to Evangelicals: ". . . they are, above all, unprepared to 'empty' God into history, and evacuate the Church in favor of the world." This conviction could very well lead to a form of "rapprochement." At the very least, it has seemed to provide a perspective from which the Evangelicals contributing to this collection have been able to evaluate the Bishops' Pastoral Letter with impressive insight.

Preface

JOHN R. DELLENBACK*

The idea for this book emerged out of the dialogue generated by "The Church and Peacemaking in the Nuclear Age" conference held in Pasadena, California, on May 25-28, 1983. Approximately 1400 evangelical Christians gathered at this historic meeting to wrestle with the issue of how to relate their biblical faith to the complex issues of the nuclear arms race. Representatives from different viewpoints explored the issues through plenary sessions, panel discussions, and workshops. For the first time, Evangelicals from a wide range of denominational backgrounds and political perspectives gathered to discuss the issue of war and peace in the nuclear age in an atmosphere nurtured by prayer and worship.

In an act of unity that in itself was encouraging, eighteen diverse evangelical organizations agreed to cooperate in sponsoring this conference. The conveners included individual churches (Bel Air Presbyterian Church, First United Methodist Church, La Canada Presbyterian Church, Lake Avenue Congregational Church, and Pasadena Covenant Church), educational institutions (Calvin College, Fuller Theological Seminary, and Westmont College), magazines (*Eternity* and *Sojourners*), para-church ministries (Voice of Calvary Ministries, Young Life International, and Youth for Christ), and national organizations

---

Dr. John R. Dellenback is president of the Christian College Coalition, the organization responsible for publishing follow-up materials for the conference "The Church and Peacemaking in the Nuclear Age."

(Christian College Coalition, Evangelicals for Social Action, National Association of Evangelicals, New Call to Peacemaking, and the Reformed Church in America).

Following the conclusion of the conference, the Board of Directors, representing the conveners, asked the Christian College Coalition to take responsibility for the conference follow-up, including the publication of materials. During numerous conversations during the months after the conference, the concept of this book developed. Under the guidance of Dr. John A. Bernbaum, who was responsible for directing the conference follow-up for the Coalition, and Dr. Dean C. Curry, who was on leave from Messiah College (Grantham, PA) for the purpose of assisting the Coalition with its postconference work, the structure of this volume was shaped and refined.

Inspired by the thought-provoking and carefully crafted work of the American Catholic Bishops, who had approved their pastoral letter "The Challenge of Peace" earlier during the same month in which the Pasadena conference was held, the idea emerged of writing a response—thoughtfully and humbly—from various evangelical perspectives. The authors of this volume are some of the most knowledgeable thinkers within Evangelicalism on this subject; most were participants at the Pasadena conference. After many years of silence on this issue, Evangelicals are now entering into the national debate on this important public policy issue.

The Christian College Coalition was honored to have a role, at the request of the conference's Board of Directors, in handling the publication of materials emerging from these meetings. We take this opportunity to thank Dr. John A. Bernbaum for directing the Coalition's overall research effort, Dr. Dean C. Curry for his expert work as volume editor, Messiah College for enabling Dr. Curry to participate in this project, and the contributors for their labor of love. It is our prayer that this book will encourage the Christian community in its efforts to integrate the Word of God with all aspects of our lives, including our perspectives on peace in the nuclear age.

Acknowledgments

Writing a book is not an isolated endeavor, and this is certainly more the case with an edited volume. I would initially thank the Christian College Coalition for the opportunity it provided me to live in Washington while working on the initial and crucial stages of this project. John A. Bernbaum and his entire staff at the American Studies Program were extremely helpful in getting this project off the ground.

At Messiah College, Dean H. David Brandt's support of my work has been ongoing. Without his generosity and assistance my work would have been made much more difficult. My student assistants, Lucinda Oswald and David Bailey, worked long and, I am sure, tedious hours. The quality of their work has been outstanding. It has been a pleasure to work so closely with two such talented young scholars. Bonnie Ganoe provided secretarial help beyond the call of duty. Always willing to type "another page"—even at the last minute—Bonnie made my work much easier.

A word of thanks is also in order to George Weigel of the World Without War Council. A Catholic social ethicist with profound insights into the issues of war and peace in general and the bishops' pastoral in particular, George's comments on various aspects of this book were invaluable. I would also acknowledge the important insights surrounding the pastoral that Phillip Lawler shared with me.

Last but certainly not least, I would like to thank all the contributors to this volume for their support of my job as editor. Working under an unusually tight deadline, the contributors made my work easier by the promptness they showed in meeting what seemed at the time of assignment to be an impossible deadline. The high quality of their scholarship is reflected in each of their chapters.

Finally, this book would not have been possible without the abiding support and encouragement of my wife, Jean. Moreover, knowing that after a long day of work I would be greeted with joyful and loving enthusiasm by my children, Ashley and Peter, made my work all the more enjoyable.

DEAN C. CURRY

List of Contributors

Mark R. Amstutz received his Ph.D. from American University and is currently Chairman of the Department of Political Science at Wheaton College in Wheaton, Illinois. Dr. Amstutz is the author of *An Introduction to Political Science: The Management of Conflict* (Scott, Foresman and Company) and has published articles in numerous journals including *Christian Scholar's Review* and *The Reformed Journal*.

John A. Bernbaum received his Ph.D. from the University of Maryland and is currently Director of the American Studies Program in Washington, D.C., and Vice President for Academic Affairs of the Christian College Coalition. Prior to his joining the Christian College Coalition, Dr. Bernbaum was employed by the U.S. Department of State as Historian–Contributing Editor of the *Foreign Relations of the United States* series. Dr. Bernbaum has contributed to numerous journals and is the editor of *Perspectives on Peacemaking: Biblical Options in a Nuclear Age* (Regal).

John S. Bray received his Ph.D. from Stanford University and is currently Senior Pastor of the Pasadena Covenant Church and Adjunct Associate Professor in Church History, Preaching, and Polity at Fuller Theological Seminary. Dr. Bray has published widely, including articles in *Church History* and *His*.

Dean C. Curry received his Ph.D. from Claremont Graduate School and is currently Chairman of the Department of History and Political Science at Messiah College in Grantham, Pennsylvania. Dr. Curry has published articles in several journals including *TSF Bulletin* and *Orbis*.

Robert L. DeVries received his Ph.D. from the University of Michigan and is currently Professor of Political Science at Calvin College in Grand Rapids, Michigan. Dr. DeVries has published articles in numerous journals including *The Reformed Journal* and *Christian Scholar's Review.*

John E. Hare received his Ph.D. from Princeton University and is currently Associate Professor of Philosophy at Lehigh University in Bethlehem, Pennsylvania. From 1981 to 1983 Dr. Hare served as full-time Staff Associate on the House Foreign Affairs Committee, Subcommittee on Europe and the Middle East. The author of numerous journal articles, Dr. Hare is the co-author (with Carey B. Joynt) of *Ethics and International Affairs* (Macmillan/St. Martin's).

Stephen P. Hoffmann received his Ph.D. from Princeton University and is currently Assistant Professor of Political Science at Taylor University in Upland, Indiana. Prior to his present position, Dr. Hoffmann served for four years in the U.S. Foreign Service. Dr. Hoffmann has contributed to *Fides et Historia.*

Ronald B. Kirkemo received his Ph.D. from American University and is currently Professor of Political Science at Point Loma College in San Diego, California. Dr. Kirkemo is the author of *Between the Eagle and the Dove* (InterVarsity Press).

John E. Lawyer received his Ph.D. from the Fletcher School of Law and Diplomacy and is currently Chairman of the Department of Political Science at Bethel College in St. Paul, Minnesota. Prior to assuming his present position, Dr. Lawyer worked as a civilian policy analyst in the Office of the Secretary of Defense and from 1972 to 1983 was a Mobilization Augmentee assigned to the Arms Control and International Negotiations Division of the Air Force's Directorate of Plans in the Pentagon. Dr. Lawyer has published widely, including articles in the *Christian Scholar's Review.*

Theodore R. Malloch received his Ph.D. from the University of Toronto, is currently Assistant Professor of Political Science at Gordon College in Wenham, Massachusetts, and will in the near future join the U.S. Department of State. Dr. Malloch has published articles in numerous journals including the *Journal*

of the American Scientific Affiliation *and is the author of* Beyond
Reductionism: Ideology and the Science of Politics *(Irvington).*

Steven E. Meyer received his Ph.D. from Georgetown University and is currently an Intelligence Analyst for the Central
Intelligence Agency. In his present capacity Dr. Meyer recently
served on rotational assignment as National Security and Arms
Control Advisor to Senator Dan Quayle of Indiana. Dr. Meyer
has written widely and has published articles in journals including *The Reformed Journal.*

Hubert Morken received his Ph.D. from Claremont Graduate
School and is currently Assistant Professor of Political Science
at Oral Roberts University in Tulsa, Oklahoma. Dr. Morken has
published articles in *The Historian* and the *American Political
Science Association News.*

Richard J. Mouw received his Ph.D. from the University of
Chicago and is currently Professor of Philosophy at Calvin Col-
lege in Grand Rapids, Michigan. A past and present editor of
several journals including *The Reformed Journal* and *TSF Bulletin,*
Dr. Mouw has published many books including *Politics and the
Biblical Drama* (Eerdmans).

James W. Skillen received his Ph.D. from Duke University and
is currently Executive Director of the Association for Public
Justice in Washington, D.C. Dr. Skillen has published widely
and is the author of *International Politics and the Demand for
Global Justice* (Welch-Dordt) and (with Rockne M. McCarthy
and William A. Harper) *Disestablishment a Second Time: Genuine
Pluralism for American Schools* (Christian University Press).

Introduction: The Origins and Relevance of the Bishops' Pastoral Letter

Dean C. Curry

On May 3, 1983, the National Conference of Catholic Bishops approved a pastoral letter on war and peace entitled "The Challenge of Peace: God's Promise and Our Response." Unlike previous pastoral letters, which received little attention even within the Catholic Church itself, "The Challenge of Peace" was the subject of national front-page headlines for months preceding its adoption. Indeed, the pastoral letter on war and peace represents what one prominent Catholic journalist has called "the most significant revolution within the American Catholic Church since its start in 1634."[1]

The significance of the pastoral letter does not lie in the fact that the bishops were addressing an issue like war and peace. For more than a half-century American Catholic bishops have collectively sought to address social issues in order to promote a more just society.[2] Moreover, the Catholic Church has a centuries-long history of thoughtful scholarship and social teaching dealing with war and peace. In the words of Thomas Shannon, the Roman Catholic Church is "the home, if not the parent, of traditional just war theory."[3]

What is significant about "The Challenge of Peace" is that it signals a fundamental change of course on the part of the leadership of the American Catholic Church. Echoing the somber assessment of Vatican II that "(t)he whole human race faces a moment of supreme crisis in its advance toward maturity," the

1

bishops argue that "[n]uclear war threatens the existence of our planet (and) this is a more menacing threat than any the world has known."[4] As a result, "(n)uclear weapons . . . and nuclear warfare as planned today raise new moral questions."[5] Their conclusion is unambiguous: "As a people we must refuse to legitimate the idea of nuclear war."[6] In reaching such a conclusion the bishops have reexamined the foundations of Church teaching on war and peace, which reach back to Augustine and Aquinas. The implications for the Church and American public policy are profound. Rejecting its nearly forty-year support for postwar U.S. defense policy, the American Catholic Church has now expressed fundamental reservations regarding the strategic posture of the U.S. government. Such an adversary position is unique in the history of the American Catholic Church.[7]

To be sure, there have always been individuals within the American Catholic Church who have rejected the just-war doctrine and have defined themselves as "pure" or selective pacifists. The earliest and most well-known of the Catholic pacifist organizations was the Catholic Worker movement co-founded by Dorothy Day in 1933.[8] The increasing U.S. involvement in Vietnam during the mid-1960s promoted highly visible protests against war by individual American Catholic clergy such as the Berrigan brothers. Subsequently, Catholic pacifism was given further institutional legitimization through such organizations as the Catholic Peace Fellowship and most recently Pax Christi U.S.A.[9]

Nevertheless, the Catholic Church itself remained committed to its traditional teaching regarding the validity of the just-war doctrine. While it is true that in the 1950s Pius XII saw in nuclear weapons a destructive capacity far exceeding that of previous military technologies, he still acknowledged the right of national self-defense against unjust aggression. The 1950s came to a close with the just-war doctrine taught by the Catholic Church as the only moral approach to warfare. Through this time, as Msgr. Joseph Gremillion points out,

> Pacifism was viewed as a quaint aberration of Quakers and Mennonite sects. U.S. Catholics, on the other hand, were patriots through and through. We fought *just* wars—when our President told us to. Presidential elections in 1952 and 1960 focused on

five-star generals and war heroes, who debated rolling back the communists, unleashing Chiang Kai-shek, and closing the missile gap.[10]

The most practical consequence of the Church's teaching on war and peace was to deny to individual parishioners a pacifist option. Catholics were free to question policy options as they related to U.S. nuclear strategy; but such objections could not call into question the moral foundations on which U.S. military policy, and nuclear strategy in particular, rested.

For reasons that are subject to diverse interpretation, the 1960s witnessed a reorientation of the Catholic Church with respect to its teaching on war and peace. In hindsight it is clear that *Pacem in Terris* and Vatican II provided the moral and theological context for the Catholic reevaluation of its teaching on war and peace. Both provided the ecclesiological authority for reconsideration of the just-war doctrine. Vatican II, in particular, legitimized a more activistic role for the Church in temporal affairs. Yet subsequent interpretations of both *Pacem in Terris* and Vatican II demonstrate that there was no clear-cut interpretation of the two that demanded a movement of the Church away from the just-war doctrine toward a more pacifistic perspective.[11]

The first step in a new direction with respect to issues of war and peace was taken by John XXIII in April 1963. In addressing the issue of the dignity and worth of every human being, *Pacem in Terris* sought to lay the groundwork for a more peaceful world. Within this context the Pope spoke directly to the issue of nuclear weapons:

> Justice, right reason and harmony . . . urgently demand that the arms race should cease; that the stockpiles which exist in various countries should be reduced equally and simultaneously by the parties concerned, that nuclear weapons should be banned, and that a general agreement should eventually be reached about progressive disarmament and an effective method of control.[12]

Moreover, in a later passage that is pregnant with implications for the traditional Catholic teaching on the moral right of self-defense, John writes that "it is hardly possible to imagine that in the atomic era war could be used as an instrument of justice."[13] Some have used this passage to assert that the Pope was establishing a new pacifist ethic for the Church, that no war could be justified in a nuclear age. Commentators with such diverse perspectives as Michael Novak and J. Bryan Hehir reject this interpretation.[14] Hence while a general consensus exists that *Pacem in Terris* did not endorse pacifism, the encyclical stands out as a clear-cut authoritative Catholic critique of nuclear weapons. In the words of Hehir, *Pacem in Terris* teaches "the toleration of the use of force, not a moral endorsement."[15]

In *Pacem in Terris* the Church was acknowledging that nuclear weapons posed a unique challenge to the traditional Church teaching on war and peace. Traditional notions of self-defense, resistance to aggression, criteria for involvement in war, and conduct in war had to be reassessed. A safe reading of *Pacem in Terris* is that while it did not represent a break with past tradition, it did signify a rethinking of Church doctrines, which had not been reevaluated in over a millennium. It represented an attempt to apply traditional Church teaching to the modern world. Clearly, different interpretations have been given to *Pacem in Terris* by Catholic bishops throughout the world. The encyclical has been interpreted as either a radical departure from traditional Church teaching or as an updated affirmation of traditional Church teaching. Regardless of these differing viewpoints, *Pacem in Terris* represented a new sensitivity on the part of the Catholic Church to the realities of the nuclear age.

Vatican II, a direct outgrowth of the pontificate of John XXIII, stands as the second major event in the postwar reevaluation of war and peace within the Catholic Church. Vatican II marked the beginning of a more socially conscious Catholic Church. In the various papal and conciliar texts that were a direct outgrowth of Vatican II, one finds the basis for the social activism that has come to characterize Roman Catholicism in the past fifteen years. Yet only one of the Vatican II documents—*Gaudium et Spes* ("The Pastoral Constitution on the Church in the Modern World")—speaks directly to issues of war and peace.

Like *Pacem in Terris* those passages are controversial and have been the subject of a host of interpretations. In Chapter V, entitled "The Fostering of Peace and the Promotion of a Community of Nations," the issues of modern warfare are addressed. While not specifically referring to nuclear weapons, the Pastoral Constitution condemns the use of a wide range of modern "scientific weapons." It is strongly implied that these weapons call into question traditional assumptions concerning the conduct of warfare. These weapons, the Pastoral Constitution states, "can inflict massive and indiscriminate destruction far exceeding the bounds of legitimate defense."[16] Therefore, in what is probably the most often quoted passage of all Vatican II documents, the Pastoral Constitution concludes that "(a)ll these considerations compel us to undertake an evaluation of war with an *entirely new attitude.*"[17] (Emphasis added.)

The Council also affirms the morality of the pacifist option:

> [W]e cannot fail to praise those who renounce the use of violence in the vindication of their rights and who resort to methods of defense which are otherwise available to weaker parties too, provided that this can be done without injury to the rights and duties of others or the community itself.[18]

Furthermore, the Council calls on the temporal order to make provisions for those who cannot participate in war:

> [I]t seems right that laws make humane provisions for the case of those who for reasons of conscience refuse to bear arms, provided . . . that they accept some other form of service to human community.[19]

It is unclear from the Council text whether or not the Council fathers intended these statements to carry the weight of moral principle or whether they were simply meant to be interpreted as a pastoral commendation;[20] nonetheless, these statements stand as an unambiguous endorsement of the pacifist option for individual Catholics. The historical significance of these statements is hard to overestimate. Yet *Gaudium et Spes* did not legitimate the notion of the Catholic Church as a pacifist church. The Council, while allowing for the pacifist option, is also just as unambiguous in its reaffirmation of traditional Church teaching concerning the moral right of self-defense. Writing after *Pacem in Terris* and with a full awareness of the implications of modern "scientific weapons," the Council stresses that "as long as the danger of war remains . . . governments cannot be denied the right to legitimate defense. . . ."[21] Moreover, the Council addresses the issue of nuclear deterrence in a seemingly approving manner in stating that scientific weapons, to be sure, are not amassed solely for use in war. The defensive strength of any nation is considered dependent upon its capacity for immediate retaliation against an adversary. Hence, this accumulation of arms . . . also serve[s], in a way heretofore unknown, as a deterrent to possible enemy attack. Many regard this state of affairs as the most effective way by which peace of a sort can be maintained between nations at the present time.[22]

Vatican II, therefore, did not signal a rejection of the just-war doctrine; the Council affirmed traditional Church teaching on the morality of self-defense. The Council did, however, endorse the option of conscientious objection for Catholics. It must be kept in mind, however, that even this endorsement of the pacifist option was qualified by the assertion that the option was available "provided that this can be done without injury to the rights and duties of others or of the community itself." In other words, the Council accepted pacifism for the *individual* provided this individual choice caused no harm to the individual nonpacifist or the community at large. The implication is that pacifism can never be an option for the state by virtue of the mandate that the state has to protect its citizens, that is, "the right to legitimate defense."

Vatican II stands as a watershed in the history of Catholic teaching on war and peace not because it rejected the morality of the just-war doctrine but because, like *Pacem in Terris,* it moved the Church further away from an unquestioning endorsement of warfare in a nuclear age. The Catholic Church was not transformed into a pacifist church by Vatican II. However, the door was opened so that those who were inclined to a traditional pacifism or a newer nuclear pacifism could enter and find support for their views as well as the necessary authority to move the Church in the direction in which they perceived it was inexorably moving.

As we have seen, Vatican II urged the Church to evaluate war with "an entirely new attitude." By the late 1960s the American Catholic Church was ready to take up this mandate. There are certainly numerous factors that have to be considered when seeking to explain why the American Catholic Church moved in the direction it did with respect to issues of war and peace from this time onward. To be sure, Vatican II provided the authoritative context for the American Catholic debate. Yet

Vatican II in itself does not explain the specific direction in which the American Catholic Church was to move in the next fifteen years. The European Church also had the mandate of Vatican II but moved in a quite different direction. To find the answer to this question one must be conscious of the sociology of the late 1960s in the United States, specifically with respect to the effect the Vietnam War had on the American psyche, and one must look at the composition of the American bishops in the post-Vatican II era.[23] Regardless of the reasons and motives behind the direction the bishops chose, the late 1960s saw the gradual movement of the American Catholic Church toward a more critical evaluation of the just-war doctrine and an increasing skepticism toward the morality of the use, threat, and, most recently, even possession of nuclear weapons.

The first step in this direction is found in the NCCB's pastoral letter of 1968, "Human Life in Our Day." The second part of this letter deals with issues relating to international politics in general and U.S. foreign policy in particular. The letter is not a radical departure from previous Church teaching but finds its primary significance in its repetition of the teachings of *Gaudium et Spes* on war and peace. As such, "Human Life in Our Day" accepts the validity of individual acts of conscientious objection (with the same reservations found in the Pastoral Constitution), affirms the right of national self-defense, and rejects a policy of unilateral disarmament. In addition, the American bishops went beyond the reaffirmation of authoritative Church teaching and made several specific policy recommendations based on their own authority.[24]

"Human Life in Our Day" is important in light of the way in which it seeks to impact the specific policy options then on the agenda of U.S. foreign policy. The American bishops, drawing on the authority of Vatican II, attempted to influence U.S. public policy through their policy statements. In doing so the bishops were embarking on the activist path that would characterize their activities for the next decade and a half. This path would arouse controversy among those in the Church who felt that in making policy statements the bishops overstepped their legitimate authority within the established ecclesiology of the Catholic Church.

By the mid-1970s the American bishops had moved beyond

a simple reaffirmation of Vatican II and had begun to chart a new and in many ways distinctly *American* Catholic response to war and peace. In "To Live in Christ Jesus: A Pastoral Reflection on the Moral Life" (1976) the NCCB reaffirmed the central teaching of Vatican II relative to war and peace. This time, however, there was a discernible urgency to the bishops' letter. Specifically, the bishops (1) questioned whether war in today's world could ever be morally justified; (2) limited the conditions under which a nation might defend itself, and (3) stated that it is not only wrong to directly attack civilian populations (a principle established in prior Church teaching) but that "it is also wrong to *threaten* to attack them (civilian populations) as part of a strategy of deterrence."[25] (Emphasis added.)

With this last statement, the American bishops had gone well beyond the teachings of *Pacem in Terris* and Vatican II, arguing for the first time not only that it was immoral and contrary to Catholic teaching to use nuclear weapons against civilians but that it was also immoral to *threaten* to use such weapons against civilians. Apart from the issue of whether or not the bishops intended in this letter to rule out counterforce strikes, it appears that the bishops were precluding a countervalue strategy; the very same strategy the United States had adhered to since the Kennedy Administration.[26] For the first time in the postwar period, the Catholic Church had gone on record as opposing the strategic policy of the United States. It must be emphasized that this policy was not a peripheral element of U.S. defense strategy; to the contrary, in characterizing deterrence as "wrong" the Catholic bishops were striking at *the* central pillar of U.S. defense strategy.

The implications of the bishops' 1976 letter was further elaborated on in Cardinal John Krol's now famous testimony before the Senate Foreign Relations Committee in support of SALT II on September 6, 1979.[27] In that testimony, and speaking for the bishops of America, Krol again emphasized that it is not only wrong to use nuclear weapons, but it is also wrong to intend to use them. Clarifying his remarks a week later before a group of religious leaders, Krol addressed the issue of whether or not nuclear weapons could ever be used even in self-defense:

> As teachers of moral truth we call for the avoidance of any use of weapons aimed indiscriminately at the destruction of entire cities or extensive areas along with their population, whatever the con-

sequences. Possession, yes, for deterrence as long as negotiation gives some hope of mutual balanced reductions. . . . But use, never.[28]

Krol's remarks signaled another movement on the part of the American bishops with respect to issues of war and peace. Having previously condemned the use and intent to use (i.e., threat), the bishops, through Cardinal Krol, were establishing a theme the variation of which has dominated American Catholic episcopal statements since; namely, nuclear weapons can never be used. Likewise, it is immoral to intend to use nuclear weapons. Yet it *is* acceptable to possess nuclear weapons while negotiations on arms reductions take place. Cardinal Krol makes it clear, however, that the episcopacy's acceptance of possession is contingent on serious arms control negotiations. Given the tenor of Cardinal Krol's remarks, some might conclude that at least Cardinal Krol (if not many of his fellow bishops) was a short step away from urging that the United States take unilateral steps to disarm—at least in September 1979. As with previous statements originating with the Catholic Church leadership, however, Krol's remarks have been the subject of much debate. Father J. Bryan Hehir, director of the U.S. Catholic Conference's Office of International Justice and Peace, sought to clarify Krol's remarks further—and, one suspects, allay fears—in testimony before the House of Representatives in the spring of 1980. According to Hehir, who would play a pivotal role in drafting the 1983 pastoral letter, "He (Krol) argued that the deterrent could be tolerated (not approved) as a 'lesser evil' than use, since it seemed that deterrence was a barrier against any use of the weapons."[29]

After Krol's controversial testimony the stage was set for a thorough and systematic study of war and peace by the NCCB. Several factors prompted the bishops to establish the committee that eventually wrote "The Challenge of Peace." The failure of SALT II to be ratified, the debate surrounding a new American nuclear war-fighting strategy that was spawned by Presidential Directive 59, and even the election of Ronald Reagan gave a sense of urgency to this issue in the minds of several bishops. Yet as significant as those factors were, the most important was very simply the emergence and influence of the so-called "Mennonite Caucus" among the American bishops.

With these immediate factors juxtaposed against the important changes that had taken place within the Catholic Church from *Pacem in Terris* to Cardinal Krol's testimony, the NCCB established an ad hoc committee in November of 1980 to draft a pastoral letter on war and peace. The committee was chaired by then Archbishop Joseph Bernardin of Chicago, who has the reputation within the Roman Catholic Church of being an effective facilitator of compromise. The rest of the five-man committee included Bishop Daniel P. Reilly of Norwich, Connecticut; Bishop George A. Fulcher of Columbus, Ohio; Bishop Thomas Gumbleton of Detroit, and Bishop John O'Connor, the Vicar General of the military vicarate of New York. While Reilly and Fulcher were appointed on the basis of their reputation as moderates, Gumbleton and O'Connor were appointed by virtue of their representing different approaches within the American Catholic Church. Gumbleton has in recent years gained a reputation as one of the Church's most outspoken pacifists, whereas O'Connor's more traditional views on just war tend to reflect his many years of military service.

In July 1981 the committee began to work on their letter. The process itself took twenty-two months of serious scholarship, reflection, and debate. All told, the committee conducted well over a dozen hearings and heard from a variety of witnesses representing a broad spectrum of backgrounds and viewpoints, from Caspar Weinberger to Gordon Zahn. Evidence suggests that even Pope John Paul II and President Reagan followed closely the drafting process.

The first draft of the letter was completed in June 1982.[30] In seventy pages the first draft carefully crafted a response to issues of war and peace in a manner that was consistent with the direction that the American Catholic Church had been moving since "To Live in Christ Jesus." Specifically, the first draft, within a theological and moral framework and with reference to the just-war tradition of the Catholic Church, rejects the first use of nuclear weapons, rejects all use of nuclear weapons against innocents, and brands deterrence a "moral evil" that can only be tolerated as the lesser of evils (unilateral disarmament being the greater evil). In addition, the first draft suggests that some justification might exist for a limited nuclear retaliatory strike against military targets.

The first draft elicited a variety of responses from the Reagan Administration and from within the Catholic Church itself.[31] It is clear from the nature of responses from Clark and Weinberger that the Administration was concerned about the direction the bishops appeared headed in their pastoral. As concerned as the Reagan Administration apparently was, in the larger context of events the most important reaction to the bishops' first draft came not from the Administration nor a member of the American Catholic episcopacy but from Pope John Paul II. In his address to the Second Special Session on Disarmament of the UN General Assembly, which was read by the Vatican Secretary of State, Cardinal Agostino Casaroli, on June 11, 1982, John Paul acknowledges, as have his predecessors since Vatican II, the dangers of the nuclear age. His message went on to say in clear and unambiguous language that

> [i]n current conditions, "deterrence" based on balance, certainly not as an end in itself but as a step on the way toward a progressive disarmament, may still be judged morally acceptable.[32]

John Paul's address was not ostensibly a response to the American bishops, but there are reasons to believe that this one sentence was inserted especially for the American bishops at the request of officials of the Vatican. Regardless of the intended audience of the sentence or its source, the fact remains that Pope John Paul, with all the Church authority he commands, reaffirmed the morality of the doctrine of nuclear deterrence— albeit in a qualified manner. As such, within the context of the Catholic Church hierarchy, the American bishops had no authoritative basis for stating in their first draft of the pastoral letter that deterrence was a "moral evil." Both the Pope's statement and the issue of deterrence itself would be matters of central concern in the debate over the final two drafts of the pastoral letter.

The first draft of the pastoral letter became the discussion draft for American Catholic episcopacy. The pastoral committee also solicited comments on the first draft from various laypersons. On the basis of these comments, the committee prepared a second draft for discussion by the full body of nearly 300 American bishops in Washington, D.C., in mid-November 1982. The November meeting marked the first time that the entire

NCCB had met together to discuss publicly the new pastoral. The meeting was dominated by various individuals and groups seeking to effect modifications and changes in the second draft.

In an effort to head off expected criticisms from some segments of the Church and the Administration, the NCCB hierarchy attempted as the meetings began to lay down the rationale behind the letter. In his opening address to the bishops, the chairman of the drafting committee, Archbishop Bernardin, argued the basis for the Church's involvement in the nuclear debate:

> [B]ecause the nuclear issue is not simply political, but also a profoundly moral and religious question, the church must be a participant in the process of protecting the world and its people from the specter of nuclear destruction. . . . It is possible to speak today of a "democratization" of the nuclear debate, a process in which the concern for keeping the peace in a nuclear age reaches far beyond the customary discussion of experts, strategists and diplomats and is taken up also by the wider public.[33]

Because nuclear weapons pose, in Bernardin's words, "a qualitatively new moral and political challenge, they are not simply an extension of the moral problem of war and peace we have known in the past."[34] Acknowledging the relevance of the Soviet threat to the United States and its impact on the nature of the U.S. defense strategy, Bernardin nonetheless stated that this does not "relieve us of the responsibility we have as American bishops to spell out the implications of Catholic teaching on modern warfare for our government and society."[35] With this background Bernardin succinctly summarized the intention of the pastoral letter: "It is to draw a strong, clear line politically and morally against resort to nuclear weapons."[36]

The second draft itself is over 50 percent longer than the initial draft.[37] Among other things, including a reaffirmation of the pacifist option for Catholics, the section on theological and moral principles was expanded, while concern for the issues of deterrence and the use of nuclear weapons remained the focal point of the second draft. In particular, the second draft contains a verbatim quote of John Paul's remarks at the United Nations. The American bishops, however, still express grave moral reservations with that strategy. They emphasize that John Paul's assent to the morality of deterrence is, in the bishops' words, "strictly conditioned."[38] Consistent with their first draft, the second draft of the letter rejects the first use of nuclear weapons, rejects countercity warfare, and continues to support the "paradox of deterrence" as an interim measure only.[39] Deterrence is acceptable only to "prevent the use of nuclear weapons by others."[40] The second draft also seems to allow for the possibility of a limited nuclear war, but the bishops remain quite skeptical that such a war could remain limited. As a result, the bishops highlight John Paul's prior statement regarding the "unacceptable moral risk of crossing the threshold to nuclear war. . . ."[41] Likewise, there is some ambiguity in the second draft concerning the moral justifiability of a limited retaliatory strike. While not directly addressing this scenario in the second draft, the tone of the latter is such that the bishops move beyond a qualified acceptance of some use (i.e., a retaliatory strike) to argue against all use whatsoever.[42]

The second draft also addresses, in a manner that the first draft did not, specific policy positions of the U.S. government and, in doing so, places the letter (and by extension, the NCCB) in opposition to U.S. policy. Besides the larger concern relative to the deterrence strategy, the second draft specifically rejects as immoral the MX missile and calls for a nuclear freeze, an "immediate . . . halt (to the) testing, production and deployment of new strategic systems."[43]

The second draft was the focus of often spirited debate among bishops representing different viewpoints during their November meeting.[44] Furthermore, the Reagan Administration made its continued disappointment apparent through a letter sent to Chairman Bernardin by William P. Clark on November 16.[45] In that letter, Clark states that he is writing on "behalf of President Reagan" and other members of the Administration. While again commending the bishops for their efforts, Clark nonetheless expresses his dismay with the second draft's general nature. "We regret," Clark writes, "that the committee's latest draft continues to reflect fundamental misreadings of American policies. . . ." Clark's letter goes on to criticize the second draft for ignoring current arms reduction negotiations with the Soviets (e.g., START), supporting a nuclear freeze, and ignoring the realities of the Soviet military buildup as well as the nature of Soviet totalitarianism. In closing, Clark writes that it is important for the bishops' conference to know our decisions on nuclear armaments and our defense posture (specifically the deterrence strategy) and guided by moral considerations as compelling as any which have faced mankind.

While Clark's letter was welcomed by the bishops, there is little evidence to suggest that it had any measurable impact on the majority of bishops. By a nearly unanimous vote, the NCCB decided to continue work on the letter. The bishops left Washington agreeing to meet in Chicago in May with the intent of approving the final draft.

In the process of working on a third draft, a remarkable meeting took place in Rome on January 18 and 19, 1983. Once again the details behind the motivation for the meeting are clouded. Some have suggested that the meeting was called by the Vatican after a visit by an envoy of the Reagan Administration. Others argue that the meeting was called simply to facilitate a friendly interchange between the Vatican (which had been sent the first and second drafts), various European bishops, and representatives of the NCCB. Regardless of its origins, one cannot read the documents that have been made available from that extraordinary meeting without realizing that the American representatives—Archbishop, now Cardinal Bernardin, Msgr. Daniel Hoye, Archbishop John Roach, and Father J. Bryan Hehir—were called to Rome to discuss several points concerning the two drafts about which the Vatican and European bishops were obviously very concerned.[46]

According to the official synthesis of the meeting prepared by a representative of the Vatican, discussion on January 18 and 19 centered around five issues: (1) the precise teaching role of the NCCB; (2) the application of fundamental moral principles to the debate surrounding nuclear weapons; (3) the use of Scripture; (4) the role of pacifism within the Catholic tradition, and (5) the morality of deterrence.[47]

In light of the aforementioned, the participants left affirming: (1) the need for future drafts to spell out more clearly at what level of authority the NCCB speaks when it addresses the various topics found in the letter; (2) that all applications of moral principles to specific policy options found in the letter (e.g., limited nuclear war) are open to other interpretations, evaluations, and "differences of moral opinions"; (3) the need for future drafts to emphasize more clearly in the sections dealing with the Scriptures that " 'believing peace is possible' expresses not a credal statement but a mere conviction that respects the eschatological nature of the kingdom"; (4) that the second draft misinterprets *Gaudium et Spes* (and is "factually incorrect") in asserting that nonviolence is part of the Catholic tradition— "there is only one Catholic tradition: the just war theory . . ."; and (5) John Paul's message to the United Nations is the basis for any moral evaluation of deterrence. It bears emphasizing that the Pope's UN address was interpreted by Cardinal Casaroli who, though ostensibly offering a personal commentary on the message, was more than likely speaking for John Paul himself.

According to a memorandum sent by Archbishop Roach and Cardinal Bernardin on January 25 to the members of the ad hoc committee on war and peace, the Rome meeting was "consultative in nature and the results of the meeting will be included in a significant way in the work of the committee as it prepares the third draft."[48] The documents available from the January meeting in Rome suggest very strongly that John Paul, not to mention many of the European bishops, were as concerned about the direction the American bishops were headed in their pastoral letter as the Reagan Administration—albeit for different reasons.

The third draft of the letter, twice as long as the first draft, was completed, given unanimous support by the members of the ad hoc committee, and sent out to the members of the NCCB in March 1983 in time for the NCCB's Chicago meeting. In an early public comment on the third draft, Cardinal Bernardin stated that

> in developing the third draft, particular attention has been given to the treatment of the Scripture, to the relationship of the "just war theory" and nonviolence in Catholic tradition, to the discussion of U.S. and Soviet policies and relationships, to the moral argumentation on the question of deterrence . . . and in particular, to the distinction between moral principles and their application to concrete circumstances in order to clarify the different levels of moral authority in the document.[49]

Bernardin's description of the essence of the third draft is nearly an exact repetition of the concerns that were raised at the Vatican meeting in January. Moreover, the third draft, in its initial form, seemed to reflect the "softening" that the Reagan Administration had been arguing for but did not receive in the first and second drafts. The important changes in the initial third draft included dropping a reference found in the second draft to the unacceptability of the MX missile, calling for a "curb" rather than a "halt" to the production, testing, and deployment of nuclear weapons, and removing any reference to the previous discussion surrounding the morality of intending and threatening to use nuclear weapons within the context of deterrence.

Because of these changes there was much talk in the American press that the committee responsible for drafting the pastoral letter had given in to the pressure of the Reagan Administration. While initially acknowledging that changes had been made to make the letter more "flexible," the ad hoc committee subsequently reversed itself and reinserted much of the "nonflexible" language that had been a part of the prior drafts. Most significant was the reinsertion of the word "halt" into the letter, replacing "curb" with respect to nuclear weapons' testing, deployment, and production.

With these changes in place, the NCCB on May 3 voted 238 to 9 to adopt the pastoral letter "The Challenge of Peace: God's Promise and Our Response."[50] The final document, nearly 45,000 words in length, is in many ways quite similar as well as quite different from the first and second drafts. Divided into four chapters, the letter begins with a theological discussion of the nature of peace and the moral basis for a just-war doctrine. This discussion is followed by an evaluation of the impact of nuclear weapons on traditional Church teachings dealing with war and peace. Within this section moral principles are applied to specific policy choices including counterpopulation warfare, first use, and limited nuclear war. It is here that the morality of deterrence is addressed. In the next section the letter offers specific policy proposals for the creation of a more peaceful world, while in the letter's final section a pastoral challenge is issued.

The final letter, like its predecessors, rejects countercity warfare, opposes any first use of nuclear weapons, and is skeptical about the possibility of "limited" nuclear war. Furthermore, the letter, while sidestepping a direct discussion of threat and intention and their relationship to the morality of deterrence, accepts deterrence on a strictly conditional basis providing it is used as a step toward disarmament. At the same time, and in contrast to prior drafts, the final letter clearly states that "not every statement in this letter has the same moral authority."[51] Moreover, it clearly states that the application of moral judgments to specific cases is "not binding on conscience."[52] In building a strong and lengthy case for the validity of a nonviolent or pacifist witness for individual Catholics, the final letter, also unlike the second draft, stops short of arguing that pacifism is part of the Catholic tradition.[53]

In short, the final draft of the pastoral letter represents the culmination of Catholic thinking on issues of war and peace that finds its roots in *Pacem in Terris* and Vatican II. The letter represents the conclusions of *American* bishops and as a result of these conclusions, as we have noted, represents different levels of authoritativeness. Just how authoritative the document is and how binding it is on the consciences of American Catholics is the subject of a great deal of controversy.[54] Yet regardless how formally authoritative the letter may be in the eyes of the Catholic Church ecclesiology, there can be little doubt that the letter carries tremendous weight simply by virtue of the fact, as Father Timothy Healy suggests, that "the bishops are not just any group of church leaders."[55]

But beyond the issue of who wrote the letter, the pastoral has and will continue to attract attention by virtue of the nature of the document itself. To be sure, the substantive conclusions of the letter have elicited a growing body of criticism from both Catholics and non-Catholics.[56] However, the sources of those criticisms and the intensity with which those objections have been expressed are a testimony to the intellectual and theological vitality of the letter. One does not have to agree with either specific or general conclusions of the letter to see that "The Challenge of Peace" represents serious intellectual and scholarly inquiry. The pastoral is not a superficial polemic for a given point of view; it is a document that is at once transparent as well as subtly nuanced.

Christians should be indebted to the bishops for the thorough and systematic manner in which they raise and address the myriad complex theological and moral issues surrounding war and peace in a nuclear age. There is within the Christian world no recent precedent to match the work of the American bishops. It is certainly not that the American bishops or the Catholic Church are any more concerned about issues of war and peace than are non-Catholics; nor is it that the American bishops are any more intellectually sophisticated. Nonetheless, one is struck by the contrast between the richness of the pastoral letter and the relative paucity of efforts on the part of other Christians— particularly Protestants—to seriously and honestly address the issues of war and peace. In part this gulf between the efforts of the Catholic Church and their Protestant counterparts is a function of the differences that exist in the structures of the Catholic and Protestant Church. There is no *one* Protestant church; there is no established Church hierarchy that authoritatively speaks for the Church. In this sense it is much easier for the bishops to speak as one—yet not without controversy—for the whole Church. But this explanation is not adequate in itself to explain the reasons behind the seeming lack of serious attention that Protestants have paid to the issues of war and peace.

Certainly, the mainline denominations have spoken to the problems of war and peace, but they have done so in what too often is a superficial manner. Resolutions condemning this or affirming that are debated and passed in various denominational assemblies. Frequently, the resolutions reflect the position of a small, vocal elite and do not represent an honest attempt to examine exhaustively the complexity of issues involved by drawing on a variety of viewpoints.[57] It is therefore not surprising that at least two of the mainline denominations have embraced the bishops' pastoral and "highly recommended" it to their members.[58]

Among evangelical Christians, the situation has not been much different. While recent years have seen Evangelicals become more socially conscious (reversing what sociologist David Moberg has called the "great reversal"—the antipathy toward social activism that characterized Evangelicalism at the turn of the century), they have remained strangely silent on issues of war and peace. To be sure, there exists among Evangelicals a diversity of perspectives dealing with the morality of Christian participation in war. But this debate—or more accurately stand-off—is an old and in many respects anachronistic debate that has not been updated to take into account the "supreme crisis" that humanity faces in the latter half of the twentieth century.

There are indications that Evangelicals have awakened to the need to reevaluate war and peace in light of the realities of modern "scientific weaponry."[59] Yet even though this recent willingness on the part of some Evangelicals to address the realities of our age has been heartening, there have been too few examples of attempts to examine seriously from a balanced perspective the full range of biblical, strategic, and moral issues that relate to war and peace in our modern world.

For this reason, therefore, Evangelicals in particular and Christians in general should welcome the efforts of the American Catholic bishops. Regardless of one's theological tradition or political vantage point, "The Challenge of Peace" addresses the issues of war and peace with an incisiveness and sensitivity unknown in the evangelical debate over this issue. Moreover, and because of the nature of the document itself, the letter has become the focal point of the national debate surrounding nuclear weapons. As we have seen, the Catholic Church has weighed into the public debate surrounding nuclear weapons; indeed, with the pastoral letter the bishops have in many ways defined the parameters of the debate—certainly in its moral dimensions. American Evangelicals, on the other hand—while an increasingly important religious as well as political force in American society—have not responded in an effective or original way to the ongoing national debate.

It is, then, with appreciation to the Catholic bishops and with a firm belief in the biblical mandate to impact the created order that this present volume is written. This book represents an effort on the part of several American Evangelicals to weigh into the current national debate in a significant way. The biblical, strategic, and moral issues that the bishops raise in their letter serve as the focus of discussion. Specifically, the essays in this book are organized around the major themes of the pastoral letter: Biblical Perspectives on War and Peace, The Just War in a Nuclear Age, The Morality of Using Nuclear Weapons, The Morality of Deterrence, and Promoting Peace in a Nuclear Age.

The authors of the essays, all highly qualified in the areas in which they write, represent a diversity of perspectives. Some write out of a traditional just-war perspective, others would refer to themselves as nuclear pacifists, while still others would have difficulty placing themselves in such traditional categories. The variety of viewpoints that emerge from this volume are both a reflection of the diversity of views on war and peace that exist among Evangelicals and a reflection of the pluralism that is the Protestant tradition. It is here that the contrast between what the American bishops have done and what American Evangelicals must do is boldly apparent. There is not, nor can there be, *one* evangelical Christian response to issues of war and peace. Most Protestants understand our God-mandated responsibility as rooted in the priesthood of all believers. Hence, while acknowledging our responsibility to be co-workers with God in the creation of a more peaceful world, we realize that we will differ in terms of how we seek to build that peace. These issues are difficult and complex, but in a nuclear age—the world in which we now live—it is imperative that all Christians confront and address "The Challenge of Peace."

I: Biblical Perspectives on War and Peace

1: Biblical Peace and the Kingdom of God

JOHN S. BRAY

The specter of nuclear war looms as the greatest danger of our day. It is essential that those who follow Jesus as Lord do their best to understand what it means to be salt and light in the midst of such difficult times. Thus the entire Christian community can rejoice in the publication of the U.S. bishops' pastoral letter on war and peace. The letter was intended not just for Roman Catholics but also for our total pluralistic society.[1] It is a model of sensitive Christian scholarship that will pay rich dividends to all those who are willing to plumb its depths.

One possible barrier for Evangelicals is the Catholic social tradition that undergirds the bishops' letter. This tradition is a mix of biblical, theological, and philosophical elements, some of which are foreign to Evangelicals and may even interfere with a proper understanding of the letter. Evangelicals will be most familiar with the biblical elements used by the bishops, but there are a number of ways in which contemporary Roman Catholic biblical scholarship differs from the scholarship of Evangelicals. The purpose of this chapter will be to explore and to evaluate the bishops' use of Scripture in this letter. To what degree and in what ways may we as Evangelicals benefit from the bishops' use of Scripture as it pertains to the questions of war and peace?

THE ROLE OF THE BIBLE

The bishops are emphatic in emphasizing the centrality of "the biblical vision of the world."[2] It is the sacred Scriptures that "provide the foundation for confronting the dilemma of war and peace today."[3] But we are also cautioned that the Scriptures are conditioned by three factors to which we must be alert in our study of war and peace.

> *First,* the term "peace" has been understood in different ways at various times and in various contexts. . . . *Second,* the scriptures as we have them were written over a long period of time and reflect many varied historical situations, all different from our own. Our understanding of them is both complicated and enhanced by these differences, but not in any way obscured or diminished by them. *Third,* since the scriptures speak primarily of God's intervention in history, they contain no specific treatise on war and peace. Peace and war must always be seen in light of God's intervention in human affairs and our response to that intervention. Both are elements within the ongoing revelation of God's will for creation.[4]

But, in spite of this complexity, the bishops "still recognize in the scriptures a unique source of revelation, a word of God which is addressed to us as surely as it has been to all preceding generations."[5] The bishops also affirm that "the sacred texts. . . . provide us with direction for our lives and hold out to us an object of hope, a final promise, which guides and directs our actions here and now."[6]

The bishops have taken a strong stand on the authority of Scripture, much stronger than that affirmed by some denominational bodies today, and we Evangelicals may applaud this position. We will now look at the way in which the bishops actually use and interpret Scripture as they wrestle with the question of war and peace.

THE OLD TESTAMENT

The bishops recognize that war and violence are part of the history of the people of God in the Old Testament, especially in the period before the monarchy. "God is often seen as the one who leads the Hebrews in battle, protects them from their enemies, makes them victorious over other armies."[7]

God himself is seen as a warrior in the Old Testament, and this image had a number of connotations for the Hebrews. The metaphor provided them with a sense of security in a time of unrest and danger: God was powerful enough to protect his people and to make them secure. He was *actively* involved in their lives. And because of his power and might, he had the right to command obedience.

But the Old Testament contains other images of God that became prominent over a period of time. The metaphor of God the warrior "was gradually transformed, particularly after the experience of the exile, when God was no longer identified with military victory and might."[8]

The Old Testament image of peace is also critical in our understanding of war and peace. In the Old Testament peace is not the result of *our* activity; it is a gift from God. Peace is understood as a unity, a right order, a harmony that extends to all of creation. The emphasis is not on an individual's personal peace. And, finally, as we move through the Old Testament drama "the images of peace and the demands upon the people for covenantal fidelity to true peace grow more urgent and more developed."[9]

In the Old Testament peace also accompanies the covenant that God would make with his people (Ezek. 37:26). This covenant peace would also be marked by justice. There can be no reign of God in the presence of injustice (Ezek. 13:16; Jer. 6:14; 8:10-12; Isa. 48:18).[10]

It was obvious to the people of God that they had not yet experienced the full peace of God. "War and enmity were still present, injustices thrived, sin still manifested itself."[11] But a final age is coming, a messianic age, in which the Spirit will be poured out on all, and "justice and peace will embrace each other" (Ps. 85:10-11). It is then that the peace that is so desperately longed for in the Old Testament will come into full bloom, and all of history will be consummated.

How do we as Evangelicals assess the bishops' use of the Old Testament? I believe there are two basic issues that must be addressed here. First, what is the level of their biblical scholarship? Does it reflect the latest insights of modern scholarship? And, second, do we agree with the theological assumptions that undergird the bishops' use of the Old Testament?

There is no question about the first issue: the level of biblical scholarship is first-rate. It is obvious that the Old Testament scholars who contributed to this letter represent the best of scholarship. They do not gloss over the violence in the Old

Testament, and they take seriously the concept of God as warrior. In fact, their conclusions in these areas are very similar to those of some evangelical scholars.[12]

The bishops are also very insightful in their understanding of the Old Testament doctrine of peace. Current evangelical scholarship also reflects the concept of peace as a gift from God and as representing unity, completeness, and right order.[13] This broad understanding of peace is also a very healthy corrective to the overly personal and privatistic idea of peace held by many Christians today.

But we discover serious problems when we look more closely at the theological assumptions that underlie the bishops' use of the Old Testament. The basic problem is one of ambiguity rather than outright disagreement. The bishops have declared the Scriptures to be a word of God that is addressed to us today.[14] But how do we harmonize that understanding with the fact that the image of God changes in the Old Testament?

The concept of God as warrior brings this question into sharp focus. Certainly the bishops are correct that "warrior" has the connotation that God is powerful and is actively involved in the lives of his people. But how do we explain the gradual transformation of this image, especially after the exile?[15] Was the earlier image simply the result of Hebrew religious insight that had not been given by God and that God had to correct later with less militaristic images? If so, then in what sense was the earlier image part of the word of God?

Some would argue that the image of God as warrior was just a human interpretation and that we are now justified to move on to a less primitive concept such as an understanding of God as love. But such a resolution is filled with problems. For example, how do we deal with the *dominance* of the theme of God as warrior in the Old Testament?[16] Peter Craigie also calls attention to a problem that this resolution presents for New Testament interpretation.

> Neither Stephen nor Paul rejected the conception of God as Warrior, as is evident from their references to God's great deliverance of Israel from Egypt, the event which marked the inauguration of the conception of God as Warrior in ancient Israel (see Acts 7:35-36; 13:17).[17]

On the other hand, if one views the motif of God as warrior as part of God's self-revelation, then how does one harmonize that image with Jesus' prohibitions against the use of force (Luke 6:27-36)? This is a critical issue for Evangelicals, and it is unfortunate that the bishops have not dealt with it more forthrightly.

THE NEW TESTAMENT

In their treatment of the New Testament the bishops focus almost exclusively on the words and works of Jesus. Very little is said about the remainder of the New Testament. The bishops acknowledge that "the characteristics of the *shalom* of the Old Testament . . . are present in the New Testament traditions" but they argue that "all discussion of war and peace in the New Testament must be seen within the context of the unique revelation of God that is Jesus Christ and of the reign of God which Jesus proclaimed and inaugurated."[18]

"Jesus proclaimed the reign of God in his words and made it present in his actions. His words begin with a call to conversion and a proclamation of the arrival of the kingdom."[19] The Sermon on the Mount describes this new reality of the reign of God. This reign is marked by a way of life that is characterized by forgiveness and by love. "He called for a love that went beyond family ties and bonds of friendship to reach even those who were enemies. . . . Such a love does not seek revenge, but rather is merciful in the face of threat and opposition."[20]

These words of Jesus could be nothing more than an abstract ideal. The difference is twofold. First, the actual example of Jesus. And, second, the fact that Jesus gave us his Spirit to empower us.

Jesus gives the gift of peace to his disciples. It is a gift that is validated by his resurrection from the dead. "Jesus gives . . . peace to his disciples, to those who had witnessed the helplessness of the crucifixion and the power of the resurrection. . . . The peace which he gives to them . . . is the fulness of salvation. It is the reconciliation of the world and God."[21]

The community of believers is called on to follow after Jesus. They are to be ministers of reconciliation. Jesus calls them to be "people who would make the peace which God has established visible through the love and the unity within their own communities."[22]

The bishops conclude their section on biblical exegesis by issuing a challenge to all believers.

> Because we have been gifted with God's peace in the risen Christ, we are called to our own peace and to the making of peace in our world. As disciples and as children of God it is our task to seek for ways in which to make the forgiveness, justice and mercy, and love of God visible in a world where violence and enmity are too often the norm.[23]

It is very difficult to evaluate the bishops' use of the New Testament. Most of what they have written is simply a restatement of biblical verses with some application to the lives of believers. We do affirm their attempt to take the New Testament so seriously.

Our critical evaluation will take two forms. First, a consideration of what the bishops appear to *assume* in terms of biblical interpretation. And, second, elements of the New Testament that the bishops have overlooked or ignored.

First, what do the bishops assume? Our focus here will be on the Sermon on the Mount, which the bishops have cited numerous times and which is the backbone of their New Testament presentation.

The bishops have taken a very simplistic approach to the Sermon on the Mount. They quote it, assume that its meaning is clear, and then use it as part of their argument. Nowhere do they acknowledge the great difficulties of interpretation that have accompanied this sermon from its very inception.[24]

For example, in the Sermon Jesus spoke often about non-violence. Were these statements intended to provide a guide to *personal* ethics? Was he saying that when we are assaulted by others our response should be nonviolent? Or, on the other hand, was Jesus formulating guidelines that should govern *public* ethics between nations?

What about the striking words uttered by Jesus and recorded in Matthew 5:43-45?

> You have heard that it was said, "You shall love your neighbor and hate your enemy." But I say to you, "Love your enemies and pray for those who persecute you, so that you may be sons of your Father who is in heaven; for he makes his sun rise on the evil and on the good, and sends rain on the just and on the unjust."

What is the meaning of "enemy" and "enemies" in this famous passage? Is "enemy" to be understood as a national enemy or as a personal enemy? The context does not make the meaning self-evident; nor do the bishops help us to interpret these words.

The basic direction of modern scholarship is to understand "enemy" not as "a personal or political foe, but [as] a persecutor of the faith, the enemy of the Messianic community formed by the first Christians."[25] As D. A. Carson has expressed it, "The particular enemies on whom Jesus focuses attention are the persecutors, presumably those who persecute his followers because of righteousness, because of Jesus himself."[26] The bishops have not considered this religious interpretation of "enemy" even though it would have a great impact on their argument if it is correct.

The bishops have treated the New Testament material in such a way that one could easily view Jesus as affirming a simple pacifism. The work of many evangelical scholars leads us toward other conclusions. For example, Robert Guelich's comment on Matthew 5:9 ("Blessed are the peacemakers") is quite appropriate.

> This Beatitude is far more profound than simply offering a social or political ideal of pacifism or passive restraint to avoid conflict. Pacifism is nowhere in sight. Yet one is not to spiritualize this Beatitude so that making peace is "evangelism" narrowly defined as reconciling another's "spiritual" alienation from God (cf. 5:13-16). To make peace is to engage actively in bringing God's redemptive purposes to bear in all our broken society. The process may be diverse, even involving conflict at times (cf. 5:10, 11-12 and Jesus' own ministry), but it is concomitant with sonship for each individual.[27]

In short, the bishops have assumed a simplistic interpretation of the Sermon on the Mount. This interpretation is not supported by modern scholarship in general nor by evangelical scholarship in particular.

Now that we have looked at some of the points of biblical interpretation that the bishops have assumed, let us move on to our second critical observation: there are elements of the New Testament that the bishops have either overlooked or ignored. The most glaring area of oversight is those passages that deal with the believer's relationship to the state and to government. For example, what does it mean to "Be submissive to rulers and

authorities" (Tit. 3:1)? Or how should we interpret Peter's commands: "Be subject for the Lord's sake to every human institution, whether it be to the emperor as supreme, or to governors
as sent by him to punish those who do wrong and to praise
those who do right" (1 Pet. 2:13-14)? Or what about the Apos-
tles' refusal to obey the Sanhedrin, a political-religious institution (Acts 4–5)? Do these passages teach us anything about the
relationship of the believer to government? Could they be applied to the issue of nuclear war? The bishops never tell us.

The most striking omission by the bishops is any discussion
of Romans 13:1-7, a classical passage concerning the believer
and the state.

> Let every person be subject to the governing authorities. For there
> is no authority except from God, and those that exist have been
> instituted by God. Therefore he who resists the authorities resists
> what God has appointed, and those who resist will incur judgment.
> For rulers are not a terror to good conduct, but to bad. Would you
> have no fear of him who is in authority? Then do what is good,
> and you will receive his approval, for he is God's servant for your
> good. But if you do wrong, be afraid, for he does not bear the
> sword in vain; he is the servant of God to execute his wrath on
> the wrongdoer. Therefore one must be subject, not only to avoid
> God's wrath, but also for the sake of conscience. For the same
> reason you also pay taxes, for the authorities are ministers of God,
> attending to this very thing. Pay all of them their dues, taxes to
> whom taxes are due, revenue to whom revenue is due, respect to
> whom respect is due, honor to whom honor is due.

A consideration of this passage creates real problems for
some of the positions taken by the bishops. For example, it is
true, as the bishops have stated, that "Jesus refused to defend
himself with force or with violence."[28] But how does one harmonize that with Paul's statement that legitimate rulers have
been instituted by God and that part of their responsibility as
the servants of God is to execute God's wrath on wrongdoers?
If these rulers are indeed God's servants, then should not we,
as the community of faith, support them and cooperate with
them as they do the work of God?

In short, the bishops have eliminated the traditional painful
tension between the Christian as the follower of Christ and the
Christian as a citizen of the state by simply ignoring those passages that deal with the state.[29] The clarity and simplicity of

their position have been attained by ignoring the complexity of the biblical data. This approach must be unacceptable to Evangelicals.

CONCLUSIONS

The bishops' letter is a beautifully crafted work that draws on scholarly resources that are far richer than anything available within our evangelical heritage. Hence the letter may be of great help to us as we strive to develop our own theology of peace. One does not have to agree with everything in the letter in order to benefit from it. The bishops themselves recognize that people of goodwill may come to different opinions.[30]

We have already suggested that there are serious problems with the way in which the bishops have interpreted some portions of Scripture. And yet we as Evangelicals may rejoice in their strong affirmation of the Scriptures as the word of God for us today.

In our world, wracked by wars and by rumors of wars, it is essential that the church make "the peace of the kingdom more visible."[31] The bishops' letter should help us, as Evangelicals, to do just that. We owe the bishops a debt of gratitude for the insights they have offered us as we seek to be light and salt in God's needy world.

2: Biblical Justice and Peace: Toward an Evangelical–Roman Catholic Rapprochement

RICHARD J. MOUW

In 1976 Father Joseph Gremillion published a volume[1] of the major "social teaching" documents that the Roman Catholic Church had produced between 1960 and 1975. This period was the era of Vatican II and its influence—a time of *aggiornamento* (updating) in Roman Catholicism. Not surprisingly, then, the Roman Church had thought it necessary to address a wide variety of social issues during this period.

Official Roman Catholic teaching has always placed a strong emphasis on continuity. Thus its official documents are typically laced with many references to previous Church documents. The aggiornamento documents are no exception to this pattern; they too give the impression of continuity with the past. And they provide very few overt signals regarding the innovations they contain. But the innovations are there, discernible to the eye of the trained observer. Father Gremillion is such an observer, and in his lengthy overview of these documents he provides important insights into the changes in social teaching that were occurring during the aggiornamento period.

Two of these innovations are worthy of note here. First of all, Gremillion argues that a modification of "natural-law" thinking became obvious in the Vatican II era. Traditional Roman Catholicism had made much of what it saw as an ability in all human beings—whether or not they had been recipients of the

32

special grace of regeneration—to grasp a common "natural morality." To be sure, the aggiornamento documents do not abandon the concept of natural law. Pope John XXIII, in *Pacem in Terris* (1963), based his case on the contention that "the Creator of the world has imprinted in man's heart an order which his conscience reveals to him and enjoins him to obey"[2]; thus in speaking of nuclear weapons, Pope John could insist that "Justice, right reason and humanity . . . urgently demand that the arms race should cease."[3] But, as Father Gremillion observes, these natural-law emphases have taken on a somewhat different tone from that of the past: "John and the aggiornamento move from a relatively static view of man's nature and reason toward human rights and fulfillment of human capacities, promoted by man's worth."[4]

A second innovation had to do with the Church's attitude toward conscientious objectors. Prior to the aggiornamento era, the modern Roman Church had been virtually silent on this subject. Pope John, in *Pacem in Terris,* continues the silence. But during the Vatican Council, the subject came to be an explicit matter of concern, with the Council calling for the humane treatment by governments of those who refused to bear arms for conscientious reasons. The 1971 Synod of Bishops took the discussion a step further: "Let a strategy of nonviolence be fostered also, and let conscientious objection be recognized and regulated by law in each nation."[5]

These are significant developments in official Roman Catholic social thought—another sign that the Roman Catholic Church of Vatican II and its aftermath is a different church than the pre-Vatican II entity. But the Roman Church has continued to change since 1975. Indeed, with regard to the two factors mentioned above, where the aggiornamento Church went beyond previous social teaching, we seem to have now gone beyond the aggiornamento period.

The American bishops' recent pastoral letter is not an aggiornamento document. It is a post-aggiornamento document. If the aggiornamento documents took a step beyond the tradition in their treatment of natural law and in their cautious recognition of the rights of conscientious objectors, then the 1983 pastoral letter has taken another giant step beyond the tradition. Except for the *pro forma* references to the documents of the past, the bishops show very little interest in basing any significant part of their case on the confident appeals to a common morality that characterized both traditionalist and aggiornamento discussions. And they are not content to call for the humane treatment of those who refuse military activity on conscientious grounds. Rather they view present conditions as presenting us with a "new moment," in which pacifist concerns must become an integral part of the Church's thinking and witness.

It is important to highlight these matters as we attempt to explore in this chapter the bishops' treatment of the relationship between justice and peace, and to interact with their discussion from an evangelical perspective. There was a time when it was extremely difficult for Roman Catholics and Evangelicals to engage in productive dialogue on matters of common concern. We have employed not only different vocabularies, but also different methodologies. Thus, even when there has been a convergence on the level of practical commitment, methodological and theological barriers have stood in the way of cooperative endeavor.

Take, for example, the issue of abortion. Many Evangelicals take a strong antiabortion stand, a commitment that gives them clear sympathies with Roman Catholicism's official position on the subject. But one can imagine a frustrating conversation between an evangelical layperson and her Roman Catholic counterpart about *why* each of them opposes abortion. The Evangelical might well quote a number of Bible verses, ones that speak of God's loving a specific person before that person was born, or about John the Baptist leaping in his mother's womb at the approach of the pregnant Mary. The Roman Catholic, on the other hand, might never think of quoting the Bible, choosing rather to talk about definitions of "life," or about "potentialities" and "viability." Each would go away wondering about the kind of thinking that informs the other person's position.

This example illustrates a problem that has afflicted Roman Catholic–evangelical dialogue (such as it was) in the past. Evangelicals have tended toward a kind of "proof-texting" approach in their appeals to biblical authority. Roman Catholics, on the other hand, have seemed to be enamored with extrabiblical arguments. If the situation were to improve—if any sort of methodological convergence were to take place—it would probably have to proceed along these lines: Roman Catholics would have to become more explicitly biblical in their thinking; and Evangelicals would have to become less "biblicistic," and more systematically and reflectively biblical, in their approach.

This convergence has in fact been taking place. A new generation of Evangelicals has been calling for a more thoughtful approach to understanding the Scriptures. And many Roman Catholics seem to be adopting a methodology in which biblical authority has a central role.

The bishops' letter is an important piece of evidence for this new, more explicitly biblical emphasis in Roman Catholic teaching. The bishops "recognize in the Scriptures a unique source of revelation, a word of God which is addressed to us as surely as it has been to all preceding generations."[6] And they do not merely offer this acknowledgment as an aside in their discussion. The past documents of Roman Catholicism were characterized by a uniquely Roman Catholic brand of biblical proof-texting: Scripture references seem to be tossed out casually as illustrations of matters that can be demonstrated on extrabiblical grounds. But the bishops' letter gives evidence of biblical seriousness. Their systematic discussion begins with a lengthy exposition of biblical themes, and this exposition serves as the foundation for everything else that is said in the letter.

This is an important point for evangelical Protestants. We are not inclined to view the magisterial deliverances of the Roman Catholic hierarchy as in any way addressed to us. If we are to take an ecclesiastical document seriously, it will not be primarily because it comes from some office in the ecclesiastical hierarchy, or because it comes from a group of people whose views are newsworthy, but because the message is grounded in God's inscripturated Word. In making their case on biblical grounds, the Roman Catholic bishops have issued a plausible invitation to Evangelicals to wrestle with what they have said.

This wrestling will be most productive if evangelical Christians are motivated by a desire to learn from the example of the Roman Catholic bishops. The bishops have clearly seen the need to address new challenges that are being raised in our technological age. As should already be obvious from the preceding remarks, they have sensed that these new challenges require new modes of thought, new ways of grappling as Christians with contemporary issues. Evangelicals have much to learn from them at this point.

It is becoming increasingly obvious that evangelical Christians must also begin to think new thoughts about contemporary challenges. When many younger evangelical scholars and activists began to struggle positively with the issues raised by the Civil Rights Movement and the protest over the Vietnam War in the 1960s and '70s, they realized that the resources available from the recent evangelical past provided very little guidance in dealing with such matters. Evangelicals had done little in the first six or seven decades of this century to lay the groundwork for a social ethic that would be adequate for contemporary social, political, and economic life.

Many Evangelicals felt it necessary, then, to explore the various traditions that lay behind nineteenth- and twentieth-century Evangelicalism: some turned to traditional Anabaptist thought, others to the writings of the Calvinist Reformation; still others explored Wesleyanism, the black church tradition, and even certain strands of Roman Catholicism. The motive for exploring these traditions has been to find resources in the past that can be used for faithful witness in the contemporary era. This also seems to be the motive that inspires the bishops' pastoral letter. Thus many Evangelicals and many Roman Catholics seem to be involved in similar projects—projects that involve the creative use of the past in speaking to the urgent issues of the present. We have much to learn from each other in these endeavors.

Indeed, Evangelicals might do well to consider the pastoral letter as the opening speech in a new Roman Catholic–evangelical dialogue. This book might be viewed, then, as an initial evangelical response. My discussion here, dealing with the way in which the bishops have treated the interaction between peace and justice, is meant as one contribution to that dialogue.

What can Evangelicals learn from the bishops on these matters? One instructive dimension of the pastoral letter has to do with matters we can loosely label "methodological." We have already referred to these matters in briefly noting some differences between the place of natural-law thinking in traditionalist and aggiornamento documents, on the one hand, and the pastoral letter, on the other. Following Father Gremillion's characterization, it can be said that traditionalist documents tend to employ a rather static notion of natural law, while the aggiornamento documents use a more dynamic conception. The pastoral letter, we have said, takes the discussion a significant step further.

The writers of the letter had to face some important issues: How does the Christian community speak to the larger society about matters of peace and justice? Can Christians assume that both church and world operate with the same, or similar, concepts of peace and justice? Roman Catholics in the past have not thought it necessary to struggle long and hard with such questions. The Roman Church taught that natural morality is common to all human beings. Everyone who thinks clearly should be able to identify some core understanding of "the common good," an understanding that will include a basic grasp of the meanings of "peace" and "justice." To be sure, these understandings will be enriched, they will be added to, by attending to the deliverances of special revelation. But such deliverances will add to what is already a common stock of notions that are embedded in our natural morality.

The more "dynamic" views of the aggiornamento documents are still variations on these traditional themes. Instead of insisting on the rational recognition of a relatively static human nature, they call for the rational recognition of human rights and they point to the value of permitting certain human potentialities to be realized.

The pastoral letter proceeds along somewhat different lines. The bishops do, of course, announce that they mean to be addressing two communities: "the Catholic faithful" and "the wider civil community, a more pluralistic audience."[7] They also make it clear that they intend to set forth, among other things, "universally binding moral principles."[8] But they choose to proceed in a manner that makes the biblical perspective the foundation of what they have to say. Having stated their desire to address both a Christian and a non-Christian audience, they chart the course of their discussion in these terms: "We propose, therefore, to discuss both the religious vision of peace among peoples and nations and the problems associated with realizing this vision in a world of sovereign states."[9]

And this is exactly the pattern of their argument: first the setting forth of the religious vision and then the wrestling with practical problems that must be faced if this biblically grounded vision is to be partially realized in our contemporary world. The bishops do not set forth two foundations for their ethical discussion: one a biblical foundation for Christians and another a rationally compelling foundation for the larger community. Their primary appeal is to a "theology of peace which should ground the task of peacemaking solidly in the biblical vision of the kingdom of God."[10] No other, more "objective," basis for their discussion is necessary:

> We believe the religious vision has an objective basis and is capable of progressive realization. Christ is our peace, for he has "made us both one, and has broken down the dividing wall of hostility . . . that he might create in himself one new man in the place of the two, so making peace, and might reconcile us both to God" (Eph. 2:14-16). We also know that this peace will be achieved fully only in the kingdom of God.[11]

Is this methodology a radical break with the Roman tradition? In one sense it is. It is simply a very different way of arguing than that which has typified past Roman Catholic documents. And it is a way of arguing that is quite compatible with many Protestant approaches, especially the style typical of Evangelicalism.

But there is also a sense in which it is a development out of the Roman Catholic past. We have already noted Father Gremillion's observation that the aggiornamento documents employed a more dynamic conception of natural law than did the traditional documents. The bishops' letter embodies an even more intensive "dynamicizing" of natural-law ideas. On the one hand the bishops want to acknowledge that it is possible for Christians to address the larger society with regard to matters of justice and peace, and to do so in a way that presupposes that there is some common understanding of "justice" and "peace." And yet they insist, at the same time, that a Christian understanding of justice and peace is deeply embedded in the biblical vision of God's kingdom. In other words, they insist on accounting for the meanings of "peace" and "justice" in pervasively biblical terms; yet they think that, in operating with these biblical understandings, they can address the practical problems of peace and justice in a way that can be grasped by the larger community.

In what way is this a "dynamicizing" of the natural-law concepts? Perhaps this can be made clearer by looking briefly at how some of these same issues have been dealt with in evangelical circles. Evangelicals have regularly insisted on a radical difference between the perspectives of "world" and "church." On a practical level these differences have been spelled in a manner shaped by pietist concerns: Christians must "flee the world"; they must not trust "worldly wisdom"; they must not make compromises with "the mind of flesh."

Theologically, these themes have been reinforced by certain strains of Calvinistic thought (although parallels can be found in the Anabaptist tradition). Many Reformed thinkers have insisted on a "radical antithesis" between Christian and non-Christian patterns of thinking. The "natural mind" is in rebellion against God. Through regenerating grace, some lost sinners are given "renewed minds." Rationality is not a "neutral" faculty. It serves the motives of "the heart." And so, some have suggested, we should not expect that the redeemed and the unredeemed will operate with the same understandings of such things as "truth," "the good," "peace," or "justice."

These ideas and emphases have been a significant presence in the attitudes and thinking of North American Evangelicals. But they have seldom been taken to the extreme. References to a "radical antithesis" have usually been accompanied by modifying statements; there is nonetheless some sort of "common ground" between believer and unbeliever, or, in other words, there are "remnants" of righteousness even in the worst of sinners.

We need not go into a detailed discussion here of the nuances of evangelical epistemology. But it is safe to say that Evangelicals have tended toward a rather dynamic understanding of the processes of reasoning and conceptualization. People reason in the context of their basic projects; and there are two very basic projects being expedited in the world: the service of God and the outworking of human rebellion. Participation in these projects gives shape to the ways in which we conceptualize such things as peace and justice. To be sure, there may be a certain created structure, or patternedness, to human thought—

"grooves" that even the worst of sinners cannot eradicate. But neither can we ignore the very basic spiritual dynamics that characterize human thought.

The bishops also have recognized—or so it would seem— these spiritual dynamics. Aggiornamento thinkers had taken one step away from a static conception of natural law, in which church and world operated with a common stock of "neutral" concepts. Now the bishops have taken a further "dynamicizing" step. They have insisted that the first words to be spoken about "peace" and "justice"—even in a letter that is addressed not only to the faithful, but also to the unbelieving world—must be biblical words. Only when the biblical message is explicated can the church go on to attempt to translate its biblically grounded vision into practical words about international relations.

And how can Evangelicals benefit from this attempt? One primary benefit is that which stems from the recognition that a kind of methodological *rapprochement* between Evangelicals and Roman Catholics is being achieved. But another benefit has to do with "modelling." The bishops have made good use of this more dynamic methodology. They have performed their magisterial task effectively. Evangelicals have not yet been very effective in speaking about societal matters in a way that is both biblically faithful and intelligible to the larger community. We have lessons to learn, and the bishops' letter is a helpful pedagogical device.

A second area where Evangelicals can learn from the pastoral letter has to do with the theological groundwork the bishops lay for understanding peace and justice. In the recent renewal of social thought among Evangelicals, evangelical social ethicists have had to combat a number of distortions and misunderstandings with regard to matters of peace and justice. More specifically, they have had to contend with two very common evangelical distortions of the biblical message regarding peace and justice: the individualizing and the eschatologizing of these themes.

Evangelicals have tended to treat peace and justice as marks of the individual life. Indeed, Evangelicals have gone through long periods in which justice—understood as a feature of social interaction—was not an important topic of discussion. Insofar as references to social justice did surface among them, they were inevitably linked to very personal relationships. Peace, on the other hand, is a favorite evangelical topic; but it has normally been thought of as an individualized "personal peace."

All of this is closely tied to the central evangelical emphasis on the relationship between the individual and God. Thus, when Evangelicals have insisted that God "is a God of justice," they have not been referring to the divine concern for the poor and the oppressed; rather, they have been signalling God's wrath toward the sins of individuals. The theological discussions of justice in evangelical circles have invariably followed the pattern described by Stephen Mott: "In classical soteriology, when God's justice, which demands death for sin, is satisfied by God's love through Christ's vicarious death, this is retributive justice, which is what justice has meant in systematic theology."[12]

This is not to say that Evangelicals have completely ignored the corporate dimensions of the Bible's message about peace and justice. No believer who reads the Scriptures can ignore the vision of a *reign* of peace and justice that is presented there. But to the degree that Evangelicals have acknowledged this dimension, they have engaged in the other distortion mentioned above: they have "eschatologized" these matters. Peace and justice, they have argued, will not appear until the future reign of Christ. One dominant strain of evangelical social thought has very explicitly tied the whole of the biblical promise of a reign of peace and righteousness to the establishment of a messianic rule in a future—literally understood—millennial period.

And so, by individualizing peace and justice, and by eschatologizing any biblical residue that cannot be squeezed into an individualizing mold, Evangelicals have gone through long periods in which they have ignored the present relevance of the biblical promise of a corporate manifestation of peace and justice. But in recent years Evangelicals have made a significant attempt to remedy these distortions, with results that are very similar to the contents of the bishops' treatment of peace and justice.

It is easy, of course, to criticize the individualizing and eschatologizing tendencies in evangelical social thought. But no assessment of these tendencies is adequate if it does not recognize that past evangelical distortions of the biblical message regarding peace and justice have been linked to some very le-

42   Richard J. Mouw

gitimate concerns. Evangelicals have been tempted to individualize and eschatologize the corporate dimensions of the biblical promise out of a proper fear of two opposing distortions that have often appeared as tendencies in the "social gospel" emphases of Protestant liberalism: a corporatizing and an immanentizing of the biblical message.

Evangelicals have not been wrong in recognizing both the importance of the individual's relationship to God and the eschatological elements of the biblical promise. Their error has consisted in the reductionistic manner in which they have often treated these themes. A healthy evangelical social ethic will not abandon the evangelical insistence that Christ Jesus came into the world to save lost sinners; nor will it ignore the marvelous biblical promise that this same Jesus will someday appear on clouds of glory to manifest his Kingship. But it will insist that redeemed sinners must engage, here and now, in acts of corporate witness, in anticipation of the New Age that is to come.

On these matters, the bishops strike the proper note. Throughout their discussion of the "religious vision" they are concerned to integrate two pairs of themes: the individual and the corporate, the here-and-now and the "not yet" of the kingdom. Each of these themes finds its proper place in this summary statement:

> The fulness of eschatological peace remains before us in hope, and yet the gift of peace is already ours in the reconciliation effected in Jesus Christ. These two profoundly religious meanings of peace inform and influence all other meanings for Christians. Because we have been gifted with God's peace in the risen Christ, we are called to our own peace and to the making of peace in our world. As disciples and as children of God it is our task to seek for ways in which to make the forgiveness, justice and mercy, and love of God visible in a world where violence and enmity are too often the norm. When we listen to God's word, we hear again and always the call to repentance and to belief: to repentance because, although we are redeemed, we continue to need redemption; to belief because, although the reign of God is near, it is still seeking its fulness.[13]

A third instructive element in the pastoral letter is its ethical treatment of the tensions between justice and peace. The shape of the bishops' treatment of these tensions is seen in this passage:

> In the kingdom of God, peace and justice will be fully realized. Justice is always the foundation of peace. In history, efforts to

pursue both peace and justice are at times in tension, and the struggle for justice may threaten certain forms of peace.

It is within this tension of kingdom and history that Catholic teaching has addressed the problem of war.[14]

The language of "tension" here is quite appropriate. It is difficult to know how to avoid it in dealing with these issues. But the bishops are careful to point out that the experience of tension in this area is a characteristic of our present place in sinful history. Ultimately the tensions can be and will be resolved in the New Age, in that kingdom wherein justice and peace will exist in a harmonious relationship. And not only must Christians acknowledge this eschatological resolution of tensions as a biblical promise, but this acknowledgment must shape our present approach to the tensions: "Peace must be built on the basis of justice in a world where the personal and social consequences of sin are evident."[15]

But this is no easy task. A concern to do justice—a concern to halt aggression and restore human rights—will in many situations require actions and policies that violate the apparent demands of peacemaking. And a concern for peacemaking may lead us to tolerate situations in which the claims of justice are violated. Ultimately, of course, there can be no real conflict here. The bishops regularly insist that "secular" definitions of peace and justice are inadequate. Peace, biblically understood, is more than the cessation of hostilities; justice, biblically understood, is more than the halting of aggression. True peace cannot be attained without true justice, and vice versa. The Christian hope is for a just peace, a peaceful justice.

In sinful history, however, Christians who hope for a harmonious reign of peace and justice will often be torn between conflicting options:

> We must recognize the reality of the paradox we face as Christians living in the context of the world as it presently exists; we must continue to articulate our belief that love is possible and the only real hope for all human relations, and yet accept that force, even deadly force, is sometimes justified and that nations must provide for their defense. It is the mandate of Christians in the face of this paradox to strive to resolve it through an even greater commitment to Christ and his message.[16]

These are noble sentiments, and they have a familiar ring to those of us who make it our business to read (and occasionally to help write) ecclesiastical documents on social issues. The virtue of the bishops' expression of these sentiments is that the expression appears, not at the end of the document, but near the beginning. Their call to a "greater commitment to Christ and his message" is not a final rhetorical flourish, but a preface to careful and detailed deliberation on some of the difficult issues of war and peace in a nuclear age.

Others in this volume will comment in detail on various aspects of their practical policy proposals. It will suffice here to comment briefly on the general pattern of the advice that they give to both state and church.

Given the present tensions of our sinful history, how should governments conduct their military policies in a nuclear age? It is important to note here that in spite of the public statements of several individual bishops, to the effect that they are "pacifists" or "nuclear pacifists" or of a mind to abandon traditional just-war doctrine, it is clear that the pastoral letter stands firmly in the just-war tradition when it discusses the obligations of governments: "force, even deadly force, is sometimes justified and . . . nations must provide for their defense"; "governments threatened by armed, unjust aggression *must* defend their people."[17] Although there are references in the letter to the need for new perspectives on war and peace in the light of the "new moment" occasioned by the nuclear threat, the basic thrust of the bishops' argument is that the traditional just-war criteria still provide a proper context for assessing military policy and strategy. And their overall conclusion is that these criteria forbid the actual use of weapons of mass destruction, and that they also raise serious doubts about the mere possession of such weapons.

But the bishops are also concerned to highlight some of the underlying concerns of just-war theory. The use of military violence may never be divorced from a desire for peace. This has important implications for a Christian perspective on modern versions of militarism and nationalism. Similarly, the bishops are insistent on the relevance of the biblical command to love one's neighbor for the conduct of military affairs. They are not happy with an ethical emphasis that bifurcates love and justice: "We should do no harm to our neighbors; how we treat our enemy is the key test of whether we love our neighbor; and the possibility of taking even one human life is a prospect we should consider in fear and trembling."[18]

The bishops are not "pacifists" in the advice that they give to governments. But they are insistent that a recognition of the legitimacy of lethal violence under certain conditions is still a far cry from endorsing the kinds of violent solutions to international problems that governments often consider. The bishops call governments to commit themselves to peacemaking. And in doing so, they show a sensitivity to the kind of concern that John Calvin expressed when he insisted that "we must perform much more than the heathen philosopher required when he wanted war to seem a seeking of peace."[19]

Within the life of the Christian community, on the other hand, the bishops endorse the legitimacy of pacifist commitments. They take great pains in stressing the acceptability of pacifism. The Church must accept both pacifism and nonpacifism as "distinct moral responses having a complementary relationship."[20] Indeed,

> the "new moment" in which we find ourselves sees the just-war teaching and non-violence as distinct but interdependent methods of evaluating warfare. They diverge on some specific conclusions, but they share a common presumption against the use of force as a means of settling disputes.[21]

Not all pacifists will appreciate being "tamed" in this manner. In fact, some defenders of nonviolence have complained that the bishops' treatment amounts to a "marginalization" of pacifism. And there is some legitimacy to this complaint. In one sense, pacifism and just-war theory are exclusive claims: either lethal violence is sometimes morally justified, or it is not. Insofar as the bishops are saying that violence is in fact morally justified under certain conditions, they are indeed rejecting a principled pacifism. And insofar as they are also insisting that pacifists must nonetheless be tolerated within the Christian community, they might be thought of as "marginalizing" that point of view.

But the bishops are doing more than advocating a mere toleration of pacifism. They are encouraging it: "it is incumbent upon us to stress to our own community and to the wider society the significance of . . . support for a pacifist option."[22] The tone of their discussion of nonviolence makes it clear that this is not a grudging support. The bishops are clearly worried about the ways in which the just-war doctrine has been used in history to provide a moral gloss for militaristic programs. This worry, along with a genuine fear of the awesome destructive potential of contemporary weaponry, leads them to go well beyond their predecessors in offering a positive appraisal of the pacifist option.

A commitment to just-war teaching has been characteristic of the mainstream of both Roman Catholicism and Evangelicalism. Indeed, a belief in the morally justified use of violence has been treated as having a virtual *status confessionis* in these communities in the past. Nonetheless, each community has included pacifist subgroups: the Catholic Workers and other organizations in Roman Catholicism, and various evangelically inclined Mennonites, Quakers, and Brethren who have functioned somewhat uneasily within the conservative-evangelical camp.

The Roman Catholic commitment to the just-war doctrine, however, has been maintained in a somewhat more nuanced manner than has been the case in Evangelicalism. The nuances have been made possible by the Roman Catholic emphasis on "special vocations" and "special vows." The existence of "orders" in Roman Catholicism has made it possible for people to pursue special lifestyles and commitments without thereby standing in judgment on all those fellow believers who do not exhibit the same patterns of living. A commitment to nonviolence has a long tradition, for example, in monastic communities. It is not a coincidence that the bishops, in discussing the merits of specific nonviolent experiments, refer to the commitment to nonviolence required of lay members of the Third Order of Franciscans.[23]

Perhaps it is better to think, then, of the pastoral letter as advocating, not a "marginalization" of nonviolence, but a "vocationalization" of pacifism. Here too Evangelicals can learn something very important from the letter. There is no need for pacifists to fear being "marginalized" in the evangelical world. If mainstream Evangelicals could be heard uttering sympathetic words about pacifism, this could only be taken as a sign of progress, given the long history of official and quasi-official condemnations of pacifism in many mainline evangelical groups.

Roman Catholicism, by virtue of its numbers and cultural diversity, has had to develop structures and attitudes in which a certain degree of pluralism could flourish. Evangelicals, because of their own unique histories of dissent, have had to learn to draw sharp boundary lines of belief and practice. A pluralistic emphasis on "special vocations" has not had the opportunity to take root in the evangelical community. But the time seems to have arrived for Evangelicals to follow the example of Roman Catholicism and encourage specific individuals and groups to specialize in nonviolent ministries of peacemaking.

These comments have focused primarily on the ways in which evangelical Christians can profit from a careful study of the pastoral letter. But, at the risk of evangelical immodesty, it must also be said that a more intense evangelical–Roman Catholic dialogue will undoubtedly be profitable for both sides. The pastoral letter is an expression of a new Roman Catholicism. There are also many indications on the present scene of a new Evangelicalism. The two parties have much to talk about.

The increasing biblical sensitivities of Roman Catholicism are introducing new themes—or at least new nuances—into its self-descriptions. At one point in their discussion, where they are describing the present Christian pattern of living between the "already" and the "not yet" of the kingdom of God, the bishops confess that "we are a pilgrim people in a world marked by conflict and injustice."[24]

This is not the first time that Roman Catholics have described their earthly mission in terms of a pilgrimage. But it is perhaps the first time that an official Roman Catholic document uses this term of self-description in a way in which evangelical Protestants will be convinced they really mean it. The bishops have created a theological context in their letter in which the words "pilgrim people" seem to flow naturally and honestly from their lips. The bishops, in writing this letter, have not set themselves up primarily as gifted interpreters of a "natural law" available to all "men of good conscience." Rather, they have chosen to speak as servants of a Word that alone can shed light on the fundamental dilemmas of human existence. They have formulated a case that will make consistent sense only to those whose consciences have been cleansed by the blood of the Cross, and whose hearts long for the coming Reign.

In the past Roman Catholics and Protestants have argued

their methodological cases in terms of how, if at all, our loyalties are to be divided between Athens and Jerusalem. But a true "pilgrim people" will identify themselves with neither of these cities. Instead, they will join their Lord at the place to which the writer to the Hebrews calls them: "Therefore let us go forth to him outside the camp, bearing abuse for him. For here we have no lasting city, but we seek the city which is to come" (Heb. 13:13-14).

Evangelicals have attempted for a long time to live "outside the camp" as a pilgrim people. But they have also gone through long periods of silence, in which they have felt no need to speak words of justice and peace to the citizens of the cities of this world. Lately, however, they have begun to prophesy about such things from "outside the camp."

And now the Roman Catholic bishops have spoken prophetic words as a "pilgrim people." Their fellow Christian pilgrims are much in their debt. Perhaps the time has come to find new ways to speak and act together as we travel together toward the City of God.

II: The Just War
in a Nuclear Age

3: Jus ad Bellum: Just-War Theory and Deterrence

HUBERT MORKEN

The Rev. Billy Graham in 1982 risked the disapproval of his friends, the contempt of his enemies, the manipulations of the Soviets, and the distortions of the world's press to speak out against nuclear war. Staking his reputation on the integrity of his appeal and the support he felt from God for this mission, our generation's greatest evangelist committed his talents and spiritual gifts to the cause of world peace.[1] Personal salvation, the primary focus of Graham's gospel message for four decades, momentarily took second place to this appeal. From the perspective of many observers, the evangelist had ineptly gone political.

However, for more than ten years now, Evangelicals have shown concern for the political implications of biblical faith. The kingdom of God clearly is not just a personal matter. Hence our God-given task, as we understand it, is to recover, with the help of the Holy Spirit and under the controlling authority of the Scriptures, the full social meaning of the gospel. Evangelicals led publicly by Billy Graham are attempting to integrate personal faith with social concern especially as we address the nuclear problem.[2]

Recently the Roman Catholic Church called for a patient and arduous construction of a mature theology of peace that will itself help to bring peace to the earth. "The Challenge of Peace," issued by the U.S. bishops in the spring of 1983, is presented as a pastoral letter, yet it is written to believer and unbeliever alike. As we interpret this letter from an evangelical perspective, we find certain evangelical themes. The complex argumentation of the bishops, which we must sort through if we are to understand them, almost obscures their conclusion, which we share, that America is largely lost. Toward the end of the letter the bishops conclude that we, as a people, are far away from God. The bishops write,

> We must ask how long a nation willing to extend a constitutional guarantee to the "right" to kill defenseless human beings by abortion is likely to refrain from adopting strategic warfare policies deliberately designed to kill millions of defenseless human beings if adopting them should come to seem "expedient."[3]

And sensing that matters will get worse before they can improve they say,

> We readily recognize that we live in a world that is becoming increasingly estranged from Christian values. In order to remain a Christian, one must take a resolute stand against many commonly accepted axioms of the world. To become true disciples, we must undergo a demanding course of induction into the adult Christian community.[4]

Getting to the core of the matter in terms familiar to Evangelicals, Pentecostals, and Fundamentalists, the bishops argue,

> All of the values we are promoting in this letter rest ultimately in the disarmament of the human heart and the conversion of the human spirit to God who alone can give authentic peace.[5]

The pastoral letter, which has many purposes, must also be read as a witnessing tract, which attempts to gain a foothold for the gospel in the minds and hearts of Americans. What thoughtful person today wants to look backward in history for the answer to a problem like nuclear weapons? Yet it is precisely that connection, the one between Jesus Christ the historical person and the present threat of war, which the bishops hope to establish in a way that is credible to modern people and to themselves.

If the gospel is true, then perhaps in its light and only in its light will the nuclear threat of our age make sense. Making sense of what is going on, that is, trying to understand how and why the human race would have reached such an impasse and finding a way out, forces us to pose essentially religious questions. The hunger to understand the meaning of war and peace will lead us to theology as the bishops understood, to the Scriptures, and ultimately to God. Conversely, by starting at this point of human need, the gospel itself will begin to make sense where otherwise it would appear irrelevant to our human destiny.[6]

In short, by writing this epistle the bishops show that more is at stake than physical survival. In his mercy, God allows our sin and its consequences to wake us up to our need for redemption. That we are in trouble, all people readily acknowledge, but the church and those who understand the biblical message view this trouble as a way to alert humankind to its need for God.

THE THREAT OF WAR—GOD'S PERSPECTIVE

Before we address the specific issue of just-war theory and deterrence, let us ask more deeply than we commonly do why we are facing the nuclear problem. The bishops' letter partly attributes the arms race to the absence of a central political authority capable of bringing peace and justice to the earth. The bishops also blame war on sin and its consequences, which permeate the whole of human history. All Christians may agree with these explanations, yet we must still wonder, in the light of God's love and power, about the perilous position we are in today. Why then have matters reached such an impasse?[7]

Modern people want peace and justice without paying the price of submission to God. We struggle mightily to resolve our immediate, tangible problems and barely lift a finger to search for our Creator. In the face of this defiance, perhaps God is not as helpless as we might suppose. Might the Lord leave us in our terrible danger as long as we prefer our independence?[8]

The most basic explanation for why we face nuclear destruction today may be in the terrible sin of idolatry that modern people commit when they ignore God, choosing to live without worship, law, and prayer. Abortion is only one consequence of this larger sin. If the threat of nuclear annihilation is total, encompassing the very earth, the sin of idolatry is also total, cutting us off from the very source of life. One and only one present reality matches in scope and importance the danger of war and that is our spiritual lostness as a civilization. "Without faith it is impossible to please God," and with unbelief war could be inevitable.[9]

We know from the Scriptures that God judges whole nations, their people, and their governments by war. Not every war is punishment for sin but some wars are. Let us ask two distinct but related questions. First, what kinds of war does God allow or support for reasons that are sufficient for him in working out his purposes on the earth? And second, what kinds of wars ought nations or the godly to fight if they must? The first question deals with the purposes of war from God's perspective and the second with the limitations of war that nations ought in humility to respect if they are to fight. We note in passing that there are wars that God supports in some sense, that are unjust wars by common definition.

In the book of Amos, which deals with both questions mentioned above, we read that for three sins of Damascus, even for four, "I will not turn back my wrath . . .; for three sins of Gaza, even for four, I will not turn back my wrath . . .; for three sins of Israel, even for four, I will not turn back my wrath." This formula, "for three sins, even for four," expresses the limited patience of God. He will not favor war against nations until they have so violated his standards that destruction alone will be sufficient to limit their evil and teach righteousness. War is not just tragedy, it is not just evil, it is not just a result of ignorance, it is not just structural or accidental, it is also a way God corrects arrogant nations full of unbelief. Pride comes before a fall.[10]

The book of Jonah is an ethical primer for prophets who favor the destruction of evil nations. In the bizarre story of Jonah's aborted mission, which turned out to be surprisingly successful, we see the depth of God's mercy when dealing with stubborn national pride. At the end of the account, the Lord explains that these Ninevites, cruel though they may be, are so ignorant in matters of morals that they are not unlike common cattle—but like the cattle they serve God's purposes better by being alive.[11]

God's instruction of the nations has just begun. We are far from learning what he intends, yet we can count on the kind of patience that allows a pirate nation like Nineveh, which was built by conquest of its neighbors, to survive at least temporarily. The unrighteous will not stand for long in history but neither will they be struck down prematurely.

In the prophets we are told that "[God] will not fail or be discouraged till he has established justice in the earth."[12] However, such promises for the kingdom hinge in part on the very presence of God. According to the Scriptures, the nations will obtain justice and peace as they receive the source of justice and peace. For this reason there should be no call for peace without a call for repentance and worship. One does sense a double concern in the bishops' call for us to read "the sign of the times"—one evangelical, calling us to repentance as a civilization; the other political, helping to prepare us to make the "conscious" choices and "deliberate" policies that will enable us to survive. In short, the requirements of peace are spiritual and political.[13]

Both Evangelicals and the Roman Catholic Church are beginning to see the connections between evangelism, social concern, and modern war. Secure in evangelism, Protestants are exploring the social implications of the gospel. Secure in their heritage of philosophic discourse, Catholics are beginning to go public with the gospel. Let us turn now to the specific matter of a just war fought for acceptable reasons. On this subject, the bishops' letter has much to teach us.

JUST WAR AND DETERRENCE—
THE PASTORAL PERSPECTIVE

According to Roman Catholic teaching the governments of nations have the obligation to protect their citizens from armed attack, and those same citizens may be required to serve in the military to preserve "peace of a sort." Defending people and nations from attack and preventing their subjugation is a duty of government before God from this perspective. Consequently a Christian citizen must not "casually disregard" his defense obligation—"faced with the fact of attack on the innocent, the presumption that we do no harm even to our enemy yielded to the command of love understood as a need to restrain an enemy who would injure the innocent."[14]

To guide governments in their duties, the church in earlier centuries formulated a set of principles to govern the conduct of war. Peace, the final purpose of God for the earth, had to give way to a secondary goal of limiting conflicts, preventing them where possible, and bringing wars to an early end. The Church argued the following about wars:

Just war—should have a just cause, that is, the protection and the preservation of a people.

Competent authority—should be engaged in only by the recognized public authorities and not by private initiative.

Comparative justice—should have issues at stake so serious that they override the terrible consequences of war.

Right intention—should be motivated by a concern and respect for the threatened victims and the aggressor.

Last resort—should come only after diplomatic and other initiatives have failed.

Probability of success—should be fought where winning is possible or losing is an honorable outcome.

Proportionality—should result in a greater good than the consequences of mere submission to the aggressor.

Discrimination—should protect the lives of noncombatant civilians.

In this theory wars should be avoided whenever possible and fought with reluctance and restraint where necessary. Patriotism remains a good thing and warrior virtues like courage and self-sacrifice are lauded.[15]

In discussing "Jus ad Bellum; Why and When Recourse to War is Permissible," the bishops conclude that there are no reasons and no circumstances that justify the use of nuclear weapons or conventional weapons that might lead to a nuclear conflict. Defensive war, once considered a duty if the lives of an innocent people were at stake, is now ruled out, precisely because its results would be to kill large numbers of innocent people. The risks involved in any war between the Soviet Union and the United States are so grave that no government of either country should for any reason decide to fight the other superpower, even on a limited scale.[16]

All the values we hold dear—peace, liberty, justice, prosperity, fraternity, religious freedom, and national independence—according to the bishops, are not sufficient in themselves to justify a nuclear holocaust, for life is the precondition, the necessary requirement, for all these values. The bishops say that we must have peace first if we are to have justice or freedom.[17]

What is the use, then, of the old just-war principles that would have no purpose once the earth were reduced to an ash heap? Might they not have value as restraining influences helping to prevent a war? Can we use them to help us steer a course out of our current nuclear stalemate toward a more peaceful world? The bishops tell us just that: just-war theory must be, in the nuclear age, not a way to fight a limited war but rather a way to prevent war. By applying just-war principles in this new way to current military practice, doctrine, strategy, and preparations, we can begin to harness the arms race, preparing the way for international peacekeeping arrangements. The bishops suggest that we follow guidelines foundational for peace.[18] The eight just-war principles used in prenuclear years as guidelines for war can now appropriately be used only to limit deterrence policy:

Just war—The goal of defense policy must be peace and not war of any kind and certainly not world conquest or the destruction of the enemy.

Competent authority—In the American context, the Congress of the United States and people of this democracy share responsibility for ensuring that no chief executive acts on his own to bring war.

Comparative justice—To prevent national arrogance and reduce the risk of war, Americans must consider the failings of our government and society and the virtues of Russian government and culture before we enter any dispute with Moscow.

Right intention—Peaceful motives well cultivated will enhance a calm and reasonable approach to potential problems with our ideological adversary.

Last resort—Looking first to international organizations for remedies to national disputes, we should rely only reluctantly and tentatively on our military deterrent systems.

Probability of success—Knowing that any serious conflict may lead to war, we must act with great caution and reserve in great power relations.

Proportionality—Deterrent systems ought to seek to minimize any potential destruction except to the exact target, and be viewed only as a necessary, temporary expedient.

Discrimination—Weapons should be aimed against military targets only and should not appear to threaten civilian lives, or even too much the armed forces of the potential adversary.

The specific problem that most alarmed the bishops is a nuclear arms race out of control. The stockpiling of thousands of warheads, the building of increasingly accurate and reliable rockets, the multiplication of delivery systems, the training of troops in tactical nuclear warfare, although all these are done in the name of deterrence, make war look more likely. According to the bishops, the paradox of deterrence is that the more effective and complete our deterrence system, the less we have a full guarantee that war will not take place. The efforts we make, built on the premise that we must have strength at all points of possible conflict, leave us vulnerable in an all-important way. Strength alone will not prevent accident, miscalculation, madness, or evil intentions; any of these may lead to war. The very deterrent strength that minimizes the chances of war cannot by itself guarantee peace. And in these circumstances the mere possibility of war is too frightening to contemplate. Sooner or later, the bishops say, we must have international control of such weapons technology and an end to the arms race. This is a sign of the times, say the bishops.[19]

JUST WAR AND DETERRENCE— SECULAR PERSPECTIVES

For a group of professors from Harvard who are expert in nuclear subjects, uncertainty about what will happen in a conflict between the superpowers is not a sign of prophetic significance at all, but rather a present constraint on Moscow and Washington that helps to keep the peace. The paradox of deterrence (that we need to have redundant nuclear weapons systems that can be used in any and all circumstances on a local or global scale, in order to make sure that we don't use them) works, these scientists claim, partly because no one knows for sure what the nuclear powers will do in a crisis. In addition, we must have weapons that are usable but not too effective, that is, not capable of winning a war cleanly, easily, with few casualties suffered by the winner. Living with nuclear weapons that are a threat but not too great a threat to the other side becomes, for the Harvard scientists, *the* requirement for peace in this period of great power struggle:

> There will continue to be an uneasy balance between the degree of control required to ensure that weapons are not used accidentally and the degree of "usability" required to ensure that the weapons can be used if needed. Preventing accidental use is an important goal, but it cannot be the only objective of a nuclear weapons policy. Nuclear weapons must be usable enough to provide credible deterrence, but not so usable as to invite unintended use.[20]

The bishops and the Harvard scientists both see deterrence as necessary to protect the West from possible assault by Moscow. The bishops see it as an ultimately self-defeating approach while the scientists view this as a necessary strategy for the foreseeable future. In specific terms, the bishops want governments to promise that they will never initiate the first use of nuclear weapons, and ask them not to make war plans or practice war games that make war look practical. The Harvard scientists, on the other hand, see deterrence as all one package. Even if a nation were to promise never to use nuclear weapons, they say, no one could be sure that that nation would live up to its word. In a world full of duplicity, the mere promise not to use the weapons could lead to one side's risking war, falsely secure in the illusion that the other side would not strike back.[21]

From a secular perspective a declaration not to use nuclear weapons would undermine the credibility of deterrence and increase the chance of war. From a religious perspective, the threat to use the bombs makes the unthinkable seem that much more plausible and, besides that, makes our expressed intentions immoral. In conclusion, the threat to use nuclear weapons may restrain an enemy but it certainly reduces restraints on the power making that threat.

JUST WAR AND DETERRENCE— COMMUNIST PERSPECTIVES

The genius of the West, according to Jacques Ellul, is that we know the whole human project is a "conscious, deliberate business." Seeing that we are not the victims of fate or history but rather a free people releases our vitality. However, this sense of freedom that has led us to take responsibility for our actions both as individuals and nations has in fact given us a "bad conscience." When we fail to live up to our principles, we are the first to know, though we may not confess it so. We proclaim peace in the West, but we build our war machines, and condemn ourselves for doing what we must do.[22]

The Chinese Communists, on the other hand, do not have such constraints. Chinese defense theory is free of reflective doubt. Moreover, for its part, China has worked very hard to sell the United States on its version of deterrence. The Chinese place great stress on the vulnerability of the Russians, claiming that ethnic minorities and the uncertain support of their East European allies make the Soviet Union far weaker than it appears. Refusing to be overawed by Russian military preparations, the Chinese suggest a tough "quid pro quo" response to any aggressive Soviet actions. China claims that Moscow will not likely risk full-scale war, East or West, but that if it did, it would lose because of U.S. technical superiority and Chinese invincibility. China is prepared to hold its own on the Russian border, and expects the United States to maintain its alliances and bases in South Korea, Japan, and the Philippines.[23]

Within this Machiavellian way of thinking, the Chinese view our second thoughts about deterrence as a corruption of the will, certainly a sign of bourgeois decline. Morality has always seemed to be the vice of the weak, especially from a Marxist perspective. Though we may reject totally this persuasion, we must know that in our dealings with that part of the world relatively untouched by biblical teaching, the bishops' call for restraint and for peace will be misinterpreted as a failure of nerve and even as an abandonment of principle.

Andrei Sakharov, like the Chinese, truly alarmed that the Soviet Union would perhaps attempt to exploit the "weakness" of the morally sensitive West, recently wrote a letter from his place of exile within the Soviet Union that was widely reported in the Western press. Sakharov reached conclusions similar to those of the bishops:

1. Large-scale nuclear war could not be a legitimately defensive war and would be collective suicide.

2. Limited nuclear war would be most difficult to control and most probably would escalate into a world war.
3. Nuclear weapons are only a temporary though necessary deterrent.[24]

Sakharov went on, however, to argue forcefully in favor of what the bishops reluctantly supported, namely, the increase of conventional forces to deter any conventional Soviet attack on Western Europe. Sakharov thinks that to protect world peace, there must be strategic parity in conventional and nuclear weapons. Clearly, he fears possible aggression by the Soviets in Europe or the Middle East in the next few years more than the immediate consequences of the arms race. The Harvard group of scientists, the Chinese Communists, and Andrei Sakharov are concerned that our domestic American debate on nuclear arms may blind us to the Soviet threat.

JUST WAR AND DETERRENCE— EVANGELICAL PERSPECTIVES

What has been the response of the evangelical community to this now worldwide debate on nuclear arms and defense policy? Polls taken by organizations using modern statistical methods attempt to give us an accurate cross section of evangelical community opinion. Articles in books and magazines as well as conferences give us some sense of how the leadership of evangelical institutions view the issues. Debate within this American Protestant tradition is largely still within just-war assumptions held in common with the Roman Catholic Church. But more credence is now being given to the nonresistance doctrines of the peace churches, Mennonite and Quaker.[25]

Much as within the Roman Catholic Church, Evangelicals divide over the extent to which current deterrence theory and practice are to be trusted. However, most Evangelicals:

1. Trust their governments' handling of the nuclear issue.
2. Are more worried about possible Russian arms supremacy than about the arms race.
3. Favor a verifiable nuclear freeze but do not expect the Russians to accept this proposal.
4. Support the possession of nuclear arms for defensive purposes only.

This sampling confirms the notion that Evangelicals, like the general public, favor both arms control and a strong defense.[26]

One can understand evangelical public opinion as simply a reflection of the general climate of opinion, which is heavily influenced by the media, by government propaganda, by the antinuclear movement, and by common sense. However, Evangelicals also take positions that are related to biblical truth. The Bible lays great stress on two somewhat contradictory teachings that condition our approach to defensive war in the nuclear age.

First, the Bible stresses submission to governmental authority as instituted by God. Believers were told by the Apostle Paul to respect and honor the very government officials who were persecuting the followers of Christ. Romans 13 has long been an anchor for the church, because it taught that government did not have to be perfect to be considered a minister or servant of the Lord. A church that understands God's laws and divine purposes for government is not allowed to reject the average or below average human institutions and leaders, who so often seem to be irresponsible, ignorant, or worse.[27]

Widespread evangelical support for President Reagan's approach to nuclear arms is partly due to our biblical perspective that leaders are to be trusted in affairs of state. Some evangelical scholars agree, perhaps especially if they have been educated or trained in government. A recent article by one of these scholars argues forcefully that the conclusions of government leaders— that the American defense system may be inadequate to deter Soviet aggression and that we ought to strengthen that system— are correct. To be in favor of a nuclear freeze and to give strong support to a nuclear buildup would seem illogical or double-minded but, given the twin challenge of resisting the arms race and the Soviet menace, this contradictory program is popular.[28]

Furthermore, some evangelical scholars are wary of the recent attacks on nuclear deterrence policy. They are convinced that the church cannot in any special way understand the complex technical problems being discussed. Mere citizens, they claim, even Christian citizens or bishops, are unable to master the delicate arts of statecraft on which peace largely depends.

> In consequence, individual citizens are likely to be placed in situations where as a practical matter they cannot make a sound decision because they lack either knowledge or power or both.

Therefore, it is all the more necessary for governments, or more specifically, for the individuals who act as rulers and make collectively binding decisions, to make the greatest possible effort not to usurp or abuse the moral integrity of the citizens by compelling them to perform actions that, if fully understood, they would reject.[29]

Widespread debate of nuclear policy from this perspective is suspect at the start. Democracy requires an alert, concerned citizenry; but if the people attempt to seize control of policy, refusing to trust their leaders, mob feelings easily manipulated will rule. God designed government, even in a corrupt world, to rely on the discretion of leaders.[30]

The first biblical teaching that we have been treating does not respect too highly the moral reasoning of philosophers, theologians, or teachers, for those charged with understanding and speaking words of truth are not to be put in charge of government. To give prophetic voices the reins of government would be disastrous. Courage and cunning, the making of plans and the discernment of motives are what we need in government, according to this perspective. Abstract reasoning in the political arena has limited value because we see through a glass darkly. Consequently, those citizens who claim to know what is to be done to bring peace are not to be followed. It is not unreasonable, from this somewhat skeptical position, to respect power, authority, and structure more than the knowledge of the few, which has so often failed in the past.

Are we as a nation to place our trust in carefully articulated moral principles or in our power? Most Evangelicals reject this dilemma and prefer to turn to government leaders, who it is hoped are so skillful and so moral that, with God's help, they will steer the ship of state through the treacherous waters ahead.

The American evangelical public continues to place great trust in the authority the American people delegate to their leaders. There is a growing sense, however, that government does not have the answers to the nuclear problem and may not be capable of preserving peace. Recent support for the nuclear freeze among Evangelicals is an indication that this sentiment is real and growing.

History teaches us that if knowledgeable moral experts so often fail, so does government. A second biblical teaching on war and government recognizes that God judges nations for how they conduct their wars. Furthermore, common people have a right to challenge the decisions of their leaders, according to the Scriptures. One of the earliest examples of a man of God resisting a decision to destroy a city is found in Genesis 19. In this passage, Abraham appeals to the Lord—"who is traveling incognito"—to save the city of Sodom from destruction, for the sake of the innocent who lived within its walls. Abraham asked a question that we now in a slightly changed form ask the nuclear planners of the great superpowers:

> Will you sweep away the righteous with the wicked? What if there are 50 righteous people in the city? Will you really sweep it away and not spare the place for the sake of 50 righteous people in it? Far be it from you to do such a thing—to kill the righteous with the wicked, treating the righteous and the wicked alike. Far be it from you! Will not the Judge of all the earth do right?[31]

This bartering for lives ends with Abraham's plea to spare the city for the sake of ten innocent residents and the Lord's response that he would indeed spare the city for the sake of ten. From this early discussion we learn that God loves to spare the righteous from the punishment that wicked cities or nations deserve, but we also learn that perhaps no one living in such places is truly innocent.

Abraham was told by the Lord to teach his children and eventually the world to understand righteousness and justice. Speaking as one who loved his brother, he fought for the future of Sodom. As private citizens evangelical scholars find themselves in the position of Abraham today. Profoundly disturbed by a policy of deterrence that threatens to destroy everyone, they challenge it, looking for a better way. However, when these scholars examine the alternatives before us, asking what we are to do—

> In a limited war with limited ends forced on us by violent aggression, when the alternatives are either to let unjust violence rampage unchecked against innocent populations or else to let others without our aid attempt to check the assault, can a Christian fight?[32]—

they have trouble coming up with definite answers because any war, even one we think God could support at least in theory, may be our last.[33]

JUST WAR AND DETERRENCE—CONCLUSION

Security once lay in the restrained use of power. Today we have security systems that are hard to restrain, and enormous power that is itself vulnerable to attack. Some press for restraint, others for invulnerability. We can be sure that this debate, raised in America to new levels of intelligent concern by the bishops' pastoral letter, will continue. Meanwhile we must continue to exercise wisely our civic duty in this matter.

God is the source of all the peace that we enjoy, whether it comes primarily through government authority or through the efforts of a peace movement led partly by religious activists. Biblical teaching encourages us to trust those in authority but it also asks that we challenge them. No single vocation has a corner on peace or its requirements.

The Bible, as the book of Proverbs indicates, would lead us into the marketplace in our search for wisdom, where neither public official nor religious teacher has full authority because neither the great nor the wise are able to either fully understand or bring peace. Human wisdom refined by philosophy and governed by the Scriptures will help. Alert and humble government leadership is vital. Yet in the end more than deliberate, conscious effort will be required of us. We need faith and the very presence of God, and they begin with the fear of the Lord, that is, the groaning of the very creation toward its Source.

We have a growing sense as Christians that there are more intimate connections between evangelism and the threat of nuclear war than we may have supposed. Evil on so massive a scale has apocalyptic significance. It may even be God's judgment on our civilization. In contrast to the world's opinion, to be fully mature on God's terms requires dependence on grace and responsible rule of the earth. Peace without submission to God appears beyond our reach by God's design.

4: Jus in Bello: Discrimination, Proportionality, and Nuclear Weapons

Theodore R. Malloch and James W. Skillen

We applaud the National Conference of Catholic Bishops for their pastoral letter on war and peace. The "just-war" framework that undergirds their serious interpretation and evaluation of contemporary military and political realities remains a powerful light illuminating the darkness of human warfare and the political strategies from which warfare arises. Most Protestants share the assumptions of the "just-war" doctrine, and thus it is possible for them to benefit greatly from the bishops' pastoral letter.[1] We have certainly gained much from it.

In our reading of the text we have found few details to criticize. Part I, dealing with Old and New Testament teaching about peace and the kingdom of God, is especially inspiring and substantial, as is the section dealing with just-war criteria (*jus ad bellum*). However, the open-ended nature of the nuclear weapons debate requires comment on two general and two particular issues of great importance in the pastoral. The first general point concerns the nature of public responsibility for government policy, and the second concerns the dilemma or ambiguity of a qualified acceptance of nuclear deterrence doctrine. The two particular issues that will concern us are the criteria of "proportionality" and "discrimination" in the "just-war" doctrine itself as they relate to deterrence strategy.

66

CHRISTIANS AS CITIZENS

The pastoral letter is written primarily as moral advice to Catholic laypeople from the bishops. This exercise recognizes morally obligating principles, morally constraining principles, and morally enlightening principles. The bishops are quick to point out that their contribution is not primarily technical or political but rather moral and religious. Their judgments are made "as moral teachers, not as technical experts."[2]

At the same time, throughout the letter the bishops express concern about some of the actual U.S. foreign and military policies that have unfolded during the last forty years, leading to the present nuclear arms spiral.[3] Why are some of the present policies so problematic? Why are we facing a crisis? At the very least it seems clear that over the past several decades the U.S. government, supported by a majority of the citizenry, has made some questionable military choices of an integral political, moral, and technical nature. It is hardly the case that the United States is solely to blame for the present nuclear spiral, but America does bear partial responsibility for the current predicament.

If U.S. policy has flaws and needs some corrections, what will be required? Obviously this demands more than some general moral advice; we need new policies of a detailed political and technical sort. Who will be responsible for these? The government, of course? How will the government come up with cogent, just, and healthy policies? Through the efforts of those who make policy in the Congress and the Administration under the influence of electoral and lobbying pressures from American citizens. What, then, do citizens and government policymakers, especially *Christian* citizens and policymakers, need in order to be able to change or continue government policies? They need to develop and support policy alternatives consistent with principles that define or qualify a just state and a just government. The crux of the issue for Christians, therefore, is a Christian understanding of the state and of their faithful service as citizens in shaping and influencing public policy.

What have the Catholic bishops offered in this regard? They have only briefly referred to the state; they have only lightly touched on the need for Christians *as citizens* to act in the body politic with a distinctive political program; and they have worked so consistently with the "moral/political" distinction that much of their general moral instruction is left up in the air because it does not display sufficient connection with the integral political/moral/technical reality of the state and interstate relations.

We are not suggesting that the bishops themselves should have tried to write a definitive policy statement for the President on nuclear arms control or adequate defense, but we are suggesting that the urgency of the present crisis should have driven them to give much more attention to the great need for contemporary, detailed, consistent Christian political action and analysis by citizens. In the absence of that, the pastoral letter tends to leave the "lay" reader with the sense that he or she is a mere respondent to the political realities that someone else shapes, and that he or she is responsible *as a Christian* primarily for certain "moral" dimensions of the nuclear problem rather than for U.S. defense policy in its full concreteness. One person reading the pastoral might decide to quit his job at an arms production plant; another might not. One person might decide to protest against plans to build the MX missile; another might not. But all of these individual responses, especially when they are mere reactions to current policies and officeholders, do not add up to a concerted effort by Christians to work communally for a new politics and a just U.S. military posture in the world.

A QUALIFIED ACCEPTANCE OF
DETERRENCE DOCTRINE

The general problem outlined above is especially apparent when it comes to the most ambiguous passage in the pastoral—the bishops' qualified acceptance of nuclear deterrence doctrine.[4] Clearly the bishops would prefer not to have a defense policy based on the use or threat to use nuclear weapons. Nowhere in the pastoral letter do they offer strong arguments to support nuclear deterrence as a healthy or preferred strategy. At best they view it as a lesser of evils. In fact, almost all of their argumentation calls into question deterrence doctrine, based as it is on the threat to use what must not be used. And yet, when it comes to the point of needing to suggest an alternative, they decide instead to accept in a qualified way deterrence doctrine while urging that the mutual disarmament process be given more energetic support.[5]

The reader is left with the impression that a great moral passion has finally smashed against the wall of political and military reality. If one is a Christian, one can rejoice that a moral concern exists; one can even give thanks that these bishops have written this letter at this time to express that concern. But for Christian *citizens,* it is not clear what they should do with the existing military and political reality, and the bishops seem to be less concerned with the long-range civic response than with an immediate ecclesiastical moral plea. This kind of moral/political distinction (built on the ecclesiastical/lay distinction, the sacred/secular distinction, and the eternal/temporal distinction) gives away too much of the political/military reality to those who do not have the same moral passion as the bishops. Justice and peace remain too general as "ideals" instead of functioning as concrete demands from God for real states and real governments. The bishops should have urged that Christians *as citizens,* not as lay church people, need to develop a distinctive Christian political witness that can produce informed policies consistent with a Christian view of the state and the primary tasks of government. Only then can the weakness of an ambiguous deterrence policy be displaced in reality by another, more just policy option.

DETERRENCE, JUST WAR, AND PROPORTIONALITY

Nuclear deterrence is based on the threat of retaliation against an enemy if that enemy dares to launch a first strike with nuclear weapons. The bishops recognize that such a stance is morally reprehensible at worst, and morally ambiguous at best. Their moral argument gives special attention to the principles of "proportionality" and "discrimination" in the historic just-war doctrine.

When a government is deciding whether or not to go to war to defend itself, "proportionality" means that "the damage to be inflicted and the costs incurred by war must be proportionate to the good expected by taking up arms."[6] The principle of proportionality also holds *during* warfare. The damage inflicted must not be out of proportion to the good being achieved. In view of the great damage that a nuclear war would bring, the bishops come down in opposition to the use of nuclear weapons. But if the bishops reject the use of nuclear weapons while retaining a conditional acceptance of the retaliatory threat, do they not leave open and even encourage the possibility of violating the principle of proportionality at some point in the future?

Nuclear weapons in the arsenals of both superpowers are of a different kind and magnitude from those of the conventional variety.[7] This does not mean that incendiary bombings or the use of gases or other types of biological and chemical weapons can ever be easily justified. The just-war criteria apply equally to conventional and nuclear warfare. But the U.S. bishops correctly recognize the special character of nuclear weapons when they state: "To destroy civilization as we know it by waging a 'total war' as today it *could* be waged would be a monstrously disproportionate response to aggression on the part of any nation."[8] Francis X. Winters actually made the same point years ago when he asked, "What is the proportion between loss and gain to be expected from the hostilities? If the losses are unpredictable, no calculation of their proportionality to political gains is feasible. Hence, policy planners and political leaders are unable to certify the preponderance of gain over loss."[9]

In an all-out nuclear war the U.S. Arms Control and Disarmament Agency (ACDA) predicts that:

- 10,000 warheads or bombs would be detonated;
- more than 200 million fatalities would result;
- 30 to 70 percent of the ozone layer would be destroyed;
- world agriculture would be severely damaged for two to three years;
- many would suffer disabling sunburn;
- communications would be disrupted on a vast scale.[10]

Other analysts have presented evidence that a total nuclear war would destroy the industrial economy of the world.[11] What, *proportionally* speaking, could ever justify a world of massive death, starvation, and suffering cut off from the possibility of recovery? The Dean of East-West relations, George Kennan, remarked, "There is no issue at stake in our political relations with the Soviets which could conceivably be worth a nuclear war."[12]

No goal could ever legitimate or justify the use of such massive violence to secure these unintentional ends. As the Catholic bishops rightly insist, "When confronting choices among specific military options, the question asked by proportionality is: once we take into account not only the military advantages that will be achieved by using this means, but also the harms reasonably expected to follow from using it, can its use still be justified?"[13] The answer to this rhetorical question leads to the conclusion that the use of nuclear weapons must be judged disproportionate to any good that might be sought.

What, then, should we make of the possession and deployment of nuclear weapons for purely deterrent purposes? Is there any such thing as "pure deterrence"? Deterrence depends on the intention to act. Can a safe and secure bluff outlast and even control an arms race? Unfortunately, as McGeorge Bundy has reminded us, fear of the bomb is not as strong as fear of the other's bomb. If anything should have changed our minds, it is the bomb, but the beam remains in both of our eyes. Since anything more than zero bombs is not quite good enough, we are constantly driven by the momentum of the arms spiral.[14]

Deterrence—that impersonal, symmetrical form of terrorism which afflicts one's own citizens as much as it does the enemy—is nothing more than the domination of fear. What we see as a present danger to us is simply modernization to the enemy. What we see as the obvious improvement of our security forces is perceived as a growing threat to the enemy. Fear, cyclically funneled back to an action/reaction arms race, becomes triumphant.[15] Deterrence theorists, and to some extent the Catholic bishops, believe that fear is not altogether a bad thing. Fear of nuclear holocaust might help to secure the conviction that nuclear wars should never be fought. But is it not odd and somewhat irrational that the very countries and leaders who insist on new and more powerful weapons are entrusted to forestall the disaster?

Philip Green argued in the most insightful book on this topic, *Deadly Logic,* that the ethical choices in deterrence are neo-Hobbesian and lead to moral relativism by:

1. presuming that no conduct is absolutely prohibited;
2. treating all violence and destruction as qualitatively indistinguishable;
3. making moral distinctions between weapons and targets difficult to justify;
4. assuming that a deep psychological and physical commitment to destructive violence on foreign civilian populations can be morally neutral;
5. tending to subordinate all political considerations to military ones;
6. sharing in the American cold war biases and therefore remaining culture bound; and
7. having an antipopular political bias.[16]

Can nonrelativistic moral reasoning on the part of the bishops outweigh this moral relativism if the bishops do not relinquish their qualified support of nuclear deterrence?

Catholics and Protestants alike have argued that nuclear weapons, especially those like the MX missile, are destabilizing weapons with first-strike capabilities, but is not deterrence itself in the long run equally destabilizing and disorderly? Will not the acceptance of deterrence, even in a qualified way, only perpetuate the present tendencies and lines of argument that keep fueling the nuclear arms race? Gargantua, in the mind of Rabelais, had an insatiable appetite, even for a giant. But his appetite is nothing compared to the superpowers' acquisition of increasingly sophisticated, deadly, technological means of warfare that at some point in time they will use.

DETERRENCE, JUST WAR, AND DISCRIMINATION

Nuclear weapons, like some modern nonnuclear weapons, cannot discriminate between civilian populations and combatants, and even limited attacks on military targets will include a substantial number of noncombatant fatalities. The principle of discriminating between combatants and noncombatants seems therefore to mandate a rejection of every conceivable form of nuclear warfare. The bishops agree.

The gradual shift in nuclear strategy from mutual assured destruction (MAD) to an emphasis on a flexible response and counterforce targeting has opened up the possibility of fighting with the aim of winning a "limited" nuclear war. But surely the newer version of protecting security is as unjust as its predecessor. Casualties resulting from any significant counterforce strike (a nuclear strike targeted only at military installations) make the prospects of a limited nuclear war very unattractive. The Congressional Office of Technology Assessment calculated that there would be *significant* civilian casualties in a limited exchange. The Department of Defense assumes that 60 percent of the population will reach the best shelter available and remain there for 30 days in case of a limited nuclear war. For this to be possible, 20 percent of the adult population would need special civil defense training. Even at that the Department of Defense has not accounted for the disruption of the interdependent components of modern society and the longer-term genetic defects in future generations.[17]

Some military strategists have long had a certain affinity for the notion of a "limited" rather than an "all-out" or "total" nuclear war. They seem to sense the power of the "discrimination" principle. And yet the belief that nuclear weapons can be discriminating on a limited scale is illusory. In 1974 James Schlesinger was asked how "limited" a nuclear exchange directed at military targets would be. He estimated that 800,000 Americans would die.[18] In other words, in one "limited" exchange the estimated deaths would surpass the deaths in all our foreign wars combined. In actuality, Schlesinger's figure assumed that the Soviets would send a single, one-megaton bomb at each strategic site and detonate each one at the optimum point on each target. Unfortunately, Soviet missiles now carry warheads much larger than one megaton. Add to this our poor civil defense preparations and the fallout patterns downwind, and the accurate fatality figures would probably be closer to between 3.5 million and 22 million persons. Nor does this take into account later incidents due to cancer, genetic damage, and congenital malformation.[19] Colin Gray and Keith Payne have confessed forthrightly that just-war criteria can never be completely fulfilled in a nuclear war—even a limited one.[20] So it is not simply Catholic bishops and Protestant commentators who claim that nuclear war would be unjust; the "war-fighting" strategists who conceive and plan for nuclear war admit the same truth.

Can "limited" nuclear warfare ever hope to meet the criterion of discrimination? Is not all nuclear warfare on the same level when it comes to moral judgments of approval? In the end, say the bishops, "our no to nuclear war must . . . be definitive and decisive."[21]

So we return to the same point once again. If the use of nuclear weapons cannot meet the test of assured discrimination, then must we not judge them to be immoral and unacceptable by traditional just-war standards? How then can a posture of nuclear deterrence be maintained if it is based on the threat to use such weapons. Will not that posture only help to sustain our national dependence on nuclear weapons? Even a highly qualified acceptance of deterrence is unlikely to be powerful enough to move citizens and policymakers in another direction, as the bishops hope will happen. Do we not need to break altogether with the endangering nuclear spiral, including its support from deterrence doctrine?

Our questions are not intended to imply that the United States can or should somehow act alone, or that the differences between the Soviet and American systems of government are of no significance. The United States and the Soviet Union are not moral equals. Repression in the Soviet Union is undeniable, and neither neutralism nor unilateralism will counter it. But is it not more just and even safer to challenge the Soviets in ways other than the ominous nuclear threat? Does not the strong moral reasoning of the bishops demand a more conclusive break with nuclearism than they have demonstrated? The just-war tradition would surely recognize the legitimacy of defense in cases of alliances, assistance under collective security agreements, and overt aggression. However, it calls for measured restraint. Do SIOP, PD-59, counterforce, and deterrence allow for the just restraints of proportionality and discrimination? Can any effort simply be rationalized as tactically necessary given Soviet aggression and expansionism? Does the fact that Marxist-Leninists think it possible to fight wars for reasons other than self-defense permit our unjust response? Certainly, the historic Christian, just-war tradition does not allow for such means-ends rationalizations. Injustice is injustice; immorality is immorality; they cannot be called something else just because another party partakes of or executes irresponsible, even evil acts. The demands of justice are binding even in a world of nearly endless injustice. It is the Christian's obligation, in obedience to God, to see that these demands are met in concrete reality.

This is the challenge to citizens that must survive all other reactions to the bishops' important and timely pastoral letter. Christians should not spend years debating the finer moral points of the bishops' argument. They should recognize that the bishops and all other Christians are faced with this predicament precisely because paths have been (and are being) chosen that have not and cannot lead to a completely just defense policy for this or other countries. What we need now is a commitment among Christian citizens in America that will sustain the kind of political perspective that will give birth to a program of defense and foreign relations that can meet God's call to do justice.

III: The Morality of Using Nuclear Weapons

5: Nuclear Targeting: Counterforce vs. Countervalue Weapons*

STEVEN E. MEYER**

In one sense, the moral dilemma faced by the bishops—and many other Christians—is not unique. The church and Christians of many persuasions have agonized for centuries over the morality of war and whether Christians may engage in warfare.

Broadly speaking, throughout history religious scholars have agreed that Christians may indeed engage in combat, but have established criteria to determine whether a war is "just" and have admonished Christians to fight only in "just wars." Not only do the bishops agree with this, drawing on centuries of Catholic tradition and the authority of the councils and the popes, but they argue that once all peaceful attempts to redress an injustice have been exhausted, Christians and the state have an "obligation," a "duty," and a "right" to take up arms. Their admonition assumes the proportions of a moral imperative.

For the bishops, then, the question is not whether we should defend against aggression by force of arms, but it is the when and "how of defending the peace which offers the moral options." The church can neither condone the use of violence un-

---

*Counterforce weapons are those with published accuracy levels that theoretically give them the capability of being used against very specific (usually military) targets, while the accuracy levels of countervalue weapons allow them to be used only against fairly broad geographic areas.

**The views expressed in this chapter are those solely of the author and do not necessarily reflect the views of the Central Intelligence Agency or Senator Dan Quayle.

conditionally, nor sanction participation in any war. For a war to be "just," it must maintain or further "justice" and oppose "unjust" aggression. The bishops suggest that the just war most likely is defensive and the intent is to secure victory and restore peace as quickly as possible. The goal is not to annihilate the enemy, no matter how heinous he may be. The massive, indiscriminate use of force is prohibited, civilians and other noncombatants must be protected as much as possible, and the destruction of property and resources must be kept to an absolute minimum. Above all, no state or government must assume it has a monopoly on justice and should, therefore, recognize and "acknowledge the limits of its *just cause* and the consequent requirements to use only limited means in pursuit of its objective." The pursuit of a "just war," in other words, must be guided by the principles of proportionality, which requires that "the damage inflicted must be proportionate to the good expected by taking up arms," and discrimination, which "prohibits directly intended attacks on noncombatants and non-military targets."

The bishops, like other concerned Christians, can firmly, although reluctantly, justify the use of arms under specific circumstances because they have a healthy appreciation for the reality of the world around them. As the letter accurately points out in several places, we live in "a world of sovereign states devoid of any central authority and divided by ideology, geography and competing claims." It is a world that recognizes no "common moral authority," acknowledges no "central political authority," and has no consistently effective international organization to prevent or mediate conflict. It is, as a result, a complex, dangerous, strife-torn, unjust world that, at least in the near term, shows no signs of becoming a fundamentally more harmonious, peaceful place. Thus, "Christians are called to live the tension between the vision of the reign of God and its concrete realization in history." In other words, we must continue to hope for, work for, and expect the fulfillment of God's promises, but at the same time we must recognize and deal competently with the grim realities of the world we live in. In practical terms this means we are called to work diligently for peace, but we must also recognize that there are values and principles worth defending, even if war is necessary.

Applying just-war criteria has never been easy. Even in the dim past, when warfare was supposed to be essentially "chivalrous," more "gentlemanly," and, presumably, more "just," there were many times when it could be argued that just-war criteria were either relaxed or abandoned. The passage of time does have a way of dulling not only our sensitivities, but also our perspectives.

Certainly, then, the dilemma in and of itself is not new, but there is no doubt that modern warfare does present us with a new twist. Technology has caught up with the just-war criteria. We do have the technical capacity today to violate these criteria on a much wider scale. Technology in and of itself will not answer the question of whether a war is being conducted to champion justice and repulse oppression, or whether it is defensive or offensive. But our awesome technology clearly does give us the capability to annihilate the enemy, to indiscriminately kill thousands of people, and to destroy massive amounts of property more easily and more thoroughly than ever before in history—to engage in total war.

If the new technology was baptized during World War I, it attained maturity during World War II. One merely has to consider the saturation bombing of Coventry and London, the firebombing of Dresden, or the *Blitzkrieg* through Poland and Russia. And Nagasaki and Hiroshima pushed the stakes even higher. With the advent of atomic and later nuclear weapons, we attained the capacity to kill even more people and destroy even more property than we could during World War II.

From the just-war perspective, however, the leap from modern conventional weapons to nuclear weapons may be less significant than the leap from a rather limited technology to one that makes massive and indiscriminate death and destruction as simple as pushing a few buttons. After all, thousands of noncombatants in Dresden, Coventry, London, and elsewhere were killed as surely by conventional bombs as they would have been from an atomic attack.

Nevertheless, today when we think of death and destruction on a vast scale we think first and foremost of nuclear weapons, thus complicating the moral dilemma even further. The bishops see a world bristling with nuclear weapons of such vast destructive power that they literally have the capability to destroy God's creation. And, indeed, there is no doubt about what full-scale, global nuclear war would mean. The point has been hammered home vividly and effectively for decades. But the bishops also fear that even a supposedly "limited" nuclear exchange would have catastrophic consequences, although they "recognize that the policy debate on this question is inconclusive." Nuclear war of any sort, therefore, cannot be seen merely as the extension of conventional war by other means. It is qualitatively different. It "threatens the existence of our planet," and "it is neither tolerable nor necessary that human beings live under this threat." It is a threat, the bishops maintain, that is fundamentally different from anything the human race has faced before, and along with many other concerned Christians the bishops are convinced that "the world is at a moment of crisis."

In the context of applying just-war criteria to concrete situations in the nuclear age, the bishops move uneasily, but necessarily, to the relationship between the United States and the Soviet Union and the nature of Soviet and other communist systems in the contemporary international arena. They point out that our system, and other Western systems, are not without flaws and, indeed, exhibit serious shortcomings. But, they say, we should have no illusions about the Soviet system and the challenge it presents. History is clear: it is a repressive system that lacks respect for human rights, forcibly keeps many people under "communist domination despite their manifest wishes to be free," exports revolution, and follows an "imperial drive for hegemony." Despite our own problems, the bishops warn, we must never lose sight of the fact that there are fundamental differences between our system and the Soviet system, and these differences present a danger to our values, our freedoms, and our very existence. If the Soviet Union has done nothing else well, it has been successful in building military might. It is an immensely powerful state that represents a danger we dare not ignore. It is a danger against which we *must* be prepared to defend ourselves.

> Free people must always pay a proportionate price and run some risks—responsibly—to preserve their freedom. It is one thing to recognize that the people of the world do not want war. It is quite another thing to attribute the same good motives to regimes or

political systems that have consistently demonstrated precisely the opposite in their behavior.[1]

The clash of such political, social, and economic systems is as old as the question of just war itself, and at least in this the differences between the United States and the Soviet Union fit a traditional pattern. As we have noted before, however, the fact that the clash between our two systems could lead to a holocaust that might destroy our planet is, to put it mildly, a nontraditional aspect. This means that despite the fact that we must defend against the Soviet challenge, we must be guided by the "solid realism which recognizes that everyone will lose in a nuclear exchange." We and the Soviets must, therefore, pursue "political dialogue and negotiations . . . in spite of the obstacles." We must make every effort to resolve our differences peacefully, negotiate an end to the arms race, and, ultimately, cooperate to rid the world of nuclear weapons. We cannot, the bishops suggest, permit the superpower rivalry to reach such a fever pitch that we and the Soviets fail "to recognize the common interest both states have in never using nuclear weapons."

> The fact that the Soviet Union now possesses a huge arsenal of strategic weapons as threatening to us as ours may appear to them does not exclude the possibility of success in such negotiations.[2]

However, because of the threat the Soviet Union and its allies pose to our values and freedoms, and because of the stark reality of nuclear weapons on both sides, the bishops see no choice but to support nuclear deterrence.[3] Implicit in their support is the recognition of four very difficult, yet absolutely pertinent, facts. First, after nearly forty years, nuclear weapons have become an intimate part of the international political-military system. Second, as deplorable as they are, nuclear weapons will be with us in some form or other for a long time to come, no matter what we do. Third, the rough equivalency or balance between the superpowers in which neither side gains superiority has led to an uneasy, yet effective, stalemate that in all likelihood has prohibited a nuclear exchange while at the same time preserving our values and freedoms.

> . . . deterrence may still be judged morally acceptable . . . (to prevent) . . . nuclear war from . . . occurring *and* to protect and preserve those key values of justice, freedom and independence which are necessary for personal dignity and national integrity.[4]

And, fourth, while the bishops argue that the United States can by itself take certain "independent initiatives" to reduce the nuclear disarmament, they recognize that unilateral disarmament—by either side—would be destabilizing, dangerous, and counterproductive. Only mutual, verifiable agreements can lead to genuine reductions in the numbers of nuclear weapons and the risk of nuclear war.

Because of the tremendous destructive power of nuclear weapons, however, the bishops are quick to add that nuclear deterrence cannot be envisioned as a permanent fixture. It must be seen as only a temporary condition dictated by necessity. Quoting Pope John Paul II, they note that ". . . deterrence based on balance is certainly not an end in itself, but is a step on the way toward a progressive disarmament." Clearly this is the hope and expectation not only of the bishops, but of every concerned human being, Christian or not. Nobody in his or her right mind wants or likes nuclear weapons; nobody in his or her right mind favors or supports the arms race.

Not only do the bishops see deterrence as temporary, but their fear of nuclear war has also driven them to develop a policy of deterrence that, in effect, attempts to conform it to just-war criteria by subjecting the "possession and deployment" of nuclear weapons to "rigid restrictions." In applying their "rigid restrictions," however, the bishops narrow deterrence options to such an extent that, if adopted as national policy, I think they could easily undermine the credibility of nuclear deterrence. And if deterrence is not believed or appears indecisive it is not credible, and if it is not credible it is much more likely to lead to exactly the kind of dangerous, unstable superpower relationship the bishops hope so fervently to avoid. If the great strength of the bishops' letter is its cogent, reasoned presentation of the moral dilemma, its great, possibly fatal, weakness, I think, is the fact that it offers us remarkably little insight into how to resolve the dilemma—into how, as a practical matter, we should develop a policy of deterrence consistent with stability and conducive to arms control and reductions. In a world groping for answers, the bishops' stance on deterrence offers little guidance for the committed policymakers who must grapple with the dilemma on a day-to-day basis and might seem dangerously confusing to the Soviet Union.

Certainly, the intent is never to have to use nuclear weapons. Ironically, however, if deterrence is to be credible, if it is to be believed, the perception by the other side must be that nuclear weapons will, in fact, be used if necessary under certain circumstances and against certain targets. In delineating what is for them an acceptable deterrence policy, the bishops focus on the two key, related questions of *intent* and *targeting* that together tell us the "when" and "how" of deterrence strategy. In particular, "targeting doctrine raises significant moral questions because it is a significant determinant of what would occur if nuclear weapons were ever to be used."[5]

The bishops begin by categorically rejecting "counter-population" or "countervalue" warfare. Under no circumstances, they say, may nuclear weapons be either targeted or used against population centers or any "predominantly civilian targets," either in a preemptive first strike or in retaliation for a strike by enemy missiles. To do so, they argue, would be a gross violation of the rules of both proportionality and discrimination. In other words, deliberate attacks against cities and other major centers where large numbers of civilians and other noncombatants are likely to gather would violate the long-standing just-war prohibition against annihilation and the massive, indiscriminate use of force. And if countervalue nuclear warfare is to be prohibited, there is no need for a countervalue targeting policy that is, if not immoral, at least unnecessary.

So far there seems to be little to argue against. I believe no Christian who takes the just-war criteria seriously or values human life as a creation of God in his own image would favor the *deliberate* (and deliberate is the operative word) annihilation of millions of people in a nuclear attack (or any other kind of attack, for that matter). Certainly, I cannot conceive of them doing so if there were viable alternative targeting options that upheld the credibility of deterrence. And, indeed, the United States abandoned a countervalue strategy when we replaced "mutually assured destruction" (MAD) with "flexible response" in 1974 and when this course was reaffirmed in 1980 by President Carter. High officials in the Reagan Administration have assured the bishops that

> For moral, political and military reasons, the United States does not target the Soviet civilian population as such. There is no de-

liberately opaque meaning conveyed in the last two words. We do not threaten the existence of Soviet civilization by threatening Soviet cities. Rather, we hold at risk the war-making capability of the Soviet Union—its armed forces, and the industrial capacity to sustain war.[6]

But the bishops go on. In addition to prohibiting the targeting or deliberate use of nuclear weapons against population centers, they "do not perceive any situation in which the deliberate initiation of nuclear warfare on however restricted a scale can be morally justified." In other words, they see no situation, however limited, in which we can justify the first use of nuclear weapons and, in fact, favor a "no-first-use" policy.

As a point of clarification, the bishops are quick to add that this prohibition on first use also extends to using "nuclear weapons to counter a conventional attack" and urge the United States and NATO to develop adequate nonnuclear defensive options. In principle, the desire to move toward greater reliance on nonnuclear defense is laudable, and when nuclear missions can be replaced by conventional ones we should do so. In a world of increasingly diverse challenges we must have the flexibility to respond well *below* the nuclear level when our interests and those of our friends and allies are threatened. Even in conflict with the Soviet Union, a credible conventional deterrent could, depending on the scenario, allow us to avoid having to rely on nuclear weapons at all (i.e., pushing the nuclear threshold higher). If a Soviet–American conventional conflict breaks out, therefore, we should not have to be faced with the choice of "going nuclear" immediately or surrendering.[7]

But a conventional defense, no matter how good, is not by itself credible against nuclear weapons. Consequently, a move toward greater reliance on conventional deterrence could be destabilizing unless both the United States and the Soviet Union shifted their emphasis. At this point in time any move in this direction would hinge in large measure on a basic, although highly unlikely, shift in Soviet war-fighting strategy, especially as it affects Western Europe. Soviet nuclear weaponry has been specifically developed to be integrated with Soviet conventional forces. There is little in Soviet military thinking that allows for a neat delineation between conventional and nuclear weapons or between conventional and nuclear strategies per se:

Today the Soviets have modernized rocket systems (SS-21, SS-22, SS-23 and the SS-20) of longer range and with an array of nuclear warheads which have been specifically adapted to the Soviet concept of offensive operations. . . . The Soviet concept of offensive operations . . . calls for the establishment of multiple, phased axes of advance . . . these attacks would include strikes by Soviet nuclear forces.[8]

Moreover, increasing our reliance on conventional weapons would be extremely expensive. Nuclear programs constitute only about 10 percent of our total defense budget, and even if credible nonnuclear defense could replace our nuclear deterrent, it would eat very heavily into money that could be channeled into social programs supported by the bishops. Perhaps most important, however, a unilateral shift toward nonnuclear programs could be detrimental to U.S. interests and would be likely to redirect the arms race into equally dangerous directions. The Soviets, content with their larger, more modern nuclear arsenal, would be encouraged to direct their energies into nonnuclear defensive and offensive systems to defeat U.S. nuclear submarines and aircraft—a luxury they have not had to date. Both the United States and the Soviet Union, moreover, would be encouraged to develop advanced nonnuclear systems such as space-based laser and particle-beam weapons that could be even more destabilizing and far more costly than the nuclear deterrent.

All that seems left for the bishops is a deterrence policy that allows nuclear weapons to be targeted only against military targets and to be used only in retaliation for a nuclear attack. That is, they can be used only as second-strike, counterforce weapons. But the bishops are highly skeptical that, despite their reputed accuracy, counterforce weapons can be used without seriously violating the basic tenets of just-war criteria. At best they are ambivalent, but their skepticism seems so profound that it casts serious doubt on whether they actually do accept any kind of deterrence or nuclear war-fighting strategy. They admonish men and women in the military to develop "battle plans and weapons systems (which) reduce violence, destruction, suffering and death to a minimum, keeping in mind especially noncombatants and other innocent people." But at the same time they urge "negotiations to halt the testing, production and deployment of new nuclear weapons systems." If such negotiations were successful we would, in effect, be frozen into a countervalue situation because most weapons currently in our strategic deterrent are not accurate enough in most situations—to be considered truly counterforce weapons. If such negotiations were to fail or, more likely, never take place, the bishops show no clear preference to proceed with the deployment and refinement of genuine counterforce weapons and, in fact, appear hostile to them.

In particular, the bishops fear that counterforce weapons could help produce a perception that nuclear war can be controlled, that it "is subject to precise rational and moral limits." Such a perception, in turn, could lead to the assumption that nuclear war is "winnable," inducing national leaders to be more willing to launch a nuclear strike. They are deeply concerned that attacking purely military targets could involve considerable "indirect," "unintended," perhaps long-term, collateral damage to civilian populations:

> . . . the problem is not simply one of producing highly accurate weapons that might cause civilian casualties in any single explosion, but one of increasing the likelihood of escalation at a level where many, even "discriminating" weapons would cumulatively kill very large numbers of civilians.[9]

Talks with U.S. government officials reinforced the bishops' fears because, despite the intention to retaliate against military targets, these officials could not guarantee that widespread collateral damage would not result and some expected it, especially in a "substantial exchange."

The bishops also fear that counterforce weapons could be destabilizing. This is so, they argue, because counterforce weapons are not only highly accurate, but if based in fixed silos they are also vulnerable to attack from equally accurate enemy counterforce weapons. In crisis situations, then, we or the Soviets may be induced to launch a preemptive first strike, each intent on preserving their own retaliatory force by destroying the other's ability to attack. Such a "use it or lose it" mentality, the bishops suggest, could, during a crisis, catapult us into World War III.

In an effort to address these concerns, it is important to examine briefly contending views about the capabilities of counterforce weapons specifically and our entire strategic deterrent in general.

As the bishops point out, the Single Integrated Operational Plan (SIOP) identifies some 40,000 military targets in the Soviet Union. Many prime targets are located in or near cities and other population centers, but many are not, and targets also vary considerably by type, including military command posts, communication centers, military choke points, ammunition dumps, industrial centers, military bases, ports, missile silos, and scores of others. Given the limits of our overall strategic capability, we would not be able to attack all targets simultaneously. We would have to be selective, and collateral damage to civilian populations would depend to a great extent on where the targets are located. But it would also depend to a great extent on the hardness of the target and the accuracy, number, and explosive yield of incoming warheads.[10] Obviously, the harder the target, the more critical are accuracy, number, and yield. Various combinations of these three variables equal, at least in theory, the "kill probability" of a warhead, that is, the probability of a warhead destroying a hardened target.

But once a target has been selected, can we in fact hit precisely what we aim at and destroy it with a minimum of collateral damage? Clearly, our most modern warheads (and those of the Soviets) are considerably more accurate than warheads were even a few years ago. Our first intercontinental ballistic missile (ICBM), the Titan, and our early Minutemen ICBMs allowed for little more than a "city-busting" strategy, as measured by their circular error probability (CEP).[11] For example, the CEP of a Titan warhead is about 4,200 feet, while that of the MX reportedly is 450 feet, which is about twice as good as the Minuteman III, the current mainstay of our land-based strategic deterrent.

Many experts, including a large number at the Department of Defense, argue that the modern counterforce missile has been fully tested and every possible contingency has been considered and programmed into the missile's computers. They are convinced that "a missile's 'accuracy' . . . really does measure how close its warheads would come to its intended target" and, depending on yield of the warhead and hardness of the target, that it would destroy the target.[12] These experts have a high degree of confidence, for example, that a warhead with a CEP of 450 feet has an excellent chance of destroying a target hardened to 2,000 PSI. As the accuracy (and yield) of the warhead decreases and/or the hardness of the target increases, we can be progressively less confident that the target will be destroyed. At the same time, increasing the accuracy of a warhead offsets decreases in yield and should, therefore, decrease the probability of widespread collateral damage. And, these experts point out, the rapid development of technology to perfect the terminal guidance of nuclear warheads (i.e., the ability to maneuver warheads right up to the time and point of impact) will enhance accuracy even more.

Other experts recognize the triumphs of modern technology and the substantial improvements in warhead accuracy. But they are considerably less confident that we can in fact launch a nuclear strike with the kind of accuracy indicated for modern counterforce weapons.

They argue first of all that detonating nuclear warheads is subject to "bias." Bias refers to the distance between the intended target and the actual point of impact of incoming warheads. It says that the CEP does not necessarily refer to the radius of a circle that includes the intended target; it merely refers to the circle where 50 percent of the warheads land, and that circle may be a considerable distance from the target. It is somewhat like the impact of a shotgun blast. When fired, the blast will hit in a more or less specific pattern, but that pattern does not necessarily correspond with the bull's-eye. Those convinced of bias argue that, although modern missile technology can successfully predict the CEP of warheads, we have not developed the technology to ensure that the CEP includes the target.

These experts are also concerned because we test our missiles on a range that runs from east to west and the Soviets test theirs on a range that runs from west to east. They argue that our ability to make the CEP and the target coincide effectively during test firings is due to the fact that we have been able after so many years of testing to make the appropriate corrections. Such adjustments would not be possible along the expected north-south path of an actual attack where weather patterns, winds, clouds, and atmospheric pressure are different and where the magnetic pull of the north pole could have an effect unknown along an east-west or west-east trajectory. Moreover, even if we had tested along a north-south trajectory, changes in natural phenomena between test time and attack time also could be quite different, and some experts question whether onboard computers can accommodate these "unknowns" sufficiently to ensure the required accuracy.

Moreover, even under the best of circumstances, they ask, how much can we count on the computers? Can we count on them to perform the thousands of intricate jobs necessary to ensure that all missiles and all warheads perform exactly the way they are supposed to? The history of the marriage of missiles and computers, they say, gives one pause to wonder.

They are also concerned about "fratricide," that is, the deleterious effects of an exploding warhead on other incoming warheads. It is normally conceded that more than one warhead will be needed to ensure the destruction of hardened targets. Can one warhead survive the blast, debris, heat, radiation, and electromagnetic pulse produced by the explosion of the warhead that precedes it? Again, some experts pause to wonder.

In sum, they wonder, given the potential problems, whether we can synchronize a counterforce attack with the kind of remarkable precision needed to ensure that hundreds or even thousands of warheads will work as planned over thousands of miles.

These same considerations have a substantial bearing on the question of whether missiles in fixed silos—such as the MX—are vulnerable to attack and are likely to be used as first-strike weapons during crisis periods. Certainly, if all the technical problems can be controlled or, more accurately, if it is perceived that they can be controlled—if, in other words, it is "possible to fine-tune an inertial guidance system to compensate for the factors that are responsible for bias,"[13] then the arguments supporting vulnerability and first-strike capability are enhanced. If, on the other hand, we cannot be sure or it is perceived we cannot be sure, crisis situations are less likely to lead to nuclear instability. Even if the claims of accuracy are correct or are believed to be correct, however, the vulnerability and first-strike arguments are suspect for other reasons.

The key to the survivability of any of our fixed land-based

systems is the diversity and interdependence, or synergism, of our strategic triad (consisting of land-, sea-, and air-based strategic weapons). It is politically naive and militarily unsound to focus so heavily on the survivability or vulnerability of our fixed land-based missiles—or any other leg of the triad—in isolation.

With their SS-18 and SS-19 missiles, the Soviets already have a counterforce capability much greater than ours. Why have they not used them, especially before we are able to replace existing systems with more accurate MX land-based missiles and D-5 (Trident II) sea-based missiles? Even if the Soviets believe they could overcome the technical difficulties associated with accuracy, they know they would not be able to destroy all the legs of our triad in one fell swoop, even if the attack were a complete surprise. Soviet planners know this full well. What Soviet planner would dream of initiating a preemptive strike knowing the Soviet Union would certainly be devastated by our air- and sea-based systems and what was left of our land-based system? In a 1979 *Pravda* article Marshal Ogarkov, Chief of the Soviet General Staff, wondered why American concern for the "vulnerability" of ICBMs so often ignored the U.S. SLBM (submarine) and bomber forces (which carry 75 percent of U.S. strategic warheads). Soviet planners and political leaders, he noted, would not be so foolish.[14]

The flip side of the vulnerability coin is the "first-strike" capability of counterforce weapons. Supposedly their improved accuracy could tempt us into a first strike against the Soviet land-based force and other critical targets or make the Soviets so fearful of the first-strike potential that they would be tempted to initiate a first strike of their own. Most experts agree, however, that even if we wanted to launch a first strike, for the foreseeable future we would not have sufficient strategic, counterforce capability to accomplish it successfully, even if we could put every warhead directly on a Soviet silo before its missiles could be launched. But, even more important, just like the Soviet planner, what American planner would dream of initiating a preemptive strike against Soviet land-based ICBMs, knowing full well that it would result in a massive counterattack from the remainder of the Soviet triad?

Where does all this leave the bishops—and us? Clearly with an agonizing dilemma.

There is no doubt that the control and eventual elimination

of nuclear weapons (and all weapons for that matter) should be our highest priority. The sanctity of God's creation demands it. But we dare not approach arms control naively or without the realities of the world etched indelibly in our minds. Nothing could be more dangerous and destabilizing. Above all, we must never lose sight of two pertinent points. First, we have values and freedoms worth defending. And, second, it is a hard, cold, unforgiving fact that nuclear weapons are here, that they will be here for some time, and that we must deal with them. It is a sad commentary on the plight of modern man, but we must, in short, have a deterrence policy that potential enemies must perceive we would employ if necessary.

Nonetheless, neither a countervalue nor a counterforce targeting policy is comfortable; neither is what anyone wants for the long term. If, however, we reject unilateral nuclear disarmament, we have no choice. Either we select countervalue or counterforce targeting or some combination of the two. Either a purely countervalue policy or a combination of the two would be the worst possible choices, because in both cases it is certain that we would not be able to limit an attack to military targets. We would wipe out everything, violating the just-war criteria in the extreme.

There are a number of uncertainties about counterforce weapons, and there are no guarantees that a counterforce strike could be limited either in scope or duration. No one knows for certain whether we could retaliate with counterforce weapons and keep such an attack from developing into full-scale nuclear war. We can do no better than talk in terms of probability. But in the reality of this world and until we can forge meaningful arms control agreements, the uncertainty of counterforce weapons is better than the certainty of countervalue weapons. And, as the technology develops (especially with regard to terminal guidance), the uncertainties of counterforce weapons may become less imposing and a counterforce targeting strategy even more credible.

In effect, the bishops never make the choice. There is no clear policy of deterrence in their letter. They leave us hanging, proclaiming peace, but not showing us how to maintain it; agonizing over the dilemma, but never showing us how to resolve it.

6: Limited Nuclear War

JOHN E. LAWYER, JR.

It is a common mistake to think we live in a time of peace, just because the grim specter of World War III that has haunted our imaginations for a generation has yet to materialize. The list of limited wars that have scarred various parts of the world in the last three years alone is as extensive as it is typical: Iraq and Iran, Britain and Argentina, Libya and Chad, the Israeli invasion of Lebanon, China's punitive incursion into Vietnam, the abortive U.S. raid into Iran, the Soviet Union's ongoing war in Afghanistan, and various insurgencies and counterinsurgencies in Central America, to name but a few. War has touched every continent except North America and Australia, and all seven nuclear powers have been direct participants in one recent conflict or another. A working group under the UN's Disarmament Commission estimates that some twenty million casualties have been incurred in such fighting since the end of World War II, but no one knows how high the real total is.

In discussing the possibility of limited war in the nuclear era the Catholic bishops have thus touched on a central issue of contemporary peacekeeping. Nuclear technology, including weapons-related knowhow and materials, has spread steadily since the 1950s, and the likelihood of further proliferation is high. It is probable that the world will witness its first small-scale nuclear war sometime before the century is out; and if a global nuclear holocaust ever does occur, by far the most likely cause will have been a limited nuclear conflict that got out of hand.

This state of more or less continuous limited war is no accident, but the predictable outcome of a political dynamic established when nuclear weapons first became a significant element in superpower arsenals in the early 1950s. As early as 1957 Henry Kissinger, in an accurate if dismal paraphrase of Woodrow Wilson, suggested that the main consequence of nuclear weapons would be to make the world safe for limited war. All-out war, he argued in *Nuclear Weapons and Foreign Policy,* has ceased to be a meaningful instrument of policy, and is in fact the least likely contingency, since it would risk the destruction of both major powers. But if all-out war is no longer a viable policy resort, neither is a diplomatic acceptance of aggression, however fierce the verbal protests that clothe it. Acquiescence would only hand a blank check to aggressors, and as we have seen there is no lack of governments that repudiate the idea of peaceful change. The gap between total war and diplomatic surrender will be filled, Kissinger argued, with near-continuous limited war. Subsequent history has more than confirmed this prediction, and as nuclear technology spreads, there is no reason to doubt that sooner or later it will find its way onto a battlefield somewhere.

The idea of limited nuclear war can be defined in various ways, depending on what sorts of limits are stressed. Generally, limited nuclear war has been considered in the West chiefly as a response to a Soviet invasion of Western Europe. More recently planners have had to think about it as a possible counter to a Soviet incursion into Iran, comparable in scale to the 1979 Soviet invasion of Afghanistan next door. In both cases the Soviets, as the aggressors, would have the initiative, which would include the initial choice of weapons. It is further assumed that the Soviet motivation would be to take advantage of a tempting opportunity, or to stave off a limited reversal of their own fortunes; in other words, that no vital Soviet interest was directly at stake. Were national survival at issue, Soviet military doctrine and force structures indicate that they would launch a preemptive attack on U.S. strategic offensive forces; thus we can assume that a Soviet attack limited to Europe or the Middle East would have limited goals, if at a high level of risk.

In both cases the United States is committed to defend the invaded territory, in Europe under the North Atlantic Treaty, and in the Persian Gulf area by the Carter Doctrine. Both commitments rest on solid geopolitical foundations. The loss of either Europe or the Persian Gulf in itself would be an intolerable blow to the West. Furthermore, the rest of our foreign policy would be discredited to the extent that we could no longer conduct our international business through diplomatic means; we would soon find ourselves turning into a beleaguered garrison state.

In addition to specifying under what sort of limited war conditions the United States might consider resorting to a limited nuclear war, we should also bear in mind the distinction between tactical and strategic operations. Generally, strategy deals with the conduct of the entire war, while tactics have to do with winning or losing individual battles. Strategic weapons are long range, large scale, and designed for use against an adversary's homeland as part of the attempt to destroy his capability to wage war. They would include ICBMs and long-range bombers assigned to permanent targets in the Soviet Union. Tactical weapons, by contrast, are more modest in design and intended use. Tactical nuclear weapons would include nuclear artillery shells, or low-yield air- or rocket-delivered warheads used against enemy troop formation on the battlefield. When discussing limited nuclear war the distinction is complicated by the fact that conventional weapons at the higher end of the spectrum of violence can deliver more firepower than some low-yield tactical nuclear weapons. A nuclear shell, for instance, has less explosive force than the conventional artillery barrages that were routine as far back as the First World War; its main advantage is that it does the job more quickly, certainly, and cheaply.

The passages of the pastoral letter that deal with limited war are "The Initiation of Nuclear War" and "Limited Nuclear War," respectively.[1] The gist of these passages is that the danger of escalation is so great that no first-use of even the lowest-yield nuclear weapon is permissible; to fill the gap we must provide an alternative defense with conventional forces, but even these should be kept to a minimum. In the meantime, it is permissible to retain tactical nuclear weapons as a deterrent to situations such as a Soviet invasion of Europe, though in all probability they could never be used, even in retaliation to Soviet first-use, without rapidly driving the conflict beyond the limits of the politically useful or morally permissible.

This skepticism is set within the context of traditional Catholic teaching on peace and war.[2] The Christian tradition has generally accepted a resort to armed force as legitimate in some cases, but has also consistently sought to define and narrow the limits as much as possible. The key criteria for the justified use of force include chance of success, proportionality to the desired end, and discrimination between combatants and noncombatants. The pacifist tradition, which interprets the gospel as forbidding all violence, is also acknowledged as a complementary witness to the just-war theory, one made all the more relevant by weapons of mass destruction. The entire letter is presented as an invitation to dialogue, though the bishops also convey a certain sense that differing conclusions have been rejected in advance. To cite but one of several similar passages: "Reflecting the complexity of the nuclear problem, our arguments in this pastoral must be detailed and nuanced; but our 'no' to nuclear war must, in the end, be definitive and decisive."[3]

While no one can fail to share the bishops' concern, particular questions arise in at least three areas that must also be considered: how inevitable is nuclear escalation from a limited to a general nuclear war; what is the "fit" between the moral doctrine advanced and the realities of the contemporary battlefield; and, third, what impact will the bishops' statement have on the ongoing debate through which U.S. policy is shaped?

The concept of a nuclear firebreak dates back to the 1950s. The metaphor is taken from fighting forest fires; as long as the blaze is kept from jumping across the cleared swath of the firebreak, the danger can be contained and the damage limited; once across, even if by only a little bit, the possibilities of destruction are close to unlimited. The idea of a nuclear firebreak reflects the fact that the political impact of nuclear weapons is more significant than the military, especially at the lower ranges of firepower. Once a conflict has gone nuclear, the fragile inhibitions against resort to higher-yield weapons by the other side may be weakened beyond repair; before long an escalating chain of nuclear response and counter-response ensues.

The pastoral correctly recognizes that while the tactical effect of small-scale nuclear weapons in a limited conflict may be quite comparable to that of conventional weapons, their political impact would be far more significant. But the bishops put far more weight on this factor than it will bear in resting their whole argument explicitly on the virtual inevitability of nuclear escalation. Throughout the letter limited nuclear war is in fact discussed as little more than a mere and inevitable prelude to general nuclear war; as an important category in its own right, it virtually drops out of sight.

By definition, limited wars are conflicts kept within definite bounds with respect to geography, weapons, and goals. As we have seen, even a Soviet attack in Iran or Europe comes within this definition, though clearly close to its upper limit. But just because one criterion is violated, it does not mean that the others will be; in fact, countervailing political pressures are quickly mobilized, both within the countries most concerned and in the international community at large, to reinforce the remaining limits. As Kissinger argued in 1957, "Both sides would have a common and overwhelming interest in keeping it from spreading—if pushed close to the limits this interest would come to replace the prior goal [of winning the limited war] as the domain and end of national strategy."

This is not just a matter of theory; we have had considerable experience with the dynamic in the past. President Nixon expanded the war in Vietnam geographically by his incursion into Cambodia; General MacArthur expanded the goals of the conflict in Korea from turning back a communist invasion of the south to total victory over the north. In each case, as in others that could be cited, the decision to go beyond the limits was fraught with political consequence, particularly for the political leaders held responsible for the breach. The ultimate response, however, was not to widen the war, as the bishops presume would be the case if the choice of weapons were expanded, but on the contrary to mobilize powerful political forces to reinforce the remaining limits and to push the shaky lid down even more firmly. As the conflagration becomes more intense, the international effort to hold the limits tends to increase proportionately; escalation to higher levels is not at all automatic.

None of this is to say that the situation after tactical nuclear weapons have been introduced is not considerably more dangerous than it was before, or, what is perhaps more relevant, that the destruction within the established limits has not increased significantly. These clearly are less than desirable outcomes. To jump the nuclear firebreak is indeed serious business; and this only means that tactical nuclear weapons will not be used in a limited conflict casually, or as a "weapon of convenience." If they are used, it would only be with extreme caution, under tight political and military control, and after it was more than apparent that nothing else would suffice to prevent the defended territory from being overrun. Thus fears that low-yield nuclear weapons would be lightly tossed about in Central America, for instance, or that the decision to employ them would be left to a computer or the proverbial "mad major" at company headquarters, are not persuasive.

A second area in which the pastoral letter presents serious difficulties is in its clash with the tactical realities of the contemporary nuclear battlefield. The classic land battles of World War II typically featured a heavily defended front, behind which offensive forces could be concentrated. The enemy's front lines would first be softened up by artillery, then tanks would spearhead the attack, followed by massed infantry. When the armor had opened a gap in the defender's front, the infantry would pour through and swing around behind the defenders. At the same time, other front-line units would move forward against enemy positions opposite them. If all went according to plan, the unfortunate adversary would be caught in a giant pincher movement. The key to victory was massive troop concentrations at the point of breakthrough; the best defense was a heavily protected front line, with sufficient reserves behind it, that could be thrown in to blunt the enemy assault wherever it should come, or perhaps even turn it back.

In a nuclear environment any such force concentrations are among the most lucrative targets. By using tactical nuclear weapons against the massed assault forces, defenders can stop an offense before it begins or plug the gap opened in their own lines, destroying a significant part of the enemy's military capability in the process. On the offensive, nuclear weapons can tear more holes in the opposite front than conventional forces can block. Beachheads secured by amphibious landings, or airfields used to fly in large amounts of troops and equipment, are also easily neutralized by a few tactical nuclear weapons. The prime consideration for battlefield commanders in any theater where tactical nuclear weapons might be used is thus to avoid massing his forces.

The nuclear battlefield emphasizes small, highly mobile, and largely self-contained units scattered along a wide front and in considerable depth behind it. Such small, dispersed units will present few targets against which an aggressor could profitably employ tactical nuclear weapons, particularly in light of the political repercussions that such a step would bring. But if a defending theater commander does deploy his forces in this pattern, and at the same time is denied the use of battlefield nuclear weapons, he will be left with only a thin screen of forces, which could be easily overrun by a conventional attack along World War II lines. In other words, to deploy forces in Europe or the Gulf as if tactical nuclear weapons will not be used against them is to invite a tactical nuclear attack on the targets so presented; and if theater commanders do deploy forces in a nuclear battle configuration, their only option would be to use tactical nuclear weapons to repel a large-scale conventional attack.

The Soviets do not face any such predicament, since NATO is politically and militarily incapable of initiating a theater conflict. Due to regional political sensitivities the West cannot put anything beyond token forces into the Gulf area unless a Soviet attack is already at hand. As the defending power we have already surrendered the initiative; the tactical problems faced by U.S. and Soviet planners are not symmetrical.

One is reminded of a parallel dilemma that confronted Stonewall Jackson. A devout Presbyterian and diligent sabbatarian, Jackson refused to fight battles on Sunday as a matter of conviction. For a while all went well, until the Union commander opposite him learned of this scruple and began to attack on Sundays. At that point Jackson surrendered his principles, rather than having to surrender his lines. Similarly, initial adherence to the principle of not using nuclear weapons in limited wars is likely to bring about the event not desired; perseverance in it would crown foolishness with defeat. If any strategy could be condemned as offering no reasonable hope of success, it would be to confront a nuclear equipped adversary with conventional tactics.

If on the other hand we deploy for limited nuclear war, and are prepared to use tactical nuclear weapons if the need arise, there is reason to believe that a Soviet attack could be successfully withstood. As long as the Soviets are capable of drawing the same conclusions, they will have every reason not to set such a futile scenario in motion. The bishops notwithstanding, it is surely more moral to seek to prevent a war by being prepared to use low-yield nuclear weapons on the battlefield if the event should nonetheless come to pass, than to invite nuclear attack and court certain disaster by renouncing the use of battlefield nuclear weapons against an adversary known to be proficient in nuclear tactics.

The third criticism that can be made of the pastoral letter has to do with the political uses to which the bishops' statement is most likely to be put. Without doubt it will be taken, as it was intended to be taken, as a rallying point for those in favor of a nuclear freeze. In such a highly polarized atmosphere, the greatest danger is a selective application of what the pastoral in fact has to say. While the bishops occasionally inclined toward a more judicious approach, the document readily lends itself to one-sided application, given its context in the current nuclear debate.

With respect to limited war, the pastoral clearly states, "We do not perceive any situation in which initiation of nuclear war on however restricted a scale can be justified. Therefore a serious moral obligation exists to develop non-nuclear defensive strategies." The first part of the pronouncement will be widely hailed; but one suspects there will be singularly little public demand to fulfill the consequent "serious moral obligation." If we are to take the bishops seriously, we have no business pushing for a nonnuclear strategy until the day after Congress reinstates the draft; but such even-handed activism is hardly likely. With the present known alignment of forces, there is little chance that we could contain a Soviet assault in Europe or the Middle East without vastly increasing conventional troop levels and military budgets. Nuclear weapons were originally developed because they are cheaper and less labor-intensive than the large-scale conventional forces they replaced. If we decide to back down from the high-tech solution, we must expect to pay the price of the politically and morally necessary equivalent.

A similar unwillingness to confront the full political implications of their stance characterizes the bishops' position on deterring limited nuclear war. The pastoral nicely brackets the impossible alternatives. Recognizing the tactical difficulties involved in defending Western Europe in the short run, it holds that the carefully controlled possession and deployment of battlefield nuclear weapons is permissible, in order to deter Soviet first-use; but it simultaneously affirms that this is no more than a temporarily valid concession to a regrettable necessity.[4] Eventually, the possession or use of such weapons, even on the battlefield, must be prohibited. In other words, we can't prudently live without them in the short run, but we can't safely or morally live with them in the long run. The letter's position on limited nuclear weapons is closely linked, conceptually and politically, with its stance on the strategic arms race, which is that global nuclear deterrence may be a temporary necessity, but is morally permissible only in the context of serious efforts at progressive disarmament, and in the expectation that the arms race will soon end with the weapons not actually used in the meantime.[5]

But what if the underlying assumption that serious arms reductions talks will result in a meaningful agreement within a reasonable time is in fact invalid? Or how long is "reasonable"? If no agreement has been negotiated by 1990, or the year 2000, may nuclear stockpiles be legitimately kept up to strength indefinitely?

This is no mere quibble; what we are prepared to do in the long run is a crucial point, for two reasons. First, serious arms control negotiations are tremendously complicated and time-consuming matters at best. SALT I took three years to complete, while SALT II was under negotiation for seven years, and even then failed of ratification. Negotiating an agreement that seriously cuts existing nuclear capabilities, which neither SALT I nor II attempted to, would take literally years to work out under the best of circumstances. Pragmatically, the chances of a meaningful disarmament in even the three- to five-year mid-range is highly unlikely.

A second and far more serious issue is that the first question a government asks itself before entering serious negotiations of any kind is, "Would we be better off with an agreement than without one?" Only if the answer is in the affirmative will policymakers turn their attention to the merits of the proposal itself. This is not unlike the case of the average citizen, who will be interested in the particulars of even the best deal on a new car only if he has already decided that he is in the market for another vehicle in the first place.

In the arms control arena, the answer to that critical first question depends directly on what the alternative political landscape would look like. We are not likely to get the Soviets to agree to a freeze or builddown of either strategic or limited war nuclear capabilities unless they are first convinced that the alternative leaves them worse off than would an agreement. Only then will they seriously consider the possible terms of an accord, though they may indeed be willing to enter negotiations for a variety of other purposes, including scoring propaganda points, exploiting tensions within the Western alliance, probing for further information on U.S. capabilities, and the like. Before there is any chance that arms reduction talks will prove fruitful, the Soviet leadership will have to have come to disturbing conclusions about what the United States will do if no accord is reached. So as long as we do not specify what we will do in the absence of an agreement, we are not likely to get one.

This is precisely the question with which the pastoral does not deal: what are we to do if, after a reasonable time and then some, no agreement appears to be in sight? If a renewed arms race in the long run is explicitly ruled out, as it is,[6] the only answer is, by implication, a unilateral freeze or builddown on the part of the West, though somewhat paradoxically the pastoral explicitly repudiates a policy of unilateral disarmament.[7] And if Soviet negotiators have followed their logic to this point, their conclusion concerning the long run would completely undercut incentives to move toward serious arms reductions in the short run, except on terms that amounted to an early diplomatic capitulation by the West. Indeed, why should we expect them to pay a price for something that is less desirable than what they believe they may eventually get anyway, and at less cost? The answer to the question, what will the United States do in 1995 if no agreement has been reached by then, *will itself determine what kind of agreement might be negotiable in 1985.* Thus the bishops have nicely undercut the negotiability of their own position.

The pastoral's insistence that limited nuclear war is but an inevitable prelude to all-out war in essence denies that limited nuclear war exists at all, as a political category significant in its own right. Though an all-out war may well start as a limited conflict, it is not the case that all limited nuclear conflicts are likely to escalate to World War III. The failure of the bishops to recognize this fact, and seriously to come to grips with limited war on its own terms, leaves us ill-equipped morally as well as conceptually to deal with what has after all been the single most pressing problem actually faced by U.S. policymakers over the past forty years.

If a government's moral and political imagination is confined to two unworkable options, total war or acquiescence in the face of aggression, its foreign policy has already failed, regardless of which alternative is chosen. In practice, if we ignore limited war as an important political category we will probably reap the worst of both of the other options: avoidable wars will in time become unavoidable, and when we reach the point of military conflict it will be at such a relative disadvantage that the costs will be immensely higher in blood and treasure, and the chances of a humane resolution all the more remote.

When large numbers of people are caught between two unpalatable realities, there is always a strong temptation to flee to painless slogans and panaceas. The assumption that seems to underlie much of the current peace movement is that the Soviets are reasonable people, more or less just like us; which means that they must want peace and an end to the arms race as much as anyone else does. If peace has not yet been arrived at, this in turn must be due to poor communications, or perhaps the moral blindness of American policymakers. In either case, the recommended prescription is a large-scale, grass-roots movement that will "send a clear signal to Moscow" that the American people want an end to the arms race, and pressure the American government out of its moral apathy and into serious negotiations. The expected result will be an agreement, and that in short time.

But the truth is that we live in more difficult and ambiguous times than that model would suggest, and the pastoral letter makes it clear that the moral differences between Soviet society and our own are real and profound.[8] Successes in arms limitations agreements have been more modest, though not to be despised. While they do make the world safer, particularly in their cumulative impact, they do not make it safe, nor can they. The bishops, like the rest of the American people, have come up against what Max Weber termed "the ethical irrationality of the world." The decision maker cannot escape responsibility for the real-world consequences of his decisions, no matter how moral his intentions; and to ignore the complexities from which the bishops repeatedly shy away (such as the technical debate on keeping a limited nuclear exchange limited,[9] or on policy and budgets for the kinds of conventional forces needed to substitute for a reduced nuclear force[10]) would only lead us closer to the dangers we most hope to avoid. Instead, we must try to learn to live with the difficulties and perils of the nuclear age, something that can be done only as we shed our illusions. Ironically, one of the most pervasive and dangerous illusions is that we can in effect "uninvent" nuclear weapons through negotiation.

A far more attractive policy, strategically and morally, than that outlined by the pastoral, is to accept limited nuclear war as a significant element in the contemporary political problem, and then to work as diligently as possible to see that such conflicts do not occur, or if they occur that they do not get out of hand. A government best serves both ends by understanding the dynamic of limited wars, and by being prepared to fight them competently, on whatever level the adversary's choice of tactics makes necessary.

Competence includes moral competence as well as battlefield professionalism, and it should be noted that limited nuclear war is entirely compatible with the traditional just-war theory. The prohibitions against the use of nuclear weapons center on the ideas of proportionality, discrimination, reasonable probability of success, and the like. Tactical nuclear weapons are designed and used precisely with such criteria in mind. Their whole point is to deliver carefully tailored, precisely discriminating destructive power on designated military targets, such as an advancing army or a highly concentrated beachhead. The probability of success when nuclear weapons are so employed is high, and the side effects relatively low. Contrary to popular belief, fallout is not much of a hazard; since the wind might be blowing in the user's direction, no commander is willing to risk high-fallout in a tactical situation, and the weapons are designed accordingly. It is sometimes argued that residual radiation or the genetic implications of nuclear weapons automatically push them beyond moral limits, but there is little technical foundation for such an argument in the case of lower-yield tactical warheads. Hiroshima was rebuilt as quickly as Tokyo, despite some residual radiation, and with no greater difficulty. Similarly it is grasping at straws to argue that the genetically damaged grandchild of a soldier exposed to radiation is more of a casualty than the grandchild not born at all because his ancestor was killed outright by a "moral" bullet.

None of this is to say that even limited nuclear war is nice, or pleasant, or what the Christian ideal is all about. War is evil, nuclear war no less than any other kind; but it also at times may be necessary to stave off worse evil. If any war can be just, limited wars in which tactical nuclear weapons are used proportionately, discriminately, against military targets, and in reasonable relation to legitimate goals, must be included in that category. Given the severe political penalties of rash use, it is not likely that otherwise responsible policymakers would use them in any other manner.

To argue that no war is just, or perhaps only that no nuclear war can be just, is always possible, but one must forsake traditional just-war theory to do so. Moreover, to take such an absolutist stance is in fact to weaken the effort to restrain the use of nuclear force through international agreement. The international community can only set limits for what it permits; it cannot prohibit and regulate at the same time, any more than one can hope to lay down rules for a "fair mugging" as one can do in the case of a prize fight.

In the end, then, it seems to be the very "nuclearness" of limited nuclear war that makes it so reprehensible to the bishops. The real weakness of the pastoral letter is that its authors have succumbed to the horrible fascination that nuclear weapons exert over the contemporary mind; they are so seduced by technology that they abandon politics. And to abandon politics is to flee the one area in which a tentative, fragile, and ambiguous safety may be constructed. We cannot expect more in this dangerous age, but we can achieve tragically less.

7: No First-Use of Nuclear Weapons

STEPHEN P. HOFFMANN

As a challenge to established nuclear weapons policy, the proposal that the United States declare never to initiate the use of nuclear weapons of any kind has received widespread attention. Only the call for a nuclear freeze has been accorded more. While the "no-first-use" idea is not new, the rather dramatic advancement of it in the spring of 1982 by four Americans with distinguished records of service in public affairs touched off a vigorous debate on the question.[1] The endorsement of no first-use in 1983 by the U.S. Catholic bishops could only enhance its visibility as an object of public discussion.

I

The focus of the bishops' pronouncement is the NATO doctrine that has assumed since the early years of the Alliance that its members must retain the option to use various types of "tactical" nuclear weapons based in Europe to repel even a conventional (nonnuclear) Soviet attack. Their argument is summarized in this statement: "We express repeatedly in this letter our extreme skepticism about the prospects for controlling a nuclear exchange, however limited the first-use might be."[2] The bishops regard the ability to maintain control as deficient in several respects. First, the tactical weapons vary widely in yield (some being more powerful than the Hiroshima bomb) and exist in great numbers. If many of these were used, such "limited" weapons themselves would "totally devastate the densely populated

107

countries of Western and Central Europe." Second, the uncertainties of command and control under battlefield conditions suggest that it would be very difficult to ensure any discriminate use. Finally, they consider the risk of escalation to all-out nuclear war to be unacceptably high. They add that their skepticism as to control "is rooted not only in the technology of our weapons systems, but in the weakness and sinfulness of human communities." Thus, there can be no question of tolerating the initial use of even the smallest nuclear weapon, no matter how desperate the defenders; the ensuing destruction in all likelihood would be so disproportionate as to make "the moral responsibility of beginning nuclear war not justified by rational political objectives."

In the closing paragraphs of their brief section on no first-use, the authors point out that they by no means wish to question the "responsibility the United States has had and continues to have in assisting allied nations in their defense against either a conventional or a nuclear attack." While they thus appear to tolerate to some extent the presence of nuclear weapons as a deterrent to "theater" nuclear attack (i.e., attack limited to Europe), their stress is on the development of an adequate nonnuclear defense against conventional attack. They readily admit that constructing such a new defense posture will be difficult in light of disagreement among members of the Alliance over what share of the burden each is to assume. In the interim, however, present NATO conventional forces and Soviet uncertainty over where a conventional attack might lead are characterized as "not inconsiderable" deterrents.

The *Foreign Affairs* article may or may not have been the primary influence on the bishops as they agreed to commit themselves to the no-first-use formula. In any case, most of the bishops' major points were first made by Bundy and his colleagues. They note the destructiveness of tactical nuclear weapons, to say nothing of the damage that such larger, longer-range theater nuclear weapons as the proposed Pershing II can cause. They are likewise skeptical about the likelihood of preventing escalation. They stress the need to develop more effective conventional forces as a necessary complement to no first-use, but they also indicate, as do the bishops, that both NATO's current conventional strength and the Soviets' own inhibitions are more significant than many would like to admit. The two groups of authors regard agreement among the allies on an enhanced conventional defense as something that is difficult, but not unattainable. The bishops' point that command and control systems do not guarantee that use can be limited is perhaps prefigured in the four authors' rejection of a compromise position prohibiting only no *early* first-use. This would retain the option to use nuclear arms if initial defense efforts failed. How else can one understand the assertion in *Foreign Affairs* that "even the most responsible choice of even the most limited nuclear actions to prevent even the most imminent conventional disaster"[3] could too easily be a wrong choice, resulting not in the timely, controlled, and effective application of force, but in chaos?

There is an important difference in tone between these two treatises in behalf of no first-use, however. Both advance no first-use as a viable policy and are motivated by an urgent concern to head off the unmitigated disaster of thermonuclear war. But as the bishops note at the outset of the no-first-use section of their letter, the *Foreign Affairs* debate has been cast in political terms, while they are concerned above all to evaluate policy in moral terms.

Bundy, Kennan, McNamara, and Smith reject the present doctrine because "both its cost to the coherence of the Alliance and its threat to the safety of the world are rising while its credibility declines."[4] Their appeal has an ethical undertone that surely must have been influenced by the moral perspective that one of its authors, Kennan, has expressed elsewhere.[5] Its immediate impetus, however, was a fear that NATO's effectiveness as a deterrent is imperiled because growing segments of the public in member countries cannot accept heavy reliance on nuclear weapons, even if only for defense. In advocating no first-use, the authors admonish their readers that even should this be adopted as policy, "it is clear that large, varied, and survivable nuclear forces will still be necessary for nuclear deterrence."[6]

The bishops acknowledge that matters of political viability and deterrent credibility are relevant, but such considerations seem to play a minor role in their argument in favor of no first-use. Their conclusion that first-use is unacceptable rests primarily on their belief that present policy fails to conform to the

criteria associated with the concept of "just war," especially proportionality and discrimination. Proportionality requires a reasonable expectation that damage can be limited. Discrimination
requires that noncombatant casualties be minimized. Considering the assumptions that escalation is highly probable and that
the use of even tactical nuclear weapons would cause heavy
civilian casualties, their conclusion is inescapable.

Heavy reliance on the just-war criteria as a basis for policy
evaluation leads the bishops to regard a posture of deterrence
as justifiable only in a very narrow sense. They would prohibit
any planning for possible use of nuclear weapons, even in retaliation for an enemy's first strike. This encourages critics of no
first-use to regard it as being on the same plane as unilateral
disarmament: a highly impractical policy that, even if implemented, could very possibly bring about the disaster that it
aimed to prevent.

Yet the bishops' letter clearly assumes that moral principle
can be reflected in political practice. Its authors did not arrive
at their consensus in favor of no first-use on the basis of a
superficial application of biblical standards. They sought out and
carefully considered the testimony of expert theorists and experienced practitioners. However they justified no first-use theoretically, the bishops first had to be convinced that it promised
in fact to make war *less* likely.

II

The case for no first-use as a viable option for policymakers is
a strong one, but the bishops' effort to make the case has some
serious limitations. Before undertaking a critical examination of
their presentation, it is necessary to establish the legitimacy of
no first-use. For this we must turn to the "raw material" with
which the bishops worked: the testimony of the "experts." What
follows is a summary of the chief criticisms of no first-use, including an assessment of each one's validity.[7]

1. *No first-use would increase the possibility of war*

The essence of this objection is that given the Warsaw Pact's
superiority in conventional forces, removal of NATO's nuclear
forces from defense against conventional attack would tempt

Soviet leaders to regard war in Europe as a calculable risk. This view does not require an assumption that the Soviet Union has always been expansionist. Indeed, acknowledging that Soviet ambitions have so far been limited for the most part to securing its rimlands and protecting its gains from World War II might give it greater force. One could argue that no first-use would actually create a new danger: a less cautious, more unpredictable adversary. Not having to disperse its troops in order to minimize damage from tactical nuclear weapons, the Warsaw Pact would be free to use massive, concentrated force (as Soviet military doctrine prefers) to break through Western defenses. Furthermore, while Central Europe would suffer massive destruction, damage to the Soviet Union would be limited.

In reply, the defenders of no first-use point out that the strengthened conventional forces their initiative presupposes would allow NATO to resist an attack from the east effectively. Even at present force levels, NATO has certain advantages (e.g., quality of equipment and training, preponderance of antitank weapons) that cannot easily be dismissed. At least as important is the fact that Soviet leaders fear the destabilizing political consequences in Eastern Europe that war would bring.[8] Moreover, it is unlikely that Soviet leaders would dismiss the possibility that, if desperate, Western commanders might rescind no first-use and employ nuclear weapons at some level. It is highly unlikely that even an unusually adventurous Soviet leadership would consider the potential gains worth the risk, if not of complete devastation, then of the kind of social disruption that could very well spell the end of the communist state.

2. No first-use would dangerously close off policy options that could keep a war limited

This criticism rests on the conviction that (a) the use of at least some nuclear weapons involves a level of destructiveness no higher than that which the use of modern conventional weapons entails, and (b) escalation through the various stages of tactical and theater nuclear weaponry, culminating in the nightmare of an all-out intercontinental exchange, is by no means inevitable. The ability to use, or credibly threaten to use, nuclear weapons at lower levels would hold out some hope of convincing the aggressor to reconsider pressing his attack before it is too late. Without the capability of using the full range of nuclear weaponry, leaders facing an attacker who is overcoming conventional defenses can only surrender or break the no-first-use pledge and "go nuclear" at the most dangerous possible time: the eleventh hour.

The four *Foreign Affairs* proponents of no first-use throw down a challenge to this objection by flatly stating that "every serious analysis and every military exercise for over 25 years has demonstrated that even the most restrained battlefield use [of nuclear weapons] would be enormously destructive to civilian life and property."[9] The assumption that nuclear war can be kept limited is made questionable by evidence that the Soviet Union has never accepted the validity of the concept of a limited nuclear conflict. That is, Soviet military doctrine is not geared to tit-for-tat response, but rather to escalating before the enemy is able.[10] Even so strong an opponent of nuclear weapons as George F. Kennan admits that modern conventional war can be as destructive as tactical nuclear weapons.[11] However, there is still the danger of escalation to reckon with. History is rife with examples of the unintended consequences of the use of force. In this light, a massive preemptive strike by the Soviet Union on the United States would seem as plausible a scenario as one positing sober reassessment and disengagement once the nuclear threshold were crossed.

3. No first-use is not politically feasible

Most participants in the debate over no first-use agree that its feasibility is heavily dependent on the existence of a strong conventional defense capability. Skeptics fear that either the United States, or NATO governments in Europe, or both would be unable to bear the dramatically higher defense costs they assume this would require. They refer not only to the difficulty that large increases in military budgets would present to efforts at ensuring stable, noninflationary growth. Perhaps more important are political resistance to giving defense higher priority while trimming government social programs, and conflict over burden-sharing.

Authoritative voices suggest that NATO's conventional defense capacity could be improved as necessary with a relatively modest increase in defense spending over a finite period (five or six years).[12] Furthermore, the prospect of wrangling over who will assume what responsibility seems no more serious than the present reality of a "crisis of confidence" among their publics over nuclear weapons policy that NATO governments cannot ignore. A no-first-use policy could certainly be formulated only after careful consultation among the Western allies. It could very well open the door to a defense posture that would be both more rational and less expensive than the present one.

4. *No first-use alone would not significantly alleviate the danger of total nuclear war*

One analyst contends that so long as the United States maintains a commitment to defend Western Europe against Soviet attack, a declaration of no first-use would do little to prevent escalation. He charges that the *Foreign Affairs* authors implicitly assume the likelihood of a desperate, "unauthorized" first-use in the event that conventional defense fails, a failure he regards as all too probable. No first-use can therefore be credible only if it is redefined as part of a policy of "war avoidance," which would prohibit the United States from undertaking overseas defense commitments.[13]

In arguing only on the basis of a "worst case" scenario (i.e., last-ditch first-use in the face of an imminent Soviet victory), this objection underestimates the possibilities that a no-first-use policy might create for the relaxation of tension and the reduction of nuclear arsenals. Moreover, it is difficult to see how retreating to a "fortress America" would be any more likely to avoid an eventual (and nuclear) confrontation than a no-first-use policy combined with a viable conventional defense.

5. *No first-use would not reduce East-West tension*

Another argument questions the efficacy of no first-use as a diplomatic icebreaker. It stresses that the Soviets are unlikely to trust any such pledge by the Western allies. A prominent French critic contends that no first-use would not merely be ineffective; it would be diplomatically disastrous. Even if the Soviets had no intention of actually using force, the credibility of their threat to do so would be much higher than it is now. This would sooner encourage hard-line demands and diplomatic showdowns than flexibility and negotiation in good faith.[14]

As we have seen, the impetus for the Bundy-Kennan-

McNamara-Smith proposal was the authors' shared conviction that the present NATO policy of *first*-use in the event of a conventional attack from the east has become less and less credible, both within the Alliance and to the Soviet Union. This lack of credibility has *already* eroded the deterrent effect of first-use. In addition, the authors assume that no first-use would be adopted only in connection with the development of adequate conventional forces, the maintenance of a second-strike capability, and on the basis of a firm political commitment by all members of the Alliance. Under these circumstances, deterrence would not be eroded; it might even be enhanced. Therefore fears of Soviet diplomatic intransigence would be unfounded. Soviet distrust of no first-use, of course, would make risk-taking even less attractive. As for the futility of diplomatic initiatives, the historical record does not require us simply to assume the worst. Both sides have in fact found it to their mutual advantage to conclude agreements within the past twenty years or so. Both sides have acknowledged that nuclear war is a very real danger. The possibility of no first-use leading to a diplomatic breakthrough should not be debunked any more than it should be exaggerated.

This assessment of objections to no first-use is not meant to suggest that they can easily be dismissed. Many of the points made on either side of this and other aspects of nuclear weapons-related issues are of necessity speculative. Successful implementation of no first-use would require a high degree of political consensus and economic commitment among NATO members. Soviet responsiveness would depend on a skillful diplomacy able to minimize misperception and maximize the opportunity for further confidence-building measures. Nevertheless, critics cannot simply dismiss no first-use as impractical. The obstacles in its way are not nearly so formidable as to justify rejecting out of hand efforts to overcome them gradually. As the inadequacy of our present policy becomes apparent, exploring seriously such an initiative as no first-use seems more and more to be the better part of wisdom.

III

The Catholic bishops are convincing when they argue that no first-use is more consistent with important biblical principles relating to peace and the use of force than is reliance on peace through strength. Peace*making* suggests activity, not passivity. No first-use recognizes that deterrence is at best a temporary solution that must be supplemented by careful but active efforts to reduce armaments. Faith involves a willingness to trust, not overemphasis on security. No first-use rejects the extreme security consciousness that accepts the "necessity" of overkill while only reluctantly conceding the possibility of workable agreement with the Soviets. Discipleship requires an acute sensitivity to the human propensity to fail; it also involves a commitment to alleviate the effects of sin. No first-use recognizes the folly of blindly assuming that nuclear weapons are not likely to be used accidentally or uncontrollably; it also recognizes the necessity of effective defense against the unjust threat or use of force.

The bishops also are effective in articulating the link between their theological analysis and public policy choice. West German Catholic bishops, in their own letter on peace, avoid comment on specific policies. Their reasoning is that they are qualified only to explicate moral criteria applicable to matters of nuclear strategy. Only political or military experts may judge whether or not a particular policy meets these criteria.[15] The American bishops, fortunately, are bolder. They are committed as pastors to guiding their charges in applying God's Word to thought and action in this area of life, as in all areas.

In doing so they avoid the temptation to claim a divine mandate for mere political opinion, however sincere or well informed. The American bishops make clear the distinction between established moral principle and their advocacy of specific policies: "When making applications of these principles we realize—and we wish readers to recognize—that prudential judgments are involved based on specific circumstances that can change or that can be interpreted differently by people of goodwill (e.g., the treatment of 'no first use')." Like the Apostle Paul in I Corinthians 7:10, 12, the bishops put their own recommendations in proper perspective even while they urge their readers to do some earnest reflection: ". . . the moral judgments that we make in specific cases, while not binding in conscience, are to be given serious attention and consideration by Catholics as they determine whether their moral judgments are consistent with the Gospel."[16]

Despite these important strengths, the bishops' articulation of no first-use is not without fault. As mentioned earlier, the letter considers nuclear deterrence as justifiable only in a very limited sense. The authors reject as morally unacceptable any strategy of deterrence that (a) contemplates the possibility of striking enemy cities "even after our own have been struck"; (b) targets military and economic objectives (since striking these would also inflict high noncombatant casualties); or (c) deploys any weapons deemed to provide "war-fighting capabilities" (counterforce or tactical nuclear weapons). Although they do not explicitly say so, the logical consequence of accepting these restrictions would seem to be an affirmation that there would be virtually no circumstances under which use of the "deterrent" could be justified. What then would be left of deterrence? More importantly, what would be left of no first-use, which presupposes the existence of a second-strike capability that is *credible* to the other side?

Another problem is the letter's failure to deal adequately with two of the most important challenges to the feasibility of no first-use: that it would endanger peace by "tempting" the Soviet Union, and that it would be politically impossible to implement. Most of the section on no first-use is devoted to refuting a third major objection: that no first-use closes off options for flexible nuclear response. In this case the bishops concisely but convincingly criticize the assumption that even low-yield nuclear weapons could be effectively controlled.

There is no comparable treatment of the other two objections, however. The bishops could have demonstrated more effectively that their recommendation of no first-use was based on careful attention to the question of feasibility had they not limited their comment on these other matters to one or two sentences. They might have pointed out, for example, that aside from fearing escalation, the Soviet Union is deterred by a fear of the political repercussions (within its own sphere) of war. They might also have demonstrated their awareness that the political consensus so crucial to the implementation of no first-use would probably require a more unequivocal U.S. commitment to the defense of Western Europe. Establishing feasibility

is crucial to any effort to go beyond mere ethical pronouncement and instead convince citizens and policymakers of the necessary connection between moral principles and political
behavior. In different parts of the pastoral letter the bishops
take pains to put their message of peace in a realistic context,
such as when they discuss the Soviet approach to politics and
the need to be critical of peace rhetoric. The section on no first-
use would have benefited from more such substantive discussion
of the questions surrounding this particular issue.

These weaknesses stem from two basic problems. First, the
just-war theory is of limited usefulness in providing ethical
guidelines for nuclear strategy, because deterrence, to be credible, requires planning for at least some actions that might or
might not be used if war actually broke out. As strong an advocate of no first-use as former Secretary of Defense McNamara
expressed the paradoxical nature of nuclear politics when trying
to explain his preference for a formula he termed "no first-use
until." Asked to clarify what he meant by "until," McNamara
replied: "Until we know exactly what our opponent intended to
do, at what level the order to use nuclear weapons originated
on his side, and whether there is any chance that the conflict
might still be confined without our resorting to nuclear retaliation."[17] "Until" implies the need to retain the option for actual
use of nuclear weapons while refusing to say in advance whether
or when they would in fact be used. Michael Novak shows that
the rigid application of the just-war theory, especially of the
criterion of "intention," can undermine, in effect, the possibility
of any viable deterrent.[18] It is significant that the German bishops consider the concept of a just war to be obsolete in the
nuclear era. They suggest it be replaced by the idea of a "just
defense."[19]

Second, in their theological exposition, the bishops stress
the need to maintain a vision of peace. They note that this vision
is "capable of progressive realization" and that, besides being a
divine gift, it is also a "human work." The pastoral letter does
caution against false, utopian visions of peace and at several
places points out the need to recognize the limitations imposed
by a fallen world. Nevertheless, the bishops seem to view their
efforts to promote peace as being part of a process of continual
movement toward the millennium. "Is it hoping too much," they

ask in reference to the prospects for world peace, "to believe that the genius of humanity, aided by the grace and guidance of God, is able to accomplish it?" The theology of hope, with its stress on human involvement in the progressive realization of the kingdom, appears to have been influential also. Thus: "a theology of peace must include a message of hope."[20]

The bishops are genuinely concerned to make the connection between moral precept and political practice in a complex world. But their enthusiastic promotion of a vision for peace may have caused them to overlook somewhat the complications associated with policies such as no first-use. They have paid less attention than they might have to promoting its viability along with its morality.

The *Foreign Affairs* advocates of no first-use state: "The day is long past when public awe and governmental secrecy made nuclear policy a matter for only the most private executive determination. The questions presented by a policy of no first use must indeed be decided by governments, but they can and should be considered by citizens."[21] The bishops eloquently remind us that discipleship is an incentive for active citizenship. Near the end of the pastoral letter, they call for educational activities designed to communicate fundamental Christian principles along with "possible legitimate options." It is in this spirit that their endorsement of one of those options, no first-use, deserves to be seconded.

8: Renouncing the Use of Nuclear Weapons: Strategic Implications

RONALD B. KIRKEMO

THE MORAL BASIS OF PEACE

God calls his people to live a life holy in devotion and righteous in love and service. "Blessed are the peacemakers" is a clear biblical mandate, but the issue of nuclear weapons presents a dilemma. What *are* peacemaking and righteousness in a world possessing the ultimate weapon but rejecting the ultimate answer? The bishops address this concern by pronouncing the use of nuclear weapons morally unacceptable. They advocate moving from the present, uneasy "peace of a sort" to a future, "genuine peace" built on justice, global disarmament, and an international "public authority."[1]

The bishops' answer relies on three fundamental, but nevertheless mistaken, views. The first is their nonhistorical view of world affairs. The bishops believe a genuine peace built on justice in a disarmed world is possible; however, such a belief disregards the nature of previous periods of peace and disarmament. History is evidence, and when the bishops dismiss the continuities of history, they lose perspective on the difference between what is desirable and what is possible. Like Jonathan Schell, who calls for "reinventing the world,"[2] so they overestimate "human potential," diplomacy, and the existence of a "new moment."[3]

The bishops also mistakenly depreciate the relationship of military power to diplomacy and peace. A nation without strength

119

will not be taken seriously in world affairs because it appears to lack the commitment seriously to confront vital issues, fulfill worldwide obligations, and discourage external threats.

Finally, the bishops hold a simplified view of morality in world affairs. Believing in a moral order from which a code of universal ethics can be deduced, the bishops overlook the paradoxes, ambiguities, and conflicts of loyalties that plague moral choice in the interlocking affairs of history, nations, and individuals.

A morality of nuclear weapons must be based not only on the call to peace, but also on the factors that create and maintain peace in our present world. There is no world community of values that binds nations together into a *consensus juris* and so directs their policies toward a common good; therefore, world unity and harmony do not exist. The world is divided, instead, by the National Factor—armed nations with their own historical pasts, cultural values, and national interests. The various resources necessary for national life are unequally distributed in the world. This Scarcity Factor requires nations either to preserve their own resources or obtain more by attempting to alter existing international arrangements. Such tension produces disagreements and further nationalizes conceptions of justice. Regulation of this international competition is difficult because power and decision making are decentralized. There is no global mechanism to provide the world with the legislative, judicial, and security services necessary to harmonize actions, promote cooperation, and prevent conflicts. When nations disagree over important issues, they will use various diplomatic tools and tactics to persuade the other nations to give in or back off from their demands. If diplomatic methods are ineffective and the issue is sufficiently important, nations will resort to the use of the Military Factor to obtain their goals. In the words of Thomas Hobbes, "When nothing else turns up, clubs are trumps."[4]

In this global system of nationalized justice and dispersed power, nations must work out voluntary, mutual agreements on the nature of their cooperation, rights, and limits. As long as nations are receiving mutual benefits from their agreements, national goals are likely to be moderate, and international relations remain orderly and stable. But the development and alteration of those agreements can be subject to coercion. If one nation attains significant new strength, or if the other nations are unwilling to enforce the mutual obligations inherent in the agreement, it will be tempting for that nation to use its new power (or lack of opposition) to demand new, more favorable agreements from the other partners. In that event, agreements will reflect what is possible, not what is just.

Peace, then, will never be based on justice, because justice continues to be defined in terms of domestic politics. Peace between nuclear nations is not the result of goodwill among leaders or of the efforts of grass-roots peace movements. In the nature of our decentralized world, peace is not built on unilateral military restraint in the realm of nuclear nations and the alliances to which they belong. Expanding power and political rifts between East and West heighten our apprehension over the hope of peace in Europe and the Middle East. Peace is stable and orderly, however, when it is based on a moderation of means and ends. That moderation cannot be safely induced by satisfying the demands of the strong alone, for the goals of the strong will expand when increased satisfaction seems possible. Peace has to be constructed on three things: first, an alignment of nations that achieves a balance of forces and prevents one nation for becoming dominant; second, a willingness to enforce agreements when one nation attempts to alter them by threats or coercion; and third, a willingness to participate in efforts to reconcile conflicting demands with procedures of peaceful resolution.

Many factors are helpful in creating and maintaining peaceful relations, including the quality of leadership, organizational procedures for negotiation and persuasion, opportunities for cooperation, and programs for developmental aid. Peace can be more than just a military balance when it contains elements of common values and cooperation, but it cannot be less than a balance. Peace is not the result of an inherent and automatic harmony of interests between nations, but the result of a deliberate networking of allies, expectations, and interests to construct a specific balance of military power and commitment. By means of this balance, nations hope to influence the cost/benefit analysis (Luke 14:31, 32) of other nations considering changes in policies to pursue and methods to employ.

The Christian will find difficulties in making moral judgments about ends, means, and consequences of military policy in this fragmented world. The degree of one's holiness is totally self-dependent. In a world of instability, where the foundation of order is a combination of balanced power, moderated aspirations, and compromised interests, righteousness is difficult. Goals are limited by what is possible, means by what is effective, and consequences by unintended or unexpected developments. The ethic of perfect righteousness must be replaced in world affairs with a morality of responsibility. This does not relegate morality to being "Pentagon theologese" or a "red-white-and-blue holiness orthodoxy."[5] It does mean, however, that what is morally possible for a nation in our fragmented world is much more limited than what is morally possible for an individual within a nation having a deep community of values and effective government.

A morality of responsibility is not a counsel of despair. It is an ethic of wisdom—knowing how the world works, avoiding policies that undercut the foundation of order, and pursuing policies that strengthen cooperation and persuasion. It is also an ethic that resists the dynamics of immorality in world politics—the unholiness of a false idolatry of ultranationalism, and the unrighteousness of glorifying violence, extending tyranny, and consenting to poverty. It is not a dual morality that justifies nations using gangster ethics; it is a morality that affirms that humans have souls capable of compassion, pride, sacrifice, endurance, courage, honor, and hope.[6] These character traits will help us to confront the challenges before us. Crises will not force decision makers to choose irrational options; nuclear danger will not drive the public to a panicked willingness to trade freedom for a security based on American paralysis and Soviet pronouncements of goodwill; military spending will not dry up aid programs for the poor.

The traditional morality of war represented by the laws of war codified at the Hague Conferences in 1899 and 1907, and by the just-war doctrine, are inadequate for establishing viable limitations on the destructive capacity of the nuclear era. The moral goals of a person dealing with nuclear weapons should be to promote specific military designs, military policies, and human attitudes that establish three goals. First, strategic balance should be preserved. Second, military danger should be minimized by eliminating unintended appearances of threat, promoting control over subordinate commanders, and limiting the extent of damage in the event of a nuclear exchange. Third, human detachment should be minimized by avoiding a closed mathematical system of strategic logic, a simplistic perception of adversaries, an isolation from the consequences of nuclear war, and a despair that abandons concern for the quality of policies and life. Sometimes these goals are mutually compatible, and sometimes they are not. The moral test of this ethic is not whether it conforms or diverges from Pentagon policy, but whether it promotes moderation and prospects for control so that the more consensual and compassionate relations of nations can be expanded.

CONTINUITIES OF HISTORY

The great danger of nuclear weapons does not come from the bombs alone, but also from the fact that they represent the ascendence of the offense in military strategy over the defense. At various times in history, technological innovations have shifted the advantage in effectiveness between the attacking and the defending forces.[7] The horrible losses along the trench lines of the Western Front in World War I reflected the superiority of the defense due to such innovations as mine fields and machine guns. Between the wars, General Giulio Douhet developed a doctrine that called for the use of air forces to launch a surprise attack on the adversary's air force. With command of the air assured, he would then deliver devastating bombing attacks on industrial and residential targets to create such tremendous psychological shock that the victim would sue for peace.[8] This strategy was not decisive in World War II because the low destructive power of conventional weapons made multiple, repeated attacks necessary. Bombers could be fought off (as in the Battle of Britain), and saturation bombing (as at Dresden) did not break the nation's morale.[9]

The development of the intercontinental ballistic missile (ICBM), which could penetrate any known defense, made nations "permeable" and open to attack. When these missiles were coupled with the high explosive yield of nuclear bombs, the advantage in war shifted decisively to the offense. This shift destabilizes world order because it places a premium on striking first. It also gives the advantage to a nation armed with these weapons and intending to revise the structure of world order to improve its status at the expense of other nations.

This latest shift in military power and international stability poses lethal danger to the United States, the Soviet Union, and potentially the entire world. It convinced the bishops that the world is at a new moment in which the common danger makes possible the establishment of a world without war. History, however, has not been transformed. No world community that can bind nations into peaceful relations has come into existence. Nations may have a common nightmare, but that does not produce common dreams.[10] The international system continues to allow Machiavellian uses of force. "Yesterday war was not necessary, but it was constant. Today, war is not inevitable, but it remains a possibility."[11] International agreements to abolish such decisive weapons are impossible.[12] Unilateral renunciation of such weapons is suicidal.

This mutual danger of nuclear war should not reduce life to the question, "When will I be blown up?" As Faulkner so eloquently reminded the world, humanity can prevail if it does not drown its courage, honor, and hope in fear.[13] The use of force cannot be eliminated, but it can be restrained. Nuclear weapons can and have been constructed and deployed to create a state of mutual deterrence that eradicates the tendency to launch a surprise attack. Nuclear deterrence has prevented a general nuclear war by convincing national leaders that launching an attack will result in their own destruction.[14] Nuclear weapons have also been deployed and controlled in a rational way to lower the risk of conventional war and have, therefore, dampened instability in areas of vital importance to the nuclear nations. Additionally, U.S. nuclear weapons have been "used" to deter attack on itself, to protect its vital allies, and to support its diplomatic leadership. So, on balance, this state of mutual deterrence has been beneficial to the forces of order and global security by moderating military means in an era of immoderate military power and political ends.

NUCLEAR WEAPONS AND DETERRENCE

Nuclear weapons are strategic in the sense that they can reach the interior of another nation's territory. They are also strategic in another sense. Strategy is the art of designing and applying military means to achieve political ends,[15] and nuclear weapons, because of the destruction they can cause to the Soviet heartland, are the basic weapons by which the United States acquires its fundamental defense and foreign policy aims. That is, by design (size and payload), deployment (location and type of launcher), and doctrine (when and how used), they are utilized to achieve the national security goals of deterring war, limiting wartime damage, facilitating an armistice, protecting crucial allies, projecting diplomatic influence, and preserving the decentralized international system of nation-states.

The most important objective of the United States is to deter a nuclear attack on its territory. To achieve that, the United States must have forces that are able to destroy an aggressor. Furthermore, those forces must be able to survive an attack, strike back, and detonate on the right target. Destructiveness, survivability, and willingness to use the so-called "second-strike capability" are the prerequisites for deterrence.

The first prerequisite is the ability to destroy, not just cripple, an opponent. The levels of unacceptable damage and the commitment to the goals sought by an attacker cannot be known, so the level of deterrence that assures unacceptable damage on the attacker cannot be calculated. The ability to destroy the nation as a functioning society eliminates any margin of error in the judgments and decisions of leaders in a time of crisis. U.S. nuclear forces are presently capable of destroying approximately 33 percent of the Soviet population and 65 percent of their "recovery resources" (political institutions, i.e., the secret police, the party cadre, local officials, etc.), although these figures represent a decline in destructive capacity in the past decades.[16]

Renouncing the use of nuclear weapons would require conventional (nonnuclear) forces of sufficient magnitude to match the nuclear arsenal presently deployed. The amount of expansion that substitution would require is staggering. The United States presently has:

4,441 nuclear warheads on 1,054 ICBMs
3,625 nuclear warheads in 46 submarines
2,640 nuclear bombs carried in 407 bombers

10,706 nuclear bombs ranging in capacity from 40 kilotons to 10 megatons[17]

Conventional bombs range in size from a few pounds to over one ton of TNT.[18] A one-megaton nuclear weapon is equal to a million tons of TNT. If we assume that all U.S. nuclear bombs and warheads were only one megaton, it would take 10,706,000 conventional bombs to match current nuclear forces. The B-52 bomber carries a maximum payload of only 70,000 pounds, and the B-1 bomber will carry only 115,000 pounds.[19] The size of the bomber and missile fleets needed to deliver enough conventional weapons to match current nuclear weapons would be beyond reason for a country to afford, deploy, and protect.

The staggering power reflected in these numbers leads to a perception that the United States has far more than enough destructive capacity, and, therefore, that it could destroy the Soviet Union thirty-six times over (at least), and the amounts of forces presently deployed are grossly unnecessary. Such a perception fails to take into account the extent of destruction to those forces that would occur from an attack.[20] It also does not consider the difficulty of second-strike forces penetrating Soviet air defenses, or the factor of damaged weapons that do not detonate even if they do survive, fire, penetrate, and reach the assigned target. To be truly strategic and effective, the nuclear forces must have built-in redundancy, unless one assumes that the United States will first attack population centers only, and the Soviet Union will employ no offensive or defensive strike on U.S. weapons. The concept of overkill is greatly overblown, and the United States is not perpetuating an arms race that is out of control. The United States has not added to its missile forces since 1964. It has increased the capacity of those missiles by adding warheads with multiple bombs (MIRVs), but the bombs have been smaller in power. The total megatonage of U.S. nuclear weapons in 1980 was only one quarter of the 1960 arsenal.[21]

Second-strike capability that would eliminate all hope of the Soviet Union's survival is required to deter an all-out nuclear war. A nation-destroying, general nuclear war is not, however, the only disaster the United States must deter. The American nation has vital interests in strategic areas like Europe, Central America, and the Middle East. If a major war erupted in one of those areas, the United States might have to become involved in such a war against the Soviet Union. To prevent or to end that intervention quickly and cheaply, Soviet leaders might launch a limited nuclear strike against some isolated U.S. military forces in the hope of "scaring" the United States into paralysis. If the United States was capable of responding only with Mutual Assured Destruction (MAD), it would either have to accommodate itself or initiate a mutually suicidal holocaust. In a situation of major crisis with the United States, the Soviets might use a limited nuclear strike to shock American leaders into accommodation. The pressure on American leaders to accept the present losses and not risk more would be tremendous. Worldwide condemnation would be swift and punitive on the Soviet Union, but that condemnation would be short-lived in any disruptive sense, and the long-term value of the new arrangements could be lucrative enough to far outweigh short-term denunciation. Although general nuclear war had been avoided, the Soviet Union would have emerged believing it could use its nuclear weapons on a very limited scale to achieve massive political goals.

Deterring limited nuclear strikes requires a different policy than MAD, one that is able to respond with equal or marginally greater nuclear reprisals. The United States has adopted a nuclear strategy that provides for the possibility of "flexible nuclear responses" to limited strikes on American targets. Flexible response deters such attacks by denying the Soviet Union the ability to use limited nuclear strikes for political coercion, and it prevents the United States from pushing a limited strike to a massive attack simply because it did not have the diversity of weapon size or targeting flexibility to do otherwise.[22]

An attack on population centers only would probably unify opinion in favor of revenge rather than surrender. Even if a nuclear exchange were limited to missile sites instead of urban areas, the damage and death would be extensive.[23] A limited war would not, however, inevitably escalate to all-out war and the end of the world. The ability to respond in kind and assure mutual levels of destruction is the only way to reduce the risk of a successful limited strike and prevent political intimidation. Nuclear weapons are necessary, then, to achieve the kind of destructive capacity at *all* levels of potential warfare in order to deter a potential nuclear attack at *any* level.

Deterrence requires more than just destructive capacity at all levels. It also requires that nuclear forces be survivable—protected to such a degree that enough will survive an attack and remain operational to launch a retaliatory strike. Substituting conventional weapons for nuclear forces would decrease survivability and increase collateral damage to urban areas, which would inevitably be closer to such an expanded number of missiles and bombers.

The last requirement for deterrence is the will to use the protected nuclear forces in a retaliatory strike, whether limited or massive. The bishops give a "strictly conditional moral acceptance of nuclear deterrence," but in the context that *any use* of nuclear weapons is unacceptable and condemned.[24] They rule out both countervalue and counterforce strikes against the Soviet Union.[25] The bishops seem to want to escape the grim reality of deterrence by assuming deterrence is somehow automatic so long as both nations have nuclear weapons. This is an evasion. To possess nuclear weapons and to proclaim that their use is immoral and not credible is to make them useless for deterrence. To oppose the possibility that the weapons might have to be used, no matter how limited, is to weaken deterrence. There is no avoiding the fact that "deterrence rests not only on how the Soviets measure the severity of retaliation if it comes, but on their judgments about its certainty."[26] If a nuclear attack is launched on the United States, deterrence guarantees that an equal or greater counterattack will be delivered. A nation that maintains nuclear forces, but indicates it will never use them, eliminates deterrence.

There is a terrible paradox here. We do not want any kind of nuclear war, yet to ensure that one does not take place, we have to threaten to use nuclear weapons. That produces great anxiety and leads to efforts to renounce the use of nuclear weapons. This weakens deterrence and makes nuclear war more possible. There is no easy way out of the paradox. Just as there is no substitute for nuclear forces, so there is no substitute for a proclaimed intention to use them in the event of an attack.

Deterrence may break down in spite of all that is done to reinforce it. A conventional war might escalate to limited strikes.

The Soviet Union might achieve enough technological sophistication that its continually growing strategic forces will become capable of attacking with impunity. The Russian leaders might come to believe that the American decision makers would be so paralyzed by a nuclear strike that they would refrain from launching even a limited counterstrike. The above developments are all possible, and one has to assume that a nuclear war might occur at some level; therefore, we must consider methods to limit damage and to terminate war, and we must ask whether they are promoted or hindered by a renunciation of the use of nuclear weapons.

Since the Soviet Union would have no reason to decrease the efficiency of its strategic forces, a policy of deterrence without nuclear weapons would have the consequences of increasing both the likelihood and the collateral damage of a nuclear strike. Nor is it practical to assume that the American public will approve a major spending program to develop civil defense shelters. Until there is a breakthrough in technology that provides a defense against nuclear weapons on ICBMs employed in a Douhet-style attack, and thereby shifts the military advantage back from the offense to the defense, the only way to limit damage and speed the termination of a nuclear war is by designing a nuclear doctrine that makes limitation and termination beneficial to the safety and security of the Soviet Union. Renouncing the use of nuclear weapons allows the attacker to determine the timing, extent, and duration of a nuclear assault. The determination of the outcome of the assault, ranging from a status quo ceasefire to an unconditional surrender, would also be decided by the attacker, since it would be safe from any destructive counterattack and would not have to limit its objectives in order to limit damage to itself.

Preserving its independence and limiting damage to its society in the event of nuclear attack requires the United States to have the weapons and doctrine that allow deliberate selection of targets, choice of levels, and types of retaliation. The goal is to make the Soviet Union aware that the United States has the ability to respond with less than an all-out retaliation, and a limited attack on the United States will not result in a countervalue attack on Soviet society. In the midst of a crisis, the strategy could be reaffirmed by issuing a "sanctuary declaration" specifying that the United States will not retaliate against Soviet cities.[27] The purpose of this strategy is to induce the Soviet Union to limit its attack both in size and to military targets alone. There is no question that a limited strike will have extensive collateral damage and will constitute a major disaster. Contrary to the arguments of the bishops, however, that should not be an argument against attempts to limit damage. Distinctions, even when blurred, remain imperative when the discussion regards the lives of people who survive. Morality is minimized if choice is limited to leaving the nation open to a crippling nuclear attack or initiating nuclear suicide.

A nuclear attack could end without retaliation if the attacker intended merely to bolster its political bargaining position and not destroy the victim nation, which decided its political losses would be more acceptable than the risks of escalation. But a successful first strike would have far-reaching consequences for the future. It is unlikely that it would strengthen the firebreak between nuclear and nonnuclear weapons. The threat of its use in the next crisis would be much more credible; the likelihood that nuclear blackmail would be used again would increase; and the likelihood that the victim nation would resolve never to give in again without retaliation would be enhanced. The successful use of nuclear weapons by one nation would probably increase the incentives for nonnuclear nations to join the nuclear club.

Termination of a nuclear exchange will depend on various factors: the character of the leadership of both nations; how the war began (accident, misunderstanding, intention); the goals of the initial attack; the intensity of the fighting; and the potential of improving one's position by continuing the war. The relevance of several of these factors depends on the amount of flexibility a nation has available in the use of its nuclear forces. At a minimum, the command, control, and communication facilities and personnel must be "spared" in order to reach an agreement on a ceasefire. The ability to inflict equal or greater destruction at any level of attack ensures that an attacker cannot improve its position by continuing the exchanges. The ability to permit a "pause" before launching a second strike in order to negotiate a favorable ceasefire in return for withholding a nuclear reprisal could be workable. The ability to induce a termination of war in these ways requires design and doctrinal preparation as well as the intention to use nuclear forces as necessary. The ability to carry out a flexible response is more likely to end a war in which one nation has crossed the nuclear threshold than is the absence of that ability. As stated earlier, renouncing use of nuclear weapons will increase the likelihood of nuclear attacks, the length of hostilities, and the degree of their destructiveness.

NUCLEAR WEAPONS AND ALLY PROTECTION

Each nuclear power considers some nations and regions vital to its own security and vision of a virtuous world order. The alignment, identity, and nature of the leadership of those select countries is a crucial stake for the nuclear powers; consequently, the United States must protect its network of vital allies pursuing moderate foreign policies. Nuclear weapons aid that policy by providing adversary deterrence and ally reassurance.

A democratic Western Europe in close alignment with the United States is crucial for American security and a world order conducive to the values of America. The United States became involved in two world wars to preserve that kind of Europe from the threat of unification under a hostile, dictatorial empire. While controversy exists about the policy goals of the Soviet Union toward Europe, the empirical evidence of the size and firepower of Soviet forces directed at Western Europe is clear and frightening.[28] In the 1950s the United States coupled its overwhelming nuclear superiority to the NATO forces relative to the Warsaw Pact forces. NATO's forces acted as a "tripwire" that, when attacked by Soviet-backed forces, would trigger an American strategic strike on the Soviet Union. The construction of Soviet nuclear forces made the continuation of that strategy untenable.

American theater nuclear forces—short ranged with relatively small yield—are stationed in Western Europe for several reasons: to deter a possible land invasion from the east; to balance Soviet theater weapons; to prevent nuclear blackmail; to forestall nuclear proliferation; and to reassure West Germany that its allies will defend it. Deploying nuclear weapons in Europe is a symbolic linkage between NATO and American strategic forces. This raises the risks for the Soviet Union that its homeland might not escape the results of a conventional, European war. Making that risk real helps hold Soviet troops behind the "iron curtain" so that invasions like those into Hungary, Czechoslovakia, and Afghanistan are not carried out west of the Berlin Wall. Unfortunately, the small nuclear forces of Great Britain and France cannot serve as a link to U.S. strategic forces, nor can they function as a deterrent for other nonnuclear nations.[29] Nuclear weapons in Europe significantly duplicate similar Soviet forces in Eastern Europe. NATO thereby has a nuclear option to deter any plan by invaders to employ nuclear weapons in a decisive, preemptive strike.

The presence of American nuclear weapons in Western Europe is both important and frightening to their citizens. In effect, if major war breaks out in Europe, nuclear war is likely to take place, and it will occur on European battlefields. That fear of being an isolated nuclear battleground can be politically disruptive, but so would withdrawal of those weapons, signaling a retreat of the American guarantee of protection. NATO conventional forces might contain an invasion by Warsaw Pact armies, but not if those forces are combined with Soviet forces and the threat of theater nuclear strikes. Balancing Soviet forces with American theater nuclear weapons, and raising the risk that strategic weapons might be used, preserves military stability in Europe.

U.S. theater nuclear weapons also perform politically oriented functions. The "long shadow of military power"[30] that Soviet forces project across Europe can be used for selective blackmail against nations. A major objective of Soviet foreign policy is the separation of Europe from the United States, and an American renunciation of nuclear weapons would make formal and informal security commitments meaningless. The basic arrangements of world order would change, as occurs "when there is a major change or turning point in the rise-decline dynamic of individual nations" and in the collective response to that fluctuation.[31] To assume that the new arrangements between Europe and the Soviet Union would only be marginally detrimental to peace and democratic values is myopic.

The European fear of massive Soviet forces undeterred by the risk of nuclear retaliation could be enough to induce accommodation of governmental policies to the demands of the Soviet

Union. Europe's value to the United States and world order could be lost without a war. This realignment would have rippling effects throughout world politics. The loss of such important allies from a paralysis of will or a decline in effective strength would be seen around the world as an unwillingness or inability of the United States to protect its own vital interests.

Or, instead of accommodation, there might be proliferation. Nations in Europe and elsewhere might adopt the "Gaullist option" and launch crash programs to cross the nuclear divide in order to replace American nuclear protection with their own. Those forces would never be sufficient to deter the Soviet Union, but they would be sufficient to destabilize regional politics in Asia, Africa, and the Middle East. Since none of these new nations could quickly achieve the survivability techniques necessary to protect their forces, they would be pressured to launch a preemptive strike in a crisis.[32]

Finally, theater nuclear forces offer protection for West Germany. The trauma of national division, coupled with the proximity of Warsaw Pact forces, could drive West Germany to one of two alternative dangers: accommodation with the Soviet Union (the fear of the United States), or resurgent nationalism (the fear of the United States *and* the Soviet Union). The U.S. nuclear umbrella and the deployment of forward-based nuclear forces have provided the measure of reassurance essential for moderate German governments to survive domestic elections and Soviet threats.[33]

A renunciation of the use of nuclear weapons would eliminate both deterrence and local defense, dramatically shifting the balance of forces in Europe. With its homeland made secure, Soviet forces would be dominant. With Europe made vulnerable, the United States would be isolated. That is not a prescription for moderation.

NUCLEAR WEAPONS AND WORLD LEADERSHIP

Peace in the nuclear era will be based on one of three alternatives: a global, social contract within the context of a shared sense of moral values; a combination of imposition and accommodation between the strong and the weak; or an epic determination by the democracies to maintain their defenses and commitments and thereby preserve a stable balance within a decentralized world system.[34] The bishops believe the common danger posed by nuclear weapons is a sufficiently strong, new historical force that it will deflect the present historical forces and move the world toward a future global community. But no historical evidence from the past centuries, or even from the recent decades of the nuclear era, exists to validate that belief. Even if it is becoming true, to proceed too early to renounce nuclear weapons will undercut the state of mutual deterrence on which the present world order rests, destabilize world harmony, and abort that historical progression. A time of troubles would develop, characterized by political realignments, regional wars, and increasing nationalism, violence, and poverty. That period would be followed, or ended, by an enforced peace organized by Soviet leaders for their own security and historical ambitions. So a kind of global unification would occur; not the kind envisioned by the bishops in the first alternative, but an international Hobbesian leviathan reflecting the second alternative.

Short of a transformation of the world into a global community, would not renunciation of nuclear weapons by both superpowers bring greater equality and allow the United Nations finally to become the global mechanism for establishing peace, security, and justice? Nuclear weapons outside UN control have certainly been one of the reasons for its impotence. Other factors, however, have been involved, including the ideological hostility of the nuclear nations, the inability of the United Nations to define and take action against aggression in the non-European world, and the enlarged membership, which makes decision making more difficult. The impotence of the United Nations is not a result of nuclear weapons, but a reflection of the deep political division in the world that the existence of these weapons also demonstrates. Neither the United States nor the Soviet Union will voluntarily give up their "trumps" before a global system that can protect the way of life of both nations has been established and is functioning satisfactorily.

Short of reforming the world by strengthening the United Nations, would not greater peace, security, and justice grow if the United States renounced the use of nuclear weapons, placed more emphasis on political persuasion through diplomacy, forced

Europe and Japan to take more responsibility for their own security, and launched a new economic recovery program for the underdeveloped world? The answer is negative. The state of nuclear deterrence not only preserves existing conditions of peace, but further makes possible an active U.S. diplomacy. Deterrence makes the United States secure, and a diplomatic leader must be secure in order to have the will and flexibility to assert leadership in trouble spots throughout the world.[35] American diplomatic intervention in conflict situations is desirable to isolate and dampen problems before they erupt into major crises. In other situations the United States can project its presence and leadership so that ceasefires and other reconciliations can be negotiated among participants without nuclear coercion from the Soviet Union. The nature of leadership in world affairs has a decisive impact on the quality and outcomes of diplomatic efforts. The loss of American leadership would weaken restraints on negative historical dynamics, leave allies exposed to new assertiveness from their adversaries, and allow the extension of Soviet military forces into strategic areas. The world balance of power would be dramatically altered.

A world leader must have the image of seriousness of purpose. A nation must be serious enough to pay the price to defend itself, its allies, and the network of obligations and expectations on which world order is based. A world leader must exhibit the capacity for a continuity of purpose and commitment in a world facing long-term struggles. Renouncing the use of weapons necessary for the security of a nation and its allies would signal a withdrawal from the burdens and risks of responsible commitment.

NUCLEAR WEAPONS AND NATIONAL RESPONSIBILITY

The "new moment" announced by the bishops, and the popularity of such slogans as "No nukes" and "End the race or end the race," reflect the inherent difficulties of democracies in pursuing a long-term policy that is dangerous, costly, and based on power and threat rather than persuasion and principle.[36] The traditional American policies of isolationism and world reform, both morally satisfying but morally primitive,[37] are being reasserted as the Soviet arms buildup reduces the U.S. military position from superiority to parity. In this context, American Evangelicals must not make the mistake of limiting the definition of morality to forbearance. Fear is not a policy. Morality and rational calculation are not antithetical. Free will and moral choice must be protected and promoted in this specific historical setting. By doing so, we preserve the relation of forces, the rationality of limitation, and the ethic of responsibility that uphold order and protect peace, democracy, opportunities for negotiated reconciliations between nations, and programs of compassion and service.

IV: The Morality of Deterrence

9: The Intention to Use Nuclear Weapons

JOHN E. HARE

The focus of this chapter will be on the section of the bishops' letter that deals with the theory of deterrence (section II.D). Within this section, the focus will be on the question of how the possession of nuclear weapons relates morally to the intention to use those weapons under certain circumstances. This chapter will first discuss this question and how it fits into deterrence theory generally. Then it will elaborate three doctrines that belong especially to Roman Catholic tradition, and will relate them to the section of the letter on deterrence theory. Finally, it will examine this section of the letter in detail to determine what is meant by a conditional acceptance of nuclear deterrence.

How does the possession of nuclear weapons relate morally to the intention to use them? One way to show the relation is to set up a series of five propositions that apparently cannot consistently be asserted together. First, it is (morally) wrong to use nuclear weapons under any circumstances. Second, if it is wrong to use nuclear weapons, it is also wrong to intend to use them. Third, if it is wrong to intend to use them, it is wrong to make preparations for using them. Fourth, if it is wrong to make preparations for using them, it is wrong to possess them, even for deterrent purposes. Fifth, it is (morally) acceptable to possess nuclear weapons for deterrent purposes.[1]

The bishops' letter does not assert any of these propositions directly. This chapter will argue, however, that it does accept the middle three, and will ask whether the qualifications made to the first and last propositions are sufficient to remove the logical unease the five unqualified propositions appear to generate when asserted together.

We will be concentrating on the third proposition, that if it is wrong to intend to use the weapons, it is wrong to make preparations for using them. Making preparations here includes the formation of nuclear strategy, explicit or implicit threats to likely opponents, training military personnel, targeting the weapons, and setting up command and control processes to ensure that the strategy could be implemented by constitutional authority. The argument behind the third proposition is that it would be inconsistent to condemn an intention and not condemn the preparations for carrying it out. Michael Walzer puts this in terms of readiness:

> No doubt killing millions of innocent people is worse than threatening to kill them. It is also true that no one wants to kill them, and it may well be true that no one expects to do so. Nevertheless, we intend the killings under certain circumstances. That is the stated policy of our government and thousands of men, trained in the techniques of mass destruction and drilled in instant obedience, stand ready to carry it out. And from the perspective of morality, the readiness is all. We can translate it into degrees of danger, high and low, and worry about the risks we are imposing on innocent people, but the risks depend on the readiness. What we condemn in our government is the commitment to murder.[2]

Before looking at this proposition more closely, it is worth examining the other four briefly in order to make clear the structure of the argument as a whole. The first involves condemning the bombing of Hiroshima and Nagasaki and any other possible use of nuclear weapons. The last involves accepting morally the possession of enough nuclear weapons to deter an opponent from nuclear attack. It does not attempt to adjudicate the question of how many nuclear weapons are enough for this purpose. The point of the second proposition is that the moral evaluation of agents has to involve an evaluation of their intentions.[3] We do not blame people for the unforeseen consequences of their actions, unless the lack of foresight was itself negligent. What is relevant is what they planned to accomplish. It is the heart that God judges, not merely the results of our actions.[4] There is a different kind of moral evaluation, of an action itself as opposed to the agent, where we can say of an action that it was the wrong thing to do even though the agent did not know any better when he or she did it.[5] But the argument behind the second proposition is that to condemn the user of nuclear weapons is to condemn the intention to use them in the circumstances in which they were used. If it is wrong to use them under any circumstances, it is wrong to intend to use them under any circumstances.

The development, production, and deployment of nuclear weapons is the most obvious way of preparing to implement the (conditional) intention to use such weapons. This is the basic point of the fourth proposition. If any preparations are wrong, the possession is wrong as well. But the proposition can also be understood as a point about deterrent effectiveness. It is a requirement of good stewardship that major equipment should not be acquired without any idea of how it would be used. Deterrent weapons are a special case; their sole "use" is to deter by being possessed. But at its simplest, the deterrent is supposed to work by posing a credible threat of retaliation. Such a threat cannot be credible unless preparations have been made for using the weapons under the threatened conditions. The mere possession of the weapons is not enough without the visible capability to use them. Having said this, however, it is very difficult to determine what degree of preparation is necessary. Making the weapons easier to use may also make the use of them more likely, which is what deterrence is supposed to avoid. Moreover, there are stages of preparedness, such as the various stages of alert, which are themselves rungs on the ladder of escalation.[6] The credibility of a threat can be seen as a function of two variables, the degree of availability of the force threatened and the size of the stake at issue.[7] It is true for battlefield weapons, for intermediate-range weapons, and for strategic weapons that the threat to use them will be credible only if the opponent can believe that a decision to use them might actually be taken for the stakes for which use has been threatened. In any case, it is plausible to say that it is wrong to possess the weapons if it is wrong to make preparations for their use; for without the preparations, the mere possession of them will not deter.

The question whether the letter accepts these propositions in any form will be left until the third section of this chapter.

But it is noteworthy that it does not discuss one possible view that would mitigate the logical unease mentioned earlier.[8] This view is that the preparation for using the weapons does not need to involve the conditional intention to use them. To accept this view would be to deny the third proposition above. For it could then be both morally wrong to intend (conditionally) to use the weapons, and morally acceptable to make the preparations for using them.[9] On this view, the threat to use the weapons may be no more than a bluff.[10] The decision may not yet have been taken whether the weapons would in fact be used or not.

This situation needs to be distinguished from one where the decision has been taken not to use the weapons. If the decision not to use them were already in place, it would certainly be difficult to sustain the whole chain of preparations that are necessary for a credible deterrent threat. This would be even more difficult in an open democracy than in a closed totalitarian society. But there is a distinction in common experience, for example, between threatening to punish a child before deciding whether to carry out the threat and threatening after resigning oneself to tolerating the child's behavior without punishment. While neither may be good child-rearing practice, the threat is more likely to be effective in the first case than in the second.[11]

In the international context it is particularly relevant that intentions are invisible. The opponent has to consider not only the likelihood of the threat being carried out but also the harm that would be done if it were carried out.[12] Since the harm done would be so great, the likelihood can be very small that the threat will be carried out and deterrence still work. As long as the force is fully available and it is conceivable that the stake at issue might be large enough for the force to be used, the threat remains credible. It is not necessary that the opponent believe that the intention to use the weapons has already been formed. Since it is impossible to know whether this intention has in fact been formed or not, it is probably not very important to deterrence whether the opponent believes it has been formed or not. What is important is the belief that it might be formed, and that it might then be implemented.[13]

It may be argued that a strategy of bluff is possible only theoretically; that in practice all Presidents and heads of state in nations with nuclear arms have to determine when they come into office what the conditions are under which they will order the use of the weapons. It may be argued further that there would not be time in a crisis for this determination to be made from scratch, and that it must therefore be made in advance. But there is a response to this objection. Any public indication of a current President's intentions in this area has to be understood as part of the rhetorical or declaratory posture necessary for effective deterrence. But the private presidential papers of those U.S. Presidents in the nuclear age whose papers are now public reveal that after Hiroshima and Nagasaki no President firmly made up his mind under what conditions to authorize massive retaliation.[14] To take just one example of a President whose papers are not yet public, Jimmy Carter had quite likely not formed a definite intention on the use of the weapons.[15] This writer, having worked in Congress, has concluded that definite conditional intentions are rare in politics, especially where the conditions in question are unprecedented. Politicians may know fairly well what they are going to do (e.g., how they are going to vote) if they have faced the issue several times before. But if the issue is a new one, especially if it is new and momentous, they will very often suspend judgment until the last possible moment.

We should consider two other objections to the bluff theory of deterrence. The first may be called the objection from the rank and file.[16] Even if the President and his advisers have not formed a conditional intention, for example, to bomb Soviet cities in retaliation for an attack on U.S. cities, what about the armed forces? A strategy of bluff requires for its implementation "thousands of men trained in the techniques of mass destruction and drilled in instant obedience."[17] Do not those "manning" the deterrent have to have formed a conditional intention to fire the missiles, for example, if so ordered? If so, then a strategy of bluff may release the top military commanders from immoral intentions while at the same time requiring these of the rank and file. For if it is immoral to intend massive retaliation, it is surely immoral to intend to carry it out if so ordered. The objection runs, then, that a strategy of bluff puts thousands of people in a morally indefensible position, treating them as means rather than ends, which is incompatible with respecting their dignity as human beings.

A response to this objection is that most of those "manning" the deterrent will not be in a position to know whether in obeying orders, through all the stages of alert, they are implementing a strategy of threat or of actual use.[18] The only people who have unambiguously been in such a position so far are those who dropped the bombs on Hiroshima and Nagasaki. There is evidence from the subsequent lives of some of them that their state of mind was unstable. Their mental health was in a sense sacrificed to the national interest.[19] It would be morally preferable if the maker of the threat could be known to be the one who would eventually have to carry it out. Developments in communications technology have made this increasingly possible by allowing the centralization of control mechanisms. If this were possible, then a satisfactory response to the objection from the rank and file would be available. Each of the innumerable antecedent decisions necessary for the use of the weapon could be taken in good faith by a member of the armed forces who supported a policy of threat but not of use. But if there do have to be people who both know that they are taking the last and irreversible step, and who are not originators of the decision, then they are indeed being asked, for the sake of effective deterrence, to form the intention to obey the order to fire the weapons. This is one moral cost of nuclear deterrence even if deterrence is explained in terms of a strategy of bluff.

There are other such costs. It may be argued that the threat of nuclear warfare is immoral in itself, whether it is accompanied by the conditional intention to use the weapons or not. Many reasons may be given for this.[20] First, there is the constant possibility that the threat may be carried out by miscalculation, accident, or madness, or because the arms race has itself destabilized deterrence. Second, the longer we rely on the deterrent, the more we become used to the idea of the destruction we are threatening against others and in the end against ourselves; we become dangerously less ready to move decisively toward arms control and disarmament. Third, the whole world has to live under the shadow of the possible destruction of civilization as we know it. Fourth, the maintenance of a credible deterrent threat requires diverting essential resources from meeting basic human needs.[21] This list is by no means exhaustive.

This is not the place to attempt a detailed response to all

these points. They can be made against any proponent of deterrence. The objection is not to the claim that deterrence works by bluff, but to the claim that this rescues deterrence from moral condemnation. Any proponent of deterrence is likely to reply that the danger of the use of nuclear weapons is decreased if both parties possess them, rather than one party alone; they have after all only been used against a nonnuclear power. This is true even though the risk of the arms race producing a new generation of weapons that destabilizes deterrence is a real one, as are the risks of accident, miscalculation, or insanity.[22] Second, the continued possession of the weapons may make us less committed to the goal of getting rid of them; but recent evidence suggests that popular commitment to arms control goes in cycles, and is now more alive than it was five years ago.[23] Third, the shadow of the destruction of civilization is real, but so is the shadow of the suppression of freedoms that are the fruit of that civilization.[24] Finally, it can be agreed that if an effective conventional deterrent, for example in Europe, can be found that consumes less resources than the nuclear deterrent, it should certainly be preferred; but at the moment this seems a distant goal of policy.[25]

To defend deterrence in this way is not to say "yes" to nuclear war or to the arms race or to deny the awfulness of nuclear weapons. But this awfulness works both ways. Suppose the goal is to secure substantial reductions in the nuclear arsenals of both superpowers. It has been claimed that the historical record shows that the Soviets do not negotiate concessions unless they are presented with a credible threat that their concessions are the only way to forestall.[26] If this is right, then by continuing to deploy our present nuclear weapons and threatening to deploy new ones, we may legitimately claim to be trying to persuade the Soviets to negotiate substantial reductions.[27] The risk is that the world will end up with twice as many and twice as deadly weapons on both sides. But the present point is that a recognition of the awfulness of nuclear weapons does not help us decide whether the possible benefits outweigh this risk. It is because they are awful that we should want to negotiate reductions; but it is also because they are awful that we should want not to end up with twice as many.

An outline of a theory of deterrence is found in the teaching of Jesus about the swords taken by the disciples to Gethsemane. In Luke 22, Jesus gives his final words in the upper room, his instructions immediately following the last supper. These are words of great significance, because they mark a transition to a time when the disciples will be (physically) without their master. Jesus here tells his disciples, in contrast to his earlier teaching, to take purse and scrip, and to buy swords.[28] The disciples have two, and Jesus says it is enough. But when one of them is used to cut off the ear of a servant of the high priest, Jesus heals the ear and says (in Matt. 26:52), "Put up again thy sword into his place; for all they that take the sword shall perish with the sword." There is an echo here of Genesis 9:6, "Whoso sheddeth man's blood, by man shall his blood be shed; for in the image of God made he man."

Why does Jesus say that his disciples should *now* buy swords (and take purse and scrip)? Probably because he recognized that they were entering into a period of persecution. While Jesus was physically present, he protected them and took the persecution for them. There was no need for sword or purse when the disciples traveled, even by themselves. Why does he tell them to get *swords?* Because the multitude would be carrying swords (and staves). Why *two* swords? Because that would be enough to deter attack on the disciples, who were indeed allowed to flee. But it was not his intention that the swords should be used for attack; only, we may guess, for self-defense.

What, then, about his words about *taking* the sword? There is a way to make this teaching either absurd or exceedingly pessimistic. It is absurd for Jesus to tell his disciples to sell their cloaks to buy swords, and then to tell them never to take the swords anywhere on pain of death. It is exceedingly pessimistic to suppose that Jesus is saying both that his disciples should take the sword and that they will therefore die by the sword. "Taking the sword" here surely means something more like living by the sword, or using it in offense (in the context of the passage).[29]

The case can be made that here is the beginning of an ethics of deterrence. The possession of the weapon, with the implied threat to use it in self-defense, is justified, but not the offensive or habitual use. At any rate the Christian exegete has the task of making clear what is right about having the sword and what is wrong about "taking" it. Those Christian commentators on

U.S. foreign policy who want to engage in the political debate where it now is have a similar task. For the political debate is not now about whether or not to abandon the deterrent, but about how large a deterrent force is enough.[30] This is not to deny a legitimate role for Christian commentators who want to refuse moral justification to nuclear deterrence altogether. One way to put this is to say that some are called to help administer and some are called to prophesy, just as Christ himself is both king and prophet. The characteristic temptation of kings is to be too much of the world; the temptation of prophets is to be too little in it. To put this another way, the temptations are improper compromise on the one hand and lack of sympathy on the other. But at least one way to be the salt, or the leaven in the lump, is to be involved in the political debate where it is happening. The Christian community should have people within it who can talk in that language, and can articulate how we get from our present to our desired future in ways that have a political chance of being implemented. The Catholic bishops are taking this role (though the letter seems to shift occasionally between roles), and are trying to speak to this debate.

The next section of this chapter deals with three doctrines used in the letter that belong especially to the Roman Catholic tradition. We can call these the doctrine of graduated episcopal authority, the doctrine of double effect, and the doctrine of the progressive realization of the kingdom. These doctrines are dealt with more fully in other chapters of this book. We will treat them here only insofar as they affect the section of the letter on deterrence theory that we are considering.

No one reading the bishops' letter can fail to be struck by the care that has been taken to distinguish the different degrees of authority with which the bishops speak. Sometimes they give us universally binding moral principles, such as the principle of noncombatant immunity. At other times they apply these principles to specific cases, and here the letter says there may be interpretations of specific circumstances or prudential judgments involved (e.g., the treatment of "no first-use"). The letter makes it clear that these conclusions, though not binding on conscience, are to be given "serious consideration by Catholics as they determine whether their moral judgments are consistent with the gospel."

But the criteria for separating out these levels of authority are not completely clear in the text. Does the degree of authority depend on the degree of specificity? Probably not, for the bishops' judgment on Hiroshima (IV.C) is both specific and apparently fully authoritative. The judgment on first use, on the other hand, does not seem to be in itself more specific than the judgment on noncombatant immunity, and yet the two are given with different degrees of moral authority. Prudential judgments are not in themselves any more specific than moral judgments, except that they sometimes include explicit or implicit reference to the interest of some particular person or persons, whereas moral judgments are supposed to refer to everyone's interest. But it is not clear why this difference should in itself affect the authority with which the bishops speak.

In any case, there are some puzzles here. The way these relate to the deterrence theory section is as follows. The letter's acceptance of deterrence is conditional. We will be looking later at the conditions put forward. The point here is that they are put forward with apparently different degrees of authority.[31] This raises a problem. Suppose a person agrees with the conditions, but thinks that whereas the first three have been met by deterrence as presently constituted, the last three have not. Does this or does this not mean that deterrence is no longer even conditionally tolerable? Are the conditions, in other words, jointly necessary? This is also a problem for Christians who do not find themselves under the bishops' authority. For they are also likely to feel different weights of authority attaching to different principles; and if they are making their acceptance of deterrence conditional, they will want to be sure that they know how much weight is attached to each condition. There is, moreover, a distinction between the weight attached to a condition and the weight attached to one's evaluation of whether a condition has been met. The more technical the subject matter, the less confidence most people will have in their own evaluation. But this need not affect the importance attached to the condition itself. To give one example, it is difficult for most people to determine the extent of civilian casualties that would be caused by the targeting of military installations; but it remains true that for most people this would be an important factor in their evaluation of any particular targeting policy. Some of the hesitation expressed in the letter attaches to the conditions, and some to the determination of whether the conditions have been met.

Second, the doctrine of double effect. This has long been a part of the tradition of Christian ethics as developed within Roman Catholicism.[32] It can be explained roughly as follows. Some actions are always condemned, such as the deliberate bombing of civilians; it is always wrong not only to do these things, but to intend to do them. But a distinction has to be made between the direct intention behind an action and the consequences that may be foreseen but are "beside" the intention. These consequences may be permitted as long as they are not seen beforehand as a means to the directly intended end, and as long as the permitted evil is not disproportionate to the (directly) intended good. For example, one might construct a justification by the doctrine of double effect for the bombing of civilians that would insist that the direct intention was to bomb a military installation, but unfortunately there were civilian casualties because civilians were "co-located" with the military targets; even if these casualties were foreseen, they were not directly intended. This justification has been characterized as "withholding the intention and dropping the bomb," and has been highly controversial.[33] In the letter the bishops make use of the requirement of proportionality between foreseen (unintended) consequences and the intended goal to rule out military targeting that would result in "massive" civilian casualties.

The doctrine of double effect is "a practical formula which synthesizes an immense amount of moral experience."[34] Most of the traditional theodicies tell us to judge the character of God by what he intends, not by what he permits, even though he foresees what he permits. But the principle is nonetheless full of philosophical obscurity. How, in particular cases, are intended means to be distinguished from foreseen consequences? Is not the distinction between acts and their consequences primarily a matter of how the acts themselves are described (e.g., raising the arm, pulling the lever, dropping the bomb, hitting a center of wartime production, or killing ten thousand civilians)?

This is not the place to go into all the problems.[35] But the relevance to deterrence theory is clear. The Reagan Administration testified several times to the bishops that there was no directly intended threat against civilians. On the principle of double effect, this would excuse the targeting of a military installation even if civilian casualties were foreseen, as long as they were not seen as a means to the directly intended goal and as long as the permitted evil was not disproportionate to the intended good. The first of these conditions can be met as long as the argument is not also made that targeting civilians is valuable in itself as a means to deterrent stability.[36] The second condition is more difficult. The intended goal is the prevention of total war. But Administration officials who testified to the bishops are reported to have agreed that even with attacks limited to "military" targets, the number of deaths "in a substantial exchange would be almost indistinguishable from what might occur if civilian centers had been deliberately and directly struck." The bishops' conditional acceptance of current deterrence strategy here seems to hinge on the word "almost." If the number of deaths were really indistinguishable, then the permitted evil would be disproportionate to the intended good. For deterrence to pass this second condition, therefore, what has to be shown is at least that less harm will probably be done by the limitation to military targets than by the direct targeting of civilian population.

The third doctrine is that of the progressive realization of the kingdom. This theme is pervasive in the letter from the first paragraph to the last. The first paragraph starts with a quotation from the Second Vatican Council: "The whole human race faces a moment of supreme crisis in its advance toward maturity." The last paragraph is a quotation from the book of Revelation, which is introduced by the comment that God's continuing work among us will "issue forth" in the final kingdom.[37] The letter talks of the religious vision of peace as capable of progressive realization, and states that it is part of the vision of the kingdom, which is itself progressively accomplished.[38]

This theology of history is reflected in the section of the letter on deterrence theory. The letter states the hope that the nuclear powers will phase out nuclear deterrence altogether; and that what will enable this progressive disarmament is a new world order, a building of peace, that will involve the endowment of an international public authority with the wideness of powers, structure, and means to enforce that peace. It is against the background of this hope that the bishops' conditional acceptance of deterrence has to be understood. Deterrence may now be tolerated as a reflection of the radical distrust that marks international politics; but in the long run the expectation is of a new order, a closer realization of the kingdom, that will remove the need for nuclear deterrence and hence its justification. A person who does not share this expectation is less likely to share the conviction that nuclear deterrence cannot be considered "adequate as a long-term basis for peace." For this conviction is partly informed by an optimism about the direction of history between now and the second coming, and hence an optimism about the availability of alternatives to deterrence.

We will now consider the extent to which the letter accepts the five propositions mentioned at the beginning of this chapter, and will discuss what the letter means by a "conditional" acceptance of deterrence. The five propositions were: first, it is (morally) wrong to use nuclear weapons under any circumstances; second, if it is wrong to use nuclear weapons, it is also wrong to intend to use them; third, if it is wrong to intend to use them, it is wrong to make preparations for using them; fourth, if it is wrong to make preparations for using them, it is wrong to possess them, even for deterrent purposes; fifth, it is (morally) acceptable to possess nuclear weapons for deterrent purposes.

The first proposition is discussed in the section of the letter before the one we are discussing, which can be summarized as follows. Nuclear use is ruled out absolutely if it involves targeting population centers directly, no situation is perceived in which the deliberate initiation of nuclear use on however restricted a scale can be morally justified, and considerable skepticism is expressed about the possibility of keeping nuclear use limited.[39] The letter states that the burden of proof remains on those who assert that meaningful limitation is possible, but it does not endorse the principle that escalation is inevitable. If it could be shown that a limited nuclear response to a limited nuclear attack would probably end hostilities, such a response might be acceptable. Even the letter's condemnation of first nuclear use is not total. There is a call for NATO to move rapidly toward the adoption of a "no-first-use" policy, but to do so in tandem with development of an adequate alternative defense posture. The letter does not explicitly rule out the maintenance of flexible response while the alternative is being developed.[40] There is thus a small residue of doubt about nuclear use. There is a firm "no" to nuclear war, but not an explicit condemnation of all uses of nuclear weapons. This residue of doubt prevents any final certainty about the consistency of the letter's moral judgment on nuclear deterrence.

The middle three propositions can each be said to be accepted in the letter by implication, although it is impossible to be confident of this. The second is the easiest. "War can be legitimately intended," the letter says, "only for the reasons set forth above as a just cause."[41] Thus if an act of war is morally excluded by the just-war criteria, the intention to perform it is likewise excluded. In the same sort of way, activities are said to be criminal if they "*deliberately* conflict with the all-embracing principles of universal natural law" (emphasis added), which is to say that a judgment on their criminality involves a judgment on the intentions of the agent.[42] This general truth is then applied to nuclear weapons. Because it is wrong to attack noncombatants, for example, "deterrence may not morally include the intention of deliberately attacking civilian populations or noncombatants."[43] Condemning the intention is involved in condemning the agent.

The letter's position on the third proposition is more obscure. Deterrence is understood to mean "dissuasion of a potential adversary from initiating an attack or conflict, often by the threat of unacceptable retaliatory damage."[44] This threat is seen to be posed by the preparations to carry it out. Thus Pope John Paul II is quoted as having given provisional approval to the old Roman saying "si vis pacem, para bellum" (if you want peace, prepare [for] war). The letter deals (in section II.D.2) with the connection between these preparations and the (conditional) intention to use the weapons. The bishops heard from the Administration that even though not targeting civilians directly, they were "prepared to retaliate in a massive way if necessary." The letter concludes that "such massive civilian casualties" would mean that "in our judgment such a strike would be deemed morally disproportionate, even though not intentionally indiscriminate." The present point is that this conclusion is used as a constraint on targeting *policy* (the same constraint on U.S. and on Soviet policy) or on deterrent strategy. In other words, the moral wrongness of the action (killing civilians) descends to the intention to perform the action, and then to the formation of the policy or strategy, which is the concrete working out of the intention. Finally, the letter urges men and women in military service, in developing battle plans and weapons systems, to ensure that these are "designed to reduce violence, destruction, suffering and death to a minimum, keeping in mind especially non-combatants and other innocent persons."[45] The formation of battle plans and the design of weapons are put under the same constraints as the formation of general deterrence strategy.

The letter does not discuss the fourth proposition directly, but it does put the development, production, and deployment of nuclear weapons under the same constraints as the preparations for the use of the weapons. This is clear from the preceding quotation and elsewhere. Moreover, the letter does recognize that deterrent effectiveness requires more than just possession of the weapons. It says that stable deterrence depends on the ability of each side to deploy its retaliatory forces in ways that are not vulnerable to attack; this means that each side has an obligation not to deploy weapons that have the capability to destroy the other side's ability to retaliate. Thus possession requires at least preparations for decreased vulnerability. The letter also puts limits on the sort of planning that is morally tolerable. It says that planning for prolonged periods of repeated nuclear strikes and counterstrikes, or "prevailing" in nuclear war, are unacceptable.[46] But within these limits it seems to be accepted that the possession of the weapons requires planning for how they might be used, and making the corresponding preparations. In any case, the implication is probably accepted that if this planning and these preparations are wrong, so is possessing the weapons, even for deterrent purposes.

There is, however, one oddity in the letter's treatment of this question. The bishops are worried about the relationship of deterrence doctrine to war-fighting strategies. Now any planning or preparing for how the weapons might be used can be described as the adoption of a war-fighting strategy. For any use of nuclear weapons might be correctly described as fighting a nuclear war.[47] But the letter talks about a war-fighting capability as something the United States should not seek and which would go beyond the limited function of deterrence described in the letter. Since the letter does not elsewhere state the conclusion that any planning or preparations for nuclear use are immoral, it is preferable to suppose that the bishops, like the general public, mean something much more limited by the phrase "war-fighting strategy." The kind of strategy they want to condemn is the targeting of civilian populations or "counterforce" targeting that threatens the viability of other nations' retaliatory forces, or which is linked with a declaratory policy that conveys the notion that nuclear war is subject to precise rational and moral limits.

But it is unclear just what kind of strategy is ruled out under these descriptions. It might still be all right to put some of the opponent's retaliatory arsenal at risk, but not enough of it so that the opponent no longer has a credible threat to retaliate.[48] It might be all right to declare that under one's adopted strategy a nuclear war would be more or less controllable in the early stages but progressively less so with escalation. But the problem here is that the bishops are highly skeptical about limiting nuclear war at all. If they had said flat out that it could not be limited, they would presumably have gone on to rule out the adoption of a strategy of limited use (as well as unlimited use). Under the fourth proposition we are considering here, this would also have meant ruling out the possession of the weapons that would have been used to implement such strategies. But since the letter does not say this flat out, we are left with the sense of logical unease with which this chapter started. The question is whether the letter has been sufficiently flexible on possibly justified use to allow room for conditionally justified possession. To put this another way, since the letter leaves the burden of proof on those who maintain that meaningful limitation of nuclear war is possible, the same burden of proof is left on the bishops to justify the possession of the weapons that would implement a meaningful limitation. The letter could have escaped this dilemma by denying the third proposition above. But it did not.

Finally, the fifth proposition. Here the bishops are explicit; deterrence is conditionally acceptable. But the relevant conditions are not systematically spelled out.[49] A list of the more substantial conditions in the letter might read as follows. The deployment of nuclear weapons for deterrent purposes

a. must be a step on the way toward progressive disarmament,
b. must not involve the targeting of civilians directly,
c. must not be maintained once the radical distrust between the world's powers has been overcome,
d. must not involve targeting that would have the effect of massive civilian casualties,
e. must not be accompanied by a declaratory policy that conveys the notion that a nuclear war is subject to precise rational and moral limits;
f. must not threaten the viability of the retaliatory capacity of either side.

Most of these conditions we have discussed before, but not the first. It might seem odd to say that maintaining nuclear deterrence is a step on the way to progressive disarmament. But the rationale is that deterrence preserves a state of equilibrium between the nuclear powers, and equilibrium is necessary for substantive progress in arms control. Those observers who believe that there is now rough parity between the superpowers tend to believe also that there is now a real opportunity for substantial reductions.[50] If the bishops' first condition is one of the conditions against which deployment of nuclear weapons is measured, those deployments that disrupt the equilibrium would be ruled out. But it would also be the case that failure to maintain the deterrent balance (e.g., by certain kinds of unilateral steps toward disarmament) would interfere with bilateral movement toward arms control. It might also lead by progressive steps to a situation where those disarming would be subject to nuclear blackmail.

The conclusions drawn from the conditional acceptance of deterrence are a mixed bag. The letter opposes planning for a "prolonged" exchange or for "prevailing" in nuclear war, on the grounds that these go beyond the mere deterrence of nuclear use. But what needs to be shown is that there is no need to preserve deterrence in the tragic event that an initial nuclear exchange takes place. If "intra-war deterrence" is necessary, then it may be necessary to plan for the ability to retaliate not just after an initial attack, but after subsequent attacks as well.[51] Second, the distinction sometimes proposed between "prevailing" and "winning" in a nuclear war has to be discussed before the notion of "prevailing" is condemned out of hand.[52] The letter goes on to oppose some specific proposals, such as the addition of weapons that are likely to be vulnerable to attack, yet also possess a "prompt hard-target kill" capability; these are said to be "first-strike" weapons. A footnote mentions the possibility that both MX and Pershing II missiles fall into this category. But the notion that these are first-strike weapons should at least be checked against the counterclaim that it is the quantity of the weapons deployed, not just the capabilities of each missile, that constitutes a first-strike threat.[53] In these cases, and in some of the other recommendations, what is missing is a demonstration of how the conclusion both meets the standard objections and follows from the stated premises. This is not fair as a criticism of the letter, which could not have filled in all the argumentation here without becoming intolerably lengthy. Rather, it is a challenge to those reading the letter who agree by and large both that deterrence is conditionally acceptable, and that the relevant conditions are what the letter says they are.

Finally, a question. If we have assessed correctly the degree of assent in the letter to the five propositions mentioned at the beginning of this chapter, is the moral judgment about deterrence contained in the letter consistent? The opinion of the present writer is that the letter does not itself tell us enough to know whether this moral judgment is consistent or not. The sense of logical unease would be much smaller if the letter had either denied that making deterrent preparations involved the (conditional) intention to use the weapons, or had been a little less skeptical about the justification for nuclear use, or a little more skeptical about the justification for nuclear possession. As it is, we are left with the need to know more. Are the possibly justified occasions of use sufficiently many or sufficiently momentous to justify the preparations for using the weapons in those ways? Are the deterrent forces currently possessed by, for example, the United States, more numerous or more powerful than is required to perform the uses the letter finds morally acceptable? Is there any targeting policy that is militarily effective and meets the conditions laid down in the letter for an acceptable deterrent strategy? The letter is as good a statement as any church body has produced on the issue, and is an important contribution to the debate. What needs to be done now is to spell out carefully and in detail which kinds of nuclear use (if any) are morally tolerable and what the conditions are for a moral acceptance of nuclear possession. Once this is done, it may turn out that the only way to achieve a consistent view is to reject the third proposition above, connecting the wrongness of intention with the wrongness of preparations for use.

10: Deterrence: An Assessment of the Bishops' Nuclear Morality

MARK R. AMSTUTZ

Ideally, the world would be safer and more tolerable if nuclear weapons had never been invented. But nuclear technology is here, and no amount of wishful thinking is going to resolve the complex and morally troubling issues posed by the nuclear and thermonuclear instruments of mass destruction.

Historically, the Catholic Church has never advocated pacifism. Rather, it has defended the right of limited force to protect national interests from unjust aggression. The teachings of the Church on the use of force have been incorporated over the centuries in what is commonly called the just-war doctrine. The problem posed by the invention of nuclear arms, however, is that they are not easily encompassed in the historic principles of just war. Whereas conventional weapons have been historically regarded as legitimate instruments of defense, thermonuclear weapons pose many difficult and troubling questions regarding their use as instruments of peacemaking. For example, may a nation possess weapons that are fundamentally instruments of mass destruction? If possession is permissible, may a state threaten their use? If threats are permissible, what declaratory policy is moral? Should nuclear arms be used to deter any unjust aggression or only nuclear attack? If nuclear aggression occurs, is it morally permissible to retaliate?

These questions are not new, but the context in which they are being raised is. The growing concern, both in Europe and the United States, about the role of nuclear arms has come about because of a growing perception that the world in which we live is becoming less stable and secure. To a significant degree, the growing popular concern with nuclear peacekeeping has been stimulated by the continued modernization of superpower nuclear arsenals. This continued arms race has been aggravated particularly by the growth in the number of strategic nuclear warheads and the accuracy and speed with which they can be delivered. At the same time the strategy and declaratory policy of the superpowers has appeared to have shifted from MAD (mutual assured destruction) toward counterforce, from the premise that any nuclear conflict would result in major, indiscriminate destruction toward the concept that limited nuclear wars are possible. The fact that technological refinements increasingly make possible the feasibility of carrying out limited, counterforce targeting is all the more unsettling to those who have historically viewed nuclear weapons not as instruments of war but as instruments of deterrence.

The changing structure of nuclear peacekeeping and the growing concern with the shifts in nuclear technology and strategy have resulted in a new opportunity, or what the bishops call "a new moment," to assess the morality of strategic policy. The aim of the U.S. bishops' pastoral on war and peace is an effort to provide moral guidance to persons who are searching for better answers to the complex issues of nuclear arms and peacemaking. The bishops observe that the nuclear age is the first generation since Genesis with the power virtually to eliminate God's creation. And in the face of such danger, the bishops note that they cannot remain silent, particularly since Christ calls his disciples to be agents of peacemaking.

The fundamental aim of the pastoral is to examine the moral issues surrounding the nuclear debate and to provide moral guidelines on the types of national security policies that should be advocated. Whether or not one agrees with the major arguments of the pastoral, the bishops' document is one of the most important statements on the morality of nuclear weapons. Despite its brevity, the document is comprehensive in scope and addresses many of the central issues of the nuclear debate, including the questions dealing with possession, threat, and use of nuclear arms. The aim of this chapter is to examine briefly the bishops' views on deterrence and to assess the impact of the bishops' recommendations regarding that policy. In order to understand the context and argument made by the pastoral I shall first review some of the essential elements of the logic of deterrence.

THE NATURE OF DETERRENCE

The basic postulate of U.S. strategic policy has been and continues to be deterrence—prevention by threat. According to deterrence theorists, the most effective way of deterring nuclear aggression is to maintain a credible threat of major destruction. For deterrence to work—that is, prevent nuclear aggression—nuclear forces need to be of sufficient size and scope to be able to carry out nuclear retaliation after having been subject to a surprise nuclear attack. In addition to the requirements in military capabilities, deterrence is based on credibility—the perception that punishment can or will be inflicted on an aggressor state.

Nuclear strategists have generally thought that the effectiveness of deterrence depends on strategic stability[1]—that is, the condition in which no adversary could perceive an advantage in resorting to nuclear war. Nuclear stability has involved three dimensions, two of them critical. The first is strategic stability—a condition in which no state has the ability of carrying out a nuclear attack without suffering unacceptable nuclear retaliation. To achieve such stability, three elements have been regarded as important: first, the people and industrial targets of an adversary state must be vulnerable to attack; second, the strategic nuclear forces must themselves be relatively invulnerable; and third, the strategic forces must be capable of carrying out assured punishment. The second dimension of stable deterrence is crisis stability. Even if both superpowers have a credible deterrent force, one state may perceive an advantage in a preemptive nuclear attack. When one or both superpowers believe that a significant part of its strategic forces is vulnerable to surprise attack, a crisis could possibly tempt a state to launch a surprise attack to avoid the loss of a major part of its strategic forces. When states assume that there is a growing possibility of preemptive attacks, then there is little crisis stability.

It is clear that the technological developments in MIRVs and warhead accuracy have decreased the perceived stability of superpower nuclear forces. Although difficult to accept, the decreasing destructive power of nuclear arms, coupled with the shift toward counterforce targeting, has resulted in a more dangerous world. As Charles Krauthammer has observed, "Weapons aimed at people lessen the risk of war; weapons aimed at weapons, increase it."[2] The modernization of nuclear arms and the refinements in strategic doctrine have unwittingly decreased nuclear stability and thereby created a new set of conditions in which to explore the ethical dimensions of nuclear peacekeeping.

It is important to stress that deterrence, the cornerstone of U.S. defense policy, was not adopted because of its clear military role or moral purity. Rather, the policy was accepted as the most prudent moral course among numerous troubling alternatives. The adoption and continued acceptance of deterrence has been based on two fundamental facts: first, nuclear arms do not provide a state with "usable" force; and second, there is no method of defending against nuclear attack except deterrence. The problem posed by the nuclear invention has been what to do with nuclear and thermonuclear weapons. To date, the answer that has been given is: deter nuclear attack.

Given the enormous destructive power of the nuclear arsenals of the superpowers, the peace and stability of the world hang precariously on a balance of terror. The condition of the world is much like a circus where two fencers are on a tightrope threatening each other. Each fencer carries a sword and explosives around his waist that will explode and kill everyone in the circus if he falls. Each fencer threatens the other in the game of fencing, knowing that his own interest is maximized by ensuring a stalemate. Each fencer knows that victory will also mean defeat, for the defeat of the fencer would result in his fall from the high wire and lead to the destruction of both fencers and observers. The game of fencing thus continues with the hope that neither player will tire, losing his footing, or undertake an action that would destroy his opponent. In this game neither party can win, although both could lose. The problem of the game is to find a way to terminate it. But nobody has been able to do so yet.

Notwithstanding the importance of deterrence, the policy

has a number of major shortcomings. First, it is paradoxical. The paradox derives from the inconsistency between the aim of deterrence—to inhibit nuclear war—and the means to achieve it— the threat of nuclear retaliation. The contradiction between goals and means becomes apparent the moment nuclear aggression occurs. Since the aim is to inhibit a nuclear attack, once a nuclear attack begins, the whole doctrine is self-cancelling. As Schell observes, it is impossible credibly to deter a first strike with a second strike whose purpose dissolves the moment the first strike arrives.[3]

A second weakness of deterrence is its ambiguity of purpose. The fundamental aim of deterrence is, of course, to prevent a nuclear war. But deterrence seeks to do more than that. Because of the nature of the international system, nuclear weapons are possessed to protect the sovereign interests of states. In his 1983 Annual Report to the Congress, Secretary of Defense Caspar Weinberger stated that U.S. strategic policy had four aims: to deter nuclear attack, to deter major conventional attack, to terminate a major war on favorable terms, and to avoid nuclear blackmail.[4] That nuclear weapons have been designed to deter more than nuclear war is clearly evident in NATO, where the possible "first-use" of tactical nuclear weapons has always been considered a possibility in a situation of national emergency. Even the bishops view deterrence ambiguously when they concede that the moral duty of Christians is not only to prevent nuclear war from happening but "to protect and preserve those key values of justice, freedom and independence which are necessary for personal dignity and national integrity."[5] Schell states the problem of ambiguity well:

> For the doctrine's central claim—that it deploys nuclear weapons only in order to prevent their use—is simply not true. Actually, it deploys them to protect national sovereignty, and if this aim were not present they could be quickly dismantled.[6]

Third, deterrence is inadequate because of its moral shortcomings.[7] It seeks to do good (achieve peace) by threatening evil (nuclear retaliation). Philosophers and strategic planners disagree over the degree of evil involved in deterrence. Some hold the view that nuclear war and deterrence—the threat of nuclear retaliation—are identical and therefore bear the same moral consequences. For example, R. A. Markus, a nuclear pacifist, writes that "if an action is morally wrong, it is wrong to intend to do it, even if one never gets the chance to carry out one's intention."[8] Others, however, tend to regard the relationship of action to threat as being far more complex.[9] It is possible to distinguish many different degrees of intention in the policy of deterrence.

At the risk of oversimplifying, it is possible to identify three levels of intention: bluffs, uncertain response, and conditional response. A bluff is a threat to retaliate with no intention of fulfilling the threat. Uncertain response involves the possibility of retaliation without any predetermined commitment to retaliate. And conditional response involves the certainty of retaliation. But even those who defend this last position minimize its evil by arguing, as does Arthur Hockaday, a British defense government official, that the response to nuclear aggression is not directly intended. The real hope in deterrence, he says, is to avoid war by threatening conditional retaliation. Retaliation is not inevitable; it is possible only if the prior condition (nuclear attack) is fulfilled.[10]

However one resolves the technical questions of intention, it is difficult to justify the claim that nuclear war is morally identical with deterrence. That the threat of nuclear retaliation poses profound moral questions no one can deny. But Walzer seems closer to the truth than nuclear pacifists denying deterrence when he observes that deterrence is a difficult condition, and though it may not be a good way, there may be no other realistic way of dealing with the existence of nuclear arms. "We threaten evil in order not to do it," he writes, "and the doing of it would be so terrible that the threat seems in comparison to be morally defensible."[11]

THE DEFENSE OF DETERRENCE

One of the major themes of the bishops' letter is the conditional acceptance of deterrence. It is obvious that the bishops are not entirely comfortable with deterrence, but view it as the most responsible policy at this time among the available alternatives. It is clear from the changes in the three drafts of the letter that the topic of deterrence was one of the most difficult subjects to assess morally. That Christians should be against nuclear war was never in dispute; the challenge was to determine how best to ensure that a nuclear war might never occur. It would have been simple for the bishops to deny deterrence or give un-qualified endorsement to the policy. But the bishops chose—and rightly so, in my opinion—to affirm deterrence while si-multaneously seeking to minimize some of the moral problems posed by such a policy. What makes the pastoral such an im-pressive document is that it seeks to reconcile the legitimate claims of national defense with the historic principles of the just war by charting an intermediary position between the extremes of principled pacifism and unprincipled realism.

The pastoral recognizes that the church is divided on this complex issue. The letter notes that for some the peace and stability of the world system since 1945 have been due in great part to the balance of terror, a balance that has inhibited war between the major powers. For others the reliance on nuclear weapons has pointed to the need to change the peacekeeping system, since one single failure could result in a holocaust. For others still, the continued dependence on deterrence provides the driving force in the superpower arms race. And finally, some see in the policy of deterrence an immoral, unacceptable means (the intention of deliberately attacking civilians) being used to achieve peace. While respecting the different views on this com-plex subject, the pastoral bases its conditional acceptance of deterrence on papal teachings and the work of Vatican II. In particular, the bishops' argument is based on the views ex-pressed by Pope John Paul II, particularly his address to the UN Second Special Session on Disarmament. In that address, Pope John Paul argues that deterrence based on a "balance of forces" may be regarded as a moral strategy while the super-powers work toward progressive disarmament. According to him, deterrence represents a minimum condition—one that is justified only as a temporary policy while nations work toward reductions in military weapons.[12]

The bishops' conditional support for deterrence is based on several interrelated assumptions. The most important founda-tional principles are: (1) nuclear war is morally unacceptable; (2) the only legitimate use of nuclear weapons is deterrence; (3) the sole aim of deterrence is to inhibit nuclear aggression;

and (4) the avoidance of nuclear war is dependent on a clear firebreak between nuclear and conventional arms.

The first assumption—that nuclear war is beyond the scope of moral and rational boundaries of conflict resolution—is based largely on the indeterminate consequences of such a war. The pastoral observes that the church has traditionally sought to prevent war and then to limit its consequences if it did occur. "Today the possibilities for placing political and moral limits on nuclear war are so minimal," the letter states, "that the moral task . . . is prevention."[13] The bishops recognize that opposing nuclear war is a difficult and complex task. It is precisely because the bishops are so profoundly concerned to renounce nuclear war that they believe that the conditional possession of nuclear weapons is permissible. Indeed, it is the balanced distribution of nuclear weapons that serves as an imperfect instrument in deterring nuclear war. Nuclear war must be renounced, say the bishops, but this is to be done not unilaterally but by progressive disarmament. In the meantime, possession and the implicit threat of use against nuclear attack are morally tolerable.

The second pillar is the legitimation of deterrence as the only use of nuclear arms. The acceptance of deterrence derives from three fundamental facts concerning thermonuclear weapons: first, such weapons are fundamentally different from conventional arms; second, the best protection against nuclear aggression is the maintenance of a balance of military forces; and third, threats and actions bear different moral consequences. We shall comment briefly on each of these propositions.

Because of their destructive power, nuclear weapons are commonly regarded as useless military instruments of force. They are useless instruments because they do not provide controlled, discriminating force to achieve military objectives. Because of their massive destructive capacity, they may be used as a deterrent of last resort, but only when ultimate interests are at stake. George F. Kennan has written eloquently about the uselessness of nuclear arms:

> A weapon is something that is supposed to serve some rational end—a hideous end, as a rule, but one related to some serious objective of governmental policy, one supposed to promote the interests of the society which employs it. The nuclear device seems to me not to respond to that description.[14]

One of the first influential strategic thinkers to grasp this truth was Bernard Brodie. In his important study *The Absolute Weapon,* he observed that the basic mission of strategic nuclear policy was to guarantee the possibility of nuclear retaliation in order to deter nuclear aggression. "Thus far," wrote Brodie, "the chief purpose of our military establishment has been to win wars. From now on its chief purpose must be to avert them. It can have almost no other useful purpose."[15] For Brodie, nuclear weapons had no military function except to deter nuclear attack. Recently, the architect of U.S. strategic policy during the 1960s, Robert McNamara, has called attention to this same truth. "Nuclear weapons," he writes, "serve no military purpose whatsoever. They are totally useless—except only to deter one's opponent from using them."[16]

It is important to emphasize this fundamental differentiation between conventional and nuclear weapons, since a significant number of strategic thinkers have gained prominence in the West by advocating the feasibility of fighting limited nuclear wars. They have sought to relate the Clausewitzian rules of warfare to nuclear technology. Thus the bishops' letter stands as an important statement upholding the differentiation of conventional and nuclear weapons.

The second reality underlying the bishops' acceptance of deterrence is the implicit support for the balance-of-power system of peacekeeping. While the bishops do not explicitly endorse such a system, they recognize that unlimited power may lead to unjust aggression and that one of the means by which such aggression might be inhibited is through the principle of countervailing power. The bishops' implicit toleration, if not acceptance, of the balance-of-power approach did not originate with the pastoral but is based on previous papal teachings and official Church documents. In particular it derives from the teachings of Vatican II and Pope John Paul II. The Second Vatican Council in its pastoral constitution "The Church in the Modern World" implicitly accepted the notion of deterrence based on balance. While not formally endorsing the system of balance of power, the Vatican II Council recognized that the amassing of nuclear arms was not designed only for war but to serve as a means of deterrence. The Council then went on to affirm deterrence, noting that such a system could not be viewed as a means to achieve genuine long-term peace but as an imperfect means to "some sort of peace."[17] The Second Vatican Council, in short, recognized that in the light of existing circumstances, deterrence based on a balance of nuclear forces could be considered an imperfect, temporary yet effective way of coping with the nuclear dilemma.

A particularly important influence on the bishops' perspective on balance of forces was Pope John Paul II's address to the UN Second Special Conference on Disarmament. Like the Vatican II Council, the Pope refused to endorse the balance-of-power system. Rather, he indicated that many persons consider the preparation for nuclear war the best safeguard for peace. He then went on to offer his moral assessment of the balance-of-power approach, particularly with reference to deterrence, in the following way:

> In current conditions "deterrence" based on balance, certainly not as an end in itself but as a step on the way towards a progressive disarmament, may still be judged morally acceptable. Nonetheless, in order to ensure peace, it is indispensable not to be satisfied with this minimum, which is always susceptible to the real danger of explosion.[18]

Taking their direction and inspiration from Vatican II and Pope John Paul, the bishops implicitly accept the balance-of-power approach to peacekeeping. They do so as an imperfect, short-term approach in seeking "peace of a sort." Authentic, long-term peace can result only as states move away from the anarchic, militaristic, competitive international system.

The third reality on which the bishops rest their conditional endorsement of deterrence is the moral differentiation between nuclear war and deterrence. The bishops do not analyze the technical questions dealing with the relationship of intention to action. As noted earlier, it is possible to make threats with or without a prior commitment to punishment. Even if a commitment to retaliation is made before aggression is carried out, many degrees of intention are involved in the determination and implementation of retaliation. Deterrence, in other words, does not involve a simple, *a priori* commitment to carry out nuclear retaliation. And even if deterrence were based on the certainty of nuclear retaliation, there can be little doubt that the threat of nuclear retaliation would involve a lesser degree of evil than nuclear war itself. This explains the bishops' unequivocal condemnation of nuclear war but their toleration of deterrence. The first is clearly immoral; the second is morally tolerable.

The third major pillar of the pastoral concerns the purpose of deterrence. According to the bishops, nuclear weapons should play a single, limited role—namely, the prevention of nuclear aggression. The aim of deterrence is not to prevent any type of conflict but to inhibit a nuclear power from ever carrying out a nuclear attack. The problem, of course, is that peace is indivisible, and any major conflict between the superpowers or their allies has the potential for involving the superpowers militarily.

Historically, the United States has sought to deter more than nuclear aggression with its strategic policy. Among other things, it has "extended" the nuclear umbrella to Western Europe to assure NATO states that vital Alliance interests are ultimately under the protection of U.S. nuclear forces. The assumption underlying NATO's "flexible response" strategy has been that the Western Alliance would use whatever military measures it judged necessary, including tactical nuclear weapons, to defend its interests from Soviet aggression. Implicit in NATO's strategy has been the option of possible first-use of nuclear weapons. When NATO first adopted this integrated nuclear-conventional policy, the West had a clear nuclear advantage. And because nuclear strategy was cheaper and involved limited personnel, it was an easy course to sustain during a period of growing conventional force imbalances. But the reliance on nuclear weapons came at a cost: it reduced the barrier to nuclear war. Robert McNamara has observed recently that to the extent that NATO's nuclear weapons contribute to European peace, they increase the risk of nuclear war.[19]

Flexible response has been an easy way to provide regional security. But by deterring conventional aggression with nuclear arms, the barrier to nuclear war has been lowered. It is important to recognize, too, that the credibility of "extended deterrence" during the early postwar years derived from the significant strategic superiority of U.S. nuclear forces. With the advent of nuclear parity in the 1970s, an increasing number of strategic thinkers have advocated a shift away from NATO's reliance on nuclear arms.[20] While recognizing that regional peace may have been strengthened by the policy of flexible response, it has also become apparent that the cost for such peace—the possibility of first-use of nuclear arms—is an unacceptable risk to bear.

Since the major message of the bishops' pastoral is to condemn nuclear war, they are particularly critical of policies, such as NATO's flexible response, that increase the possibility of nuclear war. As a result, the bishops oppose any first-use of nuclear weapons, whether tactical or strategic. The pastoral states: "We do not perceive any situation in which the deliberate initiation of nuclear warfare on however restricted a scale can be morally justified. Nonnuclear attacks by another state must be resisted by other than nuclear means."[21] The moral imperative is to keep any state from ever crossing the threshold from conventional to nuclear force. Aware of the implications of this prohibition on NATO policy, the pastoral indicates that the conventional force imbalances should be corrected in kind. While not eager to encourage a conventional arms race in Europe, the bishops acknowledge that some strengthening of conventional defense would be a proportionate price to pay if such a policy would reduce the possibility of nuclear war.[22]

The fourth major pillar of deterrence is the maintenance of a clear firebreak—that is, a well-established barrier between conventional and nuclear arms. This barrier is illustrated in Figure A (p. 170), which compares the nature of nuclear and conventional forces. The firebreak, or nuclear threshold, has become increasingly important in recent years with the advent of more accurate and more refined nuclear weapons. During the 1950s and 1960s, few weapons threatened to blur the distinction between the two weapons categories. But the advent of accurate, discriminating counterforce weapons has resulted in a much more precarious firebreak. The neutron warhead, for example, is a less destructive and, in some respects, safer tactical nuclear weapon. But precisely because this weapon is "cleaner"— to use a phrase used by many of its advocates—it potentially weakens the line of demarcation between acceptable and unacceptable force, between a weapon designed for combat and one designed to deter combat. The same could be said for other developments in the strategic arsenals.

An even greater threat to the firebreak comes from the shifting perceptions of the people as a result of modifications in declaratory policy. The increasing talk in Washington about

Figure A: Comparison of Nuclear and Conventional Forces

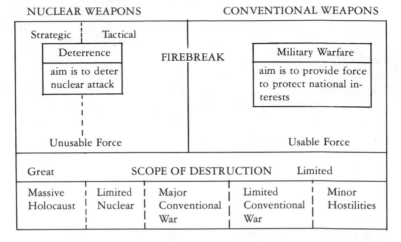

the need for "prevailing" in limited nuclear wars and for strengthening civil defense in order better to withstand a first strike has been detrimental to the psychological dimensions of the firebreak because it has conveyed the impression that the barrier between usable and nonusable force is a chimera.

While the bishops do not explicitly examine the nature of a firebreak, the need for clear differentiation between nuclear and conventional forces is central to their argument. Since the bishops doubt that a nuclear war could be maintained with moral and rational boundaries, they argue that the most effective safeguard against nuclear war is to avoid crossing the threshold. Their support of a "no-first-use" policy derives from their profound distrust of the uncontrolled and cataclysmic effects from any significant outbreak of nuclear war. "To cross the divide from conventional to nuclear combat," the pastoral states, "is to enter a realm where human beings have no experience of control."[23] If nuclear war is to be averted, therefore, it is indispensable to maintain a well-established firebreak between nuclear and conventional forces. And to be effective, such a firebreak must involve not only weapons but strategy as well. Nuclear war-fighting strategies are therefore detrimental because they undermine the psychological impediments to first use or limited use of nuclear weapons. It is for this reason that the pastoral specifically questions the counterforce strategies that have gained ascendance in Washington. While such policies may strengthen deterrence, particularly extended deterrence, they do so by weakening the historic barriers between nuclear and conventional force.

THE QUALIFICATION OF DETERRENCE

One of the important messages of the pastoral is that not all expressions of deterrence are necessarily moral. The task of Christian ethics is to provide standards by which to judge the merit of specific policies. Whether or not the declaratory strategic policy is morally acceptable will depend, therefore, on the extent to which it conforms to moral standards by which the policy is to be judged.

The bishops offer two major policy guidelines for an acceptable policy of deterrence. First, direct targeting of population centers is prohibited. Second, nuclear war-fighting strategies that increase the likelihood of nuclear war are unacceptable.

The bishops state that "it is not morally acceptable to intend to kill the innocent as part of a strategy of deterring nuclear war."[24] While the aim of deterring nuclear war by threatening retaliation is morally permissible, it is not acceptable deliberately to threaten civilian population centers. This prohibition is in accord with the just-war principle of discrimination, which holds that civilians may not be the direct target of military attack in wartime. A corollary of this principle is the doctrine of double effect, which provides that the killing of civilians in combat is justified when the deaths are not the direct result of military attack. This means that if there is no direct intention of killing civilians but people are nonetheless killed as a result of a direct attack on a military or industrial target, the civilian deaths are morally justified.

Since the major presuppositions of the bishops' letter derive from the just-war doctrine, it is understandable that the bishops should attempt to reconcile deterrence with major elements of the just-war teaching, particularly the principle of discrimination. The problem in reconciling deterrence with just-war principles is that nuclear weapons are fundamentally indiscriminate instruments of destruction. Because of their enormous power, nuclear weapons are basically nonproportional and nondiscriminatory.

There are two schools of thought on nuclear weapons targeting—countervalue and counterforce. Countervalue targeting involves massive, indiscriminate targeting of areas of "value" to an enemy society, including industrial centers, transportation depots, and communication headquarters and power sources. Since these areas are always included within or near cities, countervalue targeting involves, in effect, the targeting of populated areas. Counterforce, by contrast, involves the targeting of military and political centers with highly accurate warheads. Although U.S. strategic policy has always sought to combine both targeting strategies, countervalue targeting has generally been identified with the doctrines of assured destruction of the 1950s and 1960s, and counterforce with the flexible response and countervailing strategies of the 1970s and 1980s.

The bishops' emphasis on discriminatory targeting is clearly in opposition to the countervalue targeting of MAD and in harmony with the more recent counterforce strategic policy. But it is difficult to understand how counterforce is morally superior to a countervalue strategy. There can be no doubt that at the declaratory level the former has public relations advantages over the latter. But at the operational level it would be difficult to identify a clearly superior strategy. Indeed, the choice between countervalue and counterforce targeting is largely artificial. It matters little what targeting strategy is adopted in a major nuclear attack. For example, the U.S. strategic nuclear targeting plan (known as SIOP) has identified sixty "military targets" alone within the city of Moscow and more than 40,000 throughout the entire territory of the Soviet Union. It is difficult to understand, therefore, how a counterforce targeting policy would necessarily be more discriminating (and therefore more moral) than a countervalue strategy, particularly when the levels of destruction would be marginally different.

The bishops are correct in calling attention to the morally troubling targeting approach associated with MAD. But whereas the doctrine of double effect has meaning with conventional weapons, it has virtually no import with nuclear weapons. The problems with nuclear weapons cannot be resolved by shifting targeting from "soft" to "hard" targets. Indeed, the effort to purify the strategy is self-defeating, for any significant lowering in the destructive impact of nuclear weapons may only weaken the firebreak further, thereby increasing the possibility of nuclear war.

The bishops do not endorse counterforce. Unlike Paul Ramsey,[25] who has sought to reconcile the demands of the just war with nuclear weapons by endorsing counterforce, the bishops recognize that a narrow adherence exclusively to the principle of noncombatant immunity as a policy guideline is an inadequate moral posture. The principle of proportionality must also be taken into account. And since any limited nuclear conflict would result in massive destruction, the use of nuclear weapons would almost of necessity lead to a violation of the principle of proportionality. In short, even if nuclear weapons could be used in a discriminating fashion, the massive civilian casualties resulting from any nuclear exchange would undoubtedly violate the principle of proportionality. There can therefore be no "just" nuclear war.

What the bishops seem to be saying is this: deterrence is OK but it cannot be morally supported through policies that are themselves immoral. MAD is clearly wrong because it does not discriminate; counterforce is wrong because by discriminating it makes the use of nuclear arms more likely. And since any limited use of nuclear arms would violate the principle of proportionality, we are left with the conditional affirmation of deterrence but the denial of the strategies designed to maintain such a policy. The pastoral affirms deterrence, yet by calling into question the means to implement such a policy it weakens the very policy it seeks to promote.

The reason for the apparent confusion is that the pastoral is based on fundamentally contradictory premises. On the one hand, the document seeks to endorse nuclear deterrence. On the other hand, the application of just-war criteria to the policies of deterrence results in a condemnation of the countervalue and counterforce strategies by which deterrence has been given credibility. In the end, the bishops leave us with three irreconcilable facts about the nuclear dilemma: (1) nuclear war is immoral; (2) massive, indiscriminate threats on civilian centers are unacceptable; and (3) counterforce, war-fighting strategies that increase the probability of limited nuclear war and lower the nuclear threshold must be opposed.

The bishops' failure to resolve the nuclear dilemma or morally to purify deterrence is understandable. After all, deterrence is fundamentally a paradox in that it seeks to prevent nuclear war by threatening mutual suicide. And the paradox cannot be resolved by adjusting the threats posed by nuclear powers with criteria from the just war. The only solution is through disarmament. In the meantime sovereign nation-states must live with the reality of nuclear technology. To the bishops' credit, they affirm deterrence despite its moral and logical shortcomings. But they also unwittingly qualify the policies that have given credibility to deterrence. There may be other ways by which deterrence can be maintained, but the bishops have not told us what those other options are. But by denying both counterforce and countervalue strategies the bishops weaken deterrence and thereby decrease strategic stability—the cornerstone of peaceful superpower nuclear relations.

One way out of the dilemma is to refuse to specify the conditions under which nuclear threats can be made morally acceptable. The bishops have wisely refused to identify what should be done if deterrence fails. They have affirmed the legitimacy of threatening a retaliatory strike but have not indicated how that threat should be operationalized. But perhaps it would also have been better for the bishops to refuse to get into the specifics concerning the nature of nuclear threats themselves. What is important is to oppose nuclear war and any policies that weaken the firebreak. This the bishops have done. But by discussing the more operational dimensions of deterrence they have unnecessarily ventured into an arena that qualifies and even contradicts some of the major themes of their letter.

It should be remembered that the strength and credibility of deterrence are based not on strategic theories, targeting doctrines, declared policies, or even international commitments. It is rather, as McGeorge Bundy has observed, the result of the "existential" existence of nuclear weapons, which could be used. Writes Bundy: "As long as each side has large numbers of thermonuclear weapons that could be used against the opponent, even after the strongest possible preemptive attack, existential deterrence is strong and it rests on uncertainty about what could happen."[26]

In the last analysis, the shortcomings of the pastoral derive from the inherent tensions between the just-war doctrine and the realities of nuclear weapons. The difficulties in reconciling the just-war doctrine with deterrence are a result of their contradictory nature: just war concerns the justice of war[27] and deterrence deals with the avoidance of war. Because nuclear war would be a massive holocaust, it cannot be encompassed by the moral criteria of the just war. This is why Walzer writes that nuclear weapons "explode" the theory of just war.[28] If we are to cope successfully with the moral problems posed by nuclear arms, it will be necessary to differentiate between war and deterrence.

Nuclear war is morally unacceptable, while deterrence is morally tolerable. The toleration of deterrence does not derive from its conformity with the norms of the just war but from the conditions of supreme emergency resulting from the balance of terror. Indeed, to seek to reconcile the just war with deterrence can only result in the corruption of a historic standard that has served humankind well both in and out of war.

The pastoral is an immensely important document. It appeared at a time of growing public concern with nuclear policy, and it should prove to be a useful tool in directing and influencing the strategic debate both in and out of the church. Many will view the specific policy recommendations, including the freeze, comprehensive test ban, and deep cuts in the strategic arsenals, as the most important elements. Others will consider the review of the biblical and theological perspectives on war to be its strength. In the last analysis, the pastoral's major contribution is its unequivocal opposition to nuclear war, the qualified endorsement of deterrence, and the recommendation of policies that will help to deter nuclear war. Of these recommendations, the most important to the peace of the world are the prohibition against first-use of nuclear arms and the need to work toward genuine arms control and disarmament.

V: Promoting Peace in a Nuclear Age

11: Arms Controlled or Uncontrolled: Policy Options

ROBERT L. DEVRIES

In the third section of their pastoral letter on war and peace, the U.S. Catholic bishops discuss a number of long-range and short-range policies and proposals to promote peace. Their primary focus, and the focus of this chapter, however, is on those measures that are designed to reduce the likelihood of nuclear war, the prevention of which the bishops assert to be a "moral imperative."

In the current debate over the best way to avoid nuclear war, three basic approaches can be identified: (1) a buildup of strategic forces (the peace-through-strength approach); (2) negotiated arms control and disarmament agreements; and (3) unilateral disarmament. The second approach is clearly endorsed by the bishops.[1] Having argued that the use of nuclear weapons is morally impermissible, they believe that nuclear disarmament, best done through negotiations, is the only long-term way to avoid nuclear war. In the meantime, they reluctantly conclude that they have no choice other than to accept nuclear deterrence. But the only acceptable form is in the framework of disarmament, that is, progressively lower levels of arms.[2] The bishops rightly reject, in my view, the prevailing position of the Reagan Administration on nuclear deterrence—that new weapons with "war-fighting capabilities" strengthen nuclear deterrence. They do so on the grounds that such weapons "may seem to threaten the viability of other nations' retaliatory forces, making deterrence unstable in a crisis and war more likely."[3]

While the bishops urge nations, especially the superpowers, to pursue arms control and disarmament, they "do not advocate a policy of unilateral disarmament."[4] Yet they do favor limited arms control steps to encourage similar steps by the other side. Thus they commend the United States for unilateral actions it has taken to reduce the possibility of unauthorized firing of nuclear weapons.[5] This approach to arms control with possible examples of it will be discussed below.

The bishops do not provide a rationale for their opposition to unilateral disarmament, but I largely agree with their position. My own opposition to unilateral disarmament is based on the practical consideration that more modest and more politically realistic, negotiated agreements should be more vigorously pursued first. If these efforts prove futile, and if the risks of nuclear war appear to be greater with a continued arms race than with unilateral nuclear disarmament, then unilateral disarmament must be given more serious consideration. Some respected analysts such as George Kennan have already concluded that Americans are far less safe with their possession of thousands of nuclear weapons than they would be without any: ". . . for if there is any incentive for the Russians to use such weapons against us, it surely comes in overwhelming degree—probably, in fact, entirely—from our own enormous deployment of them."[6]

In contrast to the arms control and disarmament approach endorsed by the bishops, the Reagan Administration has, from the start, placed much greater emphasis and confidence in the peace-through-strength approach and thus has initiated a massive buildup in military forces, both nuclear and conventional. Later, perhaps partly under the pressure of public opinion in the United States and Western Europe, the Reagan Administration showed greater interest in arms control and disarmament negotiations with the Soviet Union. But it argued that this approach is viable only if it is linked with a continued arms buildup. This is the idea that more arms are needed now in order to negotiate reductions later; or more precisely, we need to show the Russians that we can outcompete them in an arms race in order to induce them to negotiate reductions.

This view, it seems to me, is not supported by the post-World War II record. There is not space here to make a detailed examination of the record, but I would assert that a general

pattern can be observed from it: the United States has led the
way with new weapons—from A-bombs and H-bombs to multiple warheads, from strategic bombers to cruise missiles and
missile-launching submarines—and the Soviet Union has tried
to catch up with similar weapons of its own. Rather than bring
the Soviet Union to the negotiating table, new American arms
have only been the occasion for a new round in the arms race.[7]

I would argue, therefore, that the attempt to promote peace
and security through linking the arms buildup and the arms
control approaches is seriously misguided. On the contrary, I
will try to show that we face a clear choice between these two
approaches in our efforts to cope with current or potential areas
of arms competition. And it is the second approach that the
bishops and I consider to offer the best, but by no means easy
or certain, way to avoid nuclear war.

The bishops do not attempt to make a comprehensive or
detailed analysis of arms control issues, but, in my judgment,
arrive at wise and prudent positions based on careful study. My
own discussion, therefore, will not critique, but rather expand
on, add to, and put into a typology, the various possible arms
control measures brought up in the bishops' letter.

Before proceeding to this discussion, it is well to be aware
of a distinction between arms control and disarmament generally
made by specialists in the field. As defined by the United States
Arms Control and Disarmament Agency,

> Arms control includes all those actions, unilateral as well as mul-
> tilateral, by which we *regulate* the levels and kinds of armaments
> in order to reduce the likelihood of armed conflicts, their severity
> and violence if they should occur, and the economic burden of
> military programs. Disarmament, a somewhat older term, de-
> scribes a particular kind of arms control—efforts specifically to
> *reduce* military force and perhaps ultimately to eliminate them.[8]

Arms control, then, is the broader term, which may or may
not include arms reductions. By this distinction, most of the
policies and proposals discussed here would be arms control
measures rather than disarmament measures in the precise
meaning of the term. Unless disarmament is meant in its narrow
sense, I will use the broader term, arms control, in my discussion.

MEASURES PROHIBITING WEAPONS FROM CERTAIN AREAS

Some agreements of this type have already been achieved. These include: the 1959 Antarctica Treaty, which establishes a demilitarized zone for the area; the 1967 Outer Space Treaty, which prohibits the placement of weapons of "mass destruction" in outer space; the 1967 Latin American Nuclear Free Zone Treaty, which prohibits nuclear weapons in this area; the 1968 Non-Proliferation Treaty, which attempts to prevent the spread of nuclear weapons to nonnuclear weapon states; and the 1971 Seabed Treaty, which bars the placement of nuclear weapons on the ocean floor beyond twelve nautical miles of the coast of parties to the Treaty.[9]

Most of these treaties accomplish what is relatively easy in the field of arms control agreements; that is, they prevent the spread of arms and arms rivalries to areas where they are presently not well developed. But the most important of these treaties, the Non-Proliferation Treaty (NPT), was controversial and difficult to achieve. It was essentially an attempt on the part of nuclear weapon states to limit their special status to themselves on the grounds that this will reduce the danger of nuclear war. Since the Treaty entered into force in 1970, only one state, India, has officially exploded a nuclear device (there are reports of a possible nuclear explosion off the coast of South Africa in 1979) while 116 nations have joined the Treaty.[10] Some of the key holdouts—Pakistan, Taiwan, South Africa, Argentina, Brazil, and Israel (most experts believe Israel has already developed nuclear weapons)—are also among the most likely candidates to join the "nuclear club." Since some of these states consider themselves to have unique defense needs, it is doubtful that any efforts to make the Treaty more attractive or effective will entice them to join it.

Yet stricter compliance with Treaty requirements may be helpful in controlling the spread of weapons in such areas as the Middle East and Latin America. One step would be a closer observance of Article III, which prohibits the supply of fissionable material to nonnuclear weapon states who refuse to accept the safeguards system of the International Atomic Energy Agency (IAEA). Several exporters of fissionable material seem to have violated this requirement, including the United States in its recent decision to allow heavy water to be sold to Argentina, which has refused to sign either the NPT or the Latin American Nuclear Free Zone Treaty and refused IAEA inspections of its nuclear facilities.[11] Some states have questioned the effectiveness of the IAEA safeguards system—as Israel apparently did when it bombed the IAEA-inspected nuclear reactor in Iraq—but it is the only Agency charged with monitoring the Treaty. If it is to gain the confidence of member states, it will need greater support from key members such as the United States.[12]

The Non-Proliferation Treaty also requires nuclear weapon states urgently to undertake measures to control and reduce their own nuclear armaments: this they have largely failed to do. If nuclear weapon states expect nonnuclear states to forego nuclear weapons they must show greater resolve in restraining their own arsenals. As the bishops have concluded, ". . . the United States should . . . seriously reexamine its policies and programs and make clear its determination to uphold the spirit as well as the letter of the treaty."[13]

Perhaps the most significant area for prohibiting new weapons developments is in space. Here the United States and the Soviet Union are on the threshold of an intensive and dangerous area of arms competition. They still have time to choose between a new weapons approach and an arms control approach to security, but it is growing short.

The arms approach, partly explained in President Reagan's so-called "Star Wars" address to the nation, March 23, 1983, envisions development of new ballistic missile defense (BMD) systems that include the possible use of high-energy lasers and charged-particle beams. BMD weapons, it is argued, promise to provide, for the first time, defense against nuclear weapons based on missiles and hence an escape from our mutual hostage predicament. This promise of defense against the most dangerous kind of nuclear weapon is certainly appealing. But what appears to one side to be defensive appears to the other side to threaten its retaliatory force; hence the prospect of BMD systems has already begun to spawn a new generation of weapons. These include: anti-satellite weapons to attack laser platforms and satellites that are used in the targeting of ballistic missiles; miniature orbiting vehicles to defend space platforms and satellites;

space cruisers to service miniature vehicles, platforms, and satellites; and space shuttles to carry cruisers, platforms, and satellites to space.[14] BMD weapons might also generate such defensive and offensive countermeasures as hardening the outer shells of missiles and satellites, adding more decoys to offensive missiles, and simply increasing the number of offensive missiles.

In short, the attempt to provide security through weapons may only leave us with an illusory defense, and a highly destabilizing and costly new dimension to the arms race.

A far more certain path to security would seem to be that of arms control. In part, this would include a reaffirmation and stricter interpretation of the Anti-Ballistic Missile (ABM) Treaty of 1972, which is generally considered to be the most significant arms control treaty between the United States and the Soviet Union.[15] Some analysts believe that U.S. BMD efforts, including the testing of lasers and beams for this purpose, already violate Article V, Section 1, of the ABM Treaty: "Each party undertakes not to develop, test, or deploy ABM systems or components which are sea-based, air-based, or mobile-based."[16] The official U.S. position, however, is that laser and beams weapons are not missiles and hence their development for ballistic missile defense would not be a technical violation of the ABM Treaty.[17] Even if the government's position—which seems contrary to the intent of the treaty—were accepted, other U.S. BMD schemes involving missiles are on a clear collision course with the ABM Treaty. In the interests of promoting strategic stability, the United States should agree with the Soviet Union on a Treaty interpretation that would prohibit both missile and laser schemes for BMD.

Another important arms control step in space would be for the United States to reenter the Anti-Satellite Weapons negotiations it had initiated in 1977 but had broken off after the Soviet invasion of Afghanistan. Talks aimed at restricting anti-satellite (ASAT) weapons are significant because satellites are both highly vulnerable to attack and the vital "eyes and ears" of strategic forces. They warn against attack, detect targets and guide missiles to them, and provide communication links with armed forces. The United States depends much more heavily on satellites for these purposes than does the Soviet Union. The United States should, therefore, carefully consider the recent proposal of Soviet Premier Yuri Andropov to ban ASAT weapons and take it as the occasion for renewing anti-satellite talks.[18] An agreement to ban anti-satellite weapons—as well as an agreement to ban BMD weapons—would save vast resources, but more importantly, promote global stability and security.[19]

MEASURES PROHIBITING CERTAIN KINDS OF NUCLEAR WEAPONS TESTS

The most important measure of this type that is achievable in the near-term is a comprehensive test ban treaty (CTBT). Ever since U.S.–Soviet negotiations on such a treaty were begun in 1958, it was regarded as a crucial step in heading off the development of new types of nuclear warheads. Had a complete test ban on warheads been achieved in 1963, instead of the Limited Test Ban Treaty which outlawed the atmospheric testing of nuclear weapons but permitted underground testing, a whole variety of warheads now used on missiles with multiple warheads, cruise missiles, and tactical battlefield weapons could not have been developed. Although this has permitted arms competition in significant areas to take place, a CTBT would still be important in stopping the further miniaturization of nuclear warheads and the development of warheads with special effects such as enhanced radiation. Preventing the development of this "third generation" of nuclear weapons is significant because they blur the difference between conventional and nuclear weapons and thus lower the threshold for the use of nuclear weapons.

A comprehensive test ban treaty seemed to be at hand in 1979 when the United States and the Soviet Union agreed on its basic terms, which included a major Soviet departure from its long-held opposition to on-site verification. Unfortunately, final agreement was delayed due to the Soviet invasion of Afghanistan, and since that time President Reagan has shown no interest in completing the treaty. Two of the reasons given for this position are questions raised about Soviet compliance with the Threshold Test Ban Treaty (explained below) and an inability to determine whether some "seismic events" in the Soviet Union were earthquakes or nuclear tests. Two experts on seismology, Lynn Sykes and Jack Evernden, believe, however, that all doubts on this matter should be put to rest. The evidence presented in

186 *Robert L. DeVries*

their *Scientific American* article shows that all unexplained "seismic events" were earthquakes and that there were no Soviet violations of treaties.[20] They conclude, therefore, that modern technical means exist that would enable the verification of a CTBT with a high degree of certainty. The only remaining obstacles to American support, they conclude, therefore, must be political rather than technical. Thus I concur with the bishops in urging "support for [an] early and successful conclusion of negotiations of a comprehensive test ban treaty."[21]

Two other treaties in this area have already been signed by the United States and the Soviet Union, but not entered into force for lack of U.S. Senate ratification. These are the 1974 Threshold Test Ban Treaty and the 1976 Peaceful Nuclear Explosions Treaty. The Threshold Treaty limits the size of underground nuclear tests to 150 kilotons, the equivalent of 150,000 tons of TNT. This Treaty would be superseded by a completed CTBT, but there is no reason to hold back from ratifying until that time. To ratify the Treaty would formally affirm what we say we already observe in practice and furthermore show good faith in the effort to achieve more ambitious restrictions on testing.

Under the terms of the Peaceful Nuclear Explosions (PNE) Treaty, the United States and Soviet Union agree to exchange data and inspect each other's nuclear explosions that are intended for strictly peaceful purposes. This treaty would nicely complement a CTBT since it would assure the parties that a ban on military testing were not violated. What is significant about the PNE Treaty is that the Soviet Union, for the first time, accepted the right of other states to inspect facilities on its territory. Again the United States should be urged formally to join this Treaty, which it has already signed and which would be a positive sign of its commitment to arms control.[22]

The most ambitious test ban proposal is that advocated by the nuclear freeze movement. Despite disclaimers of not endorsing any specific political initiatives, the bishops recommend a policy that is virtually the same, in substance and language, as the freeze proposal: "immediate, verifiable agreements to halt the testing, production and deployment of nuclear weapons systems."[23] The freeze proposal is appealing in that it calls for a straightforward, understandable, yet sweeping arms control measure. In one bold stroke, it is intended to put an end to the costly and dangerous competition in nuclear arms. Freeze negotiations, it is thought, could bypass some of the more specific arms control proposals and forums, which tend to get enmeshed in tedious and seemingly endless haggling over details. It is unlikely, however, that this is possible since some forums already concern themselves with aspects of the freeze proposal. In any case, freeze negotiations would have to face some of the same tough issues that plague other negotiations, for example, verification of production and test facilities and deciding whether to include weapons that have both conventional and nuclear capabilities, for example, cruise missiles.

As laudable as the objectives of the freeze proposal are, therefore, it seems too broad and cumbersome to be a good negotiating proposal. Instead, it would be better to pursue vigorously those related measures already proposed or under negotiation, for example, a comprehensive test ban, a cut-off of fissionable material for weapons, and quantitative and qualitative limits on nuclear weapons similar to those stipulated in SALT II and which may yet emerge from the Strategic Arms Reduction Talks.[24]

The freeze movement has nonetheless had a salutary effect in its pressuring the Reagan Administration to the nuclear arms bargaining table. This is reason enough, it seems to me, to support the freeze movement.[25]

MEASURES REDUCING THE RISKS OF THE OUTBREAK OF NUCLEAR WAR

Efforts should be made to expand on the measures already achieved in this area: the "Hotline" Agreements (1963 and 1971), which enable American and Soviet leaders to communicate directly in time of crisis; the "Accident Measures" Agreement (1971), in which the United States and the Soviet Union agreed to improve safeguards against "accidental or unauthorized use of nuclear weapons," to inform each other about any such incidents that might risk a nuclear war, and to notify each other about "planned missile" launches in the direction of the other; and the Standing Consultative Commission, which was set up to hear complaints about compliance with the SALT agreements of 1971.

Many other possible crisis-stability and confidence-building measures have been proposed. Two seem especially noteworthy. Senator Samuel Nunn (D, Georgia) has suggested the establishment of a U.S.–Soviet "crisis notification center" to coordinate responses to the unexplained or unexpected explosion of a nuclear weapon. The other proposal, by scholar and former Under Secretary of State Joseph Nye, is the establishment of regular meetings between high-level Soviet and American officials to explain and discuss nuclear weapons policy.[26] The U.S. Chairman of the Joint Chiefs of Staff and his Soviet counterpart, for example, could meet to discuss ambiguities about doctrine, strategy, and posture of nuclear weapons.

The important aim of all these proposals is to avoid any misunderstandings about each other's plans and intentions and hopefully arrive at a consensus about which plans and strategies are most likely to prevent nuclear war.

MEASURES REDUCING RELIANCE ON NUCLEAR WEAPONS IN MILITARY STRATEGY

As explained earlier in connection with the CTBT, one important step in reducing reliance on nuclear weapons—especially early resort to the use of nuclear weapons—would be to stop the development of "third generation" nuclear weapons. The major concern about such weapons, which the bishops also explain in their opposition to them, is that their use on a battlefield would quickly escalate into an uncontrolled nuclear war.

The achievement of a CTBT would prevent the development of such weapons, but in the absence of a completed treaty, the United States and the Soviet Union should be urged to undertake unilateral restraint on their development, or better yet, reach informal, joint agreement to undertake such restraint. Two small but hopeful signs of movement in this direction are reports that a NATO nuclear planning group will recommend the removal of old nuclear battlefield weapons in Europe and that the U.S. Congress has rejected the Administration's 1984 defense authorization request for a new nuclear artillery shell.[27]

The bishops also suggest two related, specific steps in reducing reliance on nuclear weapons:

1. Removal by all parties of short-range nuclear weapons
   that multiply dangers disproportionate to their deterrent
   value.
2. Removal by all parties of nuclear weapons from areas
   where they are likely to be overrun in the early stages
   of war, thus forcing rapid and uncontrollable decisions
   on their use.[28]

These proposals have special relevance for the NATO Alliance, which has relied heavily on the use of nuclear weapons
in its planning for the defense of Western Europe and whose
members have refused to endorse a "no-first-use" policy. This
is not the place to evaluate this policy or limited nuclear war
doctrine as they are discussed in other chapters of this volume.
Suffice it to say that those who urge a reduction in reliance on
nuclear weapons believe that their use in crowded Western Europe would be disastrous and that their use could not be contained in Europe.[29]

Another dimension of the debate over nuclear weapons
strategy for Europe is its relationship to conventional force levels. The commonly accepted argument is that NATO nuclear
forces are needed to compensate for superior conventional forces
of the Warsaw Pact. Consequently many supporters of a reduction in nuclear forces—from "no-first-use" advocate George
Kennan, to NATO commander, General Bernard Rogers—also
urge a buildup of conventional forces.[30] The bishops take note
of this argument without passing judgment on its merits, but
reluctantly concede that if the argument is valid, then "strengthening of conventional defense would be a proportionate price
to pay if this will reduce the possibility of a nuclear war."[31]

The case for increased conventional forces, however, is in
fact not nearly as clear-cut as a simple balance sheet comparing
various kinds of NATO and Warsaw Pact weapons and force
levels would make it out to be. For one thing, such comparisons
often leave out French forces since they are no longer part of
NATO's integrated force structure although they are still pledged
to the defense of Western Europe. More importantly, these balance sheets do not calculate qualitative factors such as training

and readiness of troops, weapons effectiveness, and reliability of Alliance partners. With these factors taken into account, my own view and that of many experts is that a Warsaw Pact advantage in conventional forces is often exaggerated.[32]

Even if this were the case, it would be better, in my view, to try to negotiate reductions in conventional forces on both sides than to try to match a supposed Warsaw Pact advantage. Negotiations on this matter have, in fact, already been underway for some time at the Mutual and Balanced Force Reduction talks in Vienna. They have proven to be very difficult partly because of disputes over counting force levels, but the goal of conventional force reductions deserves renewed diplomatic effort. One indicator of some progress in these talks was a recent Soviet proposal on means to monitor troop withdrawals that is being given serious study by the West.[33]

The reduction of conventional arms, not just in Europe, but worldwide, is a matter of great importance for many reasons: conventional weapons are, as recent wars have shown, increasingly destructive; they are very costly—nuclear powers spend much more on them than on nuclear weapons; the sale of arms to third world states has risen dramatically and added to the tension and destruction of regional rivalries; and finally conventional wars may usher in nuclear war both in Europe and in other parts of the world where nuclear powers have rival client states or where rival states begin to acquire their own nuclear weapons.

This interrelationship of conventional and nuclear arms leads the bishops to conclude

> that any program directed at reducing reliance on nuclear weapons is not likely to succeed unless it includes measures to reduce tensions and to work for the balanced reduction of conventional forces.[34]

MEASURES LIMITING THE SIZE AND TYPE OF NUCLEAR ARMAMENTS

At the present time, two major forums are devoted to limiting the size of national arsenals: the Intermediate-Range Nuclear Force (INF) talks and the Strategic Arms Reduction Talks (START). The bishops have little to say about specific issues at these negotiating forums, but they do urge the achievement of strategic arms reduction agreements.

The INF talks are concerned with limiting the planned deployment of new American missiles (108 Pershing II ballistic missiles and 464 Tomahawk cruise missiles) and the already deployed Soviet intermediate-range missiles, especially the new SS20 missile, which carries three warheads. The NATO plan to deploy the American missiles, first decided in 1979, partly in response to Soviet SS20's, was ironically made contingent on simultaneous negotiations with the Soviet Union to reduce the levels of intermediate-range missiles on both sides.

The NATO decision to deploy the American missiles, however, has less to do with military strategy than with political factors, both within and outside NATO. The missiles do not appear to have any clear military purpose since other American weapons from central strategic forces can cover the same targets. They have little value as retaliatory weapons because they are highly vulnerable to attack and only marginally augment U.S. strategic forces. (They would increase the estimated 9,500 warheads in the U.S. strategic arsenal about 6 percent.) To the extent that the missiles, especially the Pershing IIs, are useful, it is as first-strike weapons, since they are highly accurate and give the Soviets a short warning time. Their deployment, therefore, would have a destabilizing effect on the nuclear balance. For these reasons even hawkish Assistant Secretary of State Richard Perle has reportedly called the planned missile deployment an "error."[35]

But for the Western European governments, especially the West German government under Helmut Schmidt, which first requested the missiles in 1977, the weapons have a political significance. They provide yet another visible sign of the American commitment to defend Europe. By wedding American nuclear weapons, including strategic weapons, to its defense, the fate of America is linked to the fate of Europe.

The missile deployment issue is also embroiled in political competition between the United States and the Soviet Union. Both want to appear as greater champions of peace than the other but neither is willing to make concessions on missile reductions under pressure from the other.

No deployment of American missiles would be highly desirable in terms of reducing reliance on nuclear weapons and removing a highly contentious public issue in Western Europe, but by this time the NATO governments are too deeply committed to the plan to turn back except through negotiations with the Soviet Union. Hopefully, greater flexibility on both sides will at least result in sharp reductions in the missiles on both sides. Perhaps an acceptable formula can be found that counts warheads rather than missiles, which the West favors, and takes some account of British and French forces, on which the Soviets insist.

On the strategic level, SALT negotiations have been succeeded by START negotiations. The Reagan Administration rejected the SALT II Treaty as "fatally flawed" mainly on the grounds that it was not equitable and that it did not require real reductions in force levels. Whether SALT II was equitable is a moot point, but the first American and Soviet START proposals have failed another standard of successful arms talks, that of negotiability. The first proposals of each side were so clearly unfavorable and objectionable to the other that there was little basis for further negotiation. American proposals required deep cuts in Soviet land-based missiles, which comprise 75 percent of its strategic forces, and Soviet proposals required cuts in submarine-based missiles where the United States has a significant advantage. Since then there have been some encouraging reports of greater flexibility and narrowing differences on both sides.[36]

A meaningful START agreement should include restrictions on types of weapons as well as levels of weapons. In particular it should include those that are hard to verify (e.g., cruise missiles that are small and easily moved and concealed) and those that might be perceived as first-strike weapons (e.g., U.S. MX missiles and Soviet SS18s, both of which have multiple warheads).

Missiles with multiple warheads that have high accuracy and yield are ideal first-strike weapons because a single missile could theoretically destroy several land-based missiles, especially those based on vulnerable fixed sites. The MX missile, for example, which carries ten warheads, could theoretically destroy five missiles, each of which carries several warheads itself. (The Pentagon calculates that two warheads are needed to ensure destruction of a hardened missile silo.) In short, missiles with multiple warheads give the side that attacks first a very big advantage. This fact may arouse fears on each side about the intentions of the other side, and thereby prompt each to put its forces on a "hair trigger" to avoid their destruction on the ground or even attempt a preemptive first strike.

It is unfortunate, therefore, that the Reagan Administration decided to proceed with the deployment and production of the MX missile. Soviet deployment of similar missiles is not a sufficient reason to deploy our own when the likely results are considered. That is, putting greater numbers of Soviet land-based missiles at risk is not as likely to force the Soviets to abandon them in favor of less vulnerable, missile-carrying submarines (since their submarines are inferior to American submarines and easily tracked) as it is to push them to increase the number of their land-based missiles.[37]

Because of the complexities of negotiating a comprehensive treaty on strategic arms and the inherent difficulties of negotiating in a highly visible, formal setting, Joseph Nye has recommended supplementing formal START negotiations with informal but regular "Force Structure Discussions."[38] In part, the purpose of such discussions would be to determine those arms programs that might be limited by "restraint arrangements" based on informal reciprocity rather than formal treaties. An example of one possible reciprocal "restraint arrangement" would be a ban on space-based laser technology for anti-satellite purposes. The significance of such a move is discussed above and might be undertaken in the absence of a formal anti-satellite agreement.

Yet another means to supplement formal negotiations for nuclear arms reductions is that of limited unilateral initiatives. Steps initiated by one side are designed to stimulate similar steps on the other side. If they are not reciprocated, they can be taken back or reversed without much danger or loss.[39] For the United States some possible initiatives might include:

1. A decision not to deploy cruise missiles with nuclear warheads at sea (to do this before the Soviet Union develops the capacity to deploy such weapons might preclude a potentially significant area of arms competition—

and one that poses a greater threat to the United States as we have a longer coastline with more major cities along it;)[40]

2. a delay of scheduled production and deployment of weapons such as the MX missile, B-1 bomber, or the 5-D warhead on Trident II submarines that has hard-target accuracy;

3. a small but clearly documented reduction in spending levels for strategic forces.

The main point of all these informal talks, reciprocal arrangements, and unilateral initiatives would be to augment and encourage formal treaty negotiations without binding arms control progress to their slow pace.

CONCLUSION

There must be no illusions about the difficulties of achieving arms control and disarmament agreements. The difficulties are due, in part, to the technical complexities of the issues, but more fundamentally they are rooted in the ideological and political difference between the United States and the Soviet Union. Indeed, it is the antipathy between the two political systems that fuels the arms race in the first place. But it is also true that the arms race itself contributes to this antipathy and makes it more dangerous.

We have no choice, therefore, but to renew our arms control efforts. Some modest progress has been made, but much more remains to be done. Whether the nuclear arms race is contained and reversed or expands out of control will depend on the choices and actions that are made in the critical arms control areas outlined in this chapter.

Because of their inherent importance, arms control and disarmament negotiations should not be made a condition of resolving all of our differences with the Soviet Union. The United States can and should oppose Soviet policy and action in some areas while cooperating in others of mutual interest and benefit. President Reagan's response to the shooting down of a Korean commercial airliner by a Soviet fighter is a case in point. He was right to condemn it for what it was—"a barbaric . . . cold-blooded act." But he was also right to assert that arms talks with the Soviets must go on.

Yet arms negotiations cannot take place in a political vacuum. Specific actions like the destruction of the Korean plane and the Afghanistan invasion, as well as the overall state of Soviet–American relations, are bound to have an impact on arms control. Improved relations should, then, be a matter of high priority. Here we need to heed the advice of the bishops:

> Negotiation on arms control agreements . . . , without persistent and parallel efforts to reduce the political tensions which motivate the buildup of arms, will not suffice. The United States, therefore, should have a policy of maximum political engagement with governments of potential adversaries, providing for repeated, systematic discussion and negotiation of areas of friction.[41]

We must not expect such negotiations to have any immediate or large impact on the deep-seated differences between the Soviet and American systems or on the onerous, sometimes brutal, side of the Soviet state. At the same time, we must not consider the Soviet Union to be the source of all evil in the world. To do so makes it impossible to see that we still have some objective common interests, the most important of which is avoiding a nuclear war that both would lose. To adapt a phrase of Reinhold Niebuhr, our differences with the Soviet Union make arms control necessary, but our common interests make it possible.

12: Shaping a Peaceful World

JOHN A. BERNBAUM

The bishops' call for a "moral about-face"[1] in light of the crisis the world is experiencing because of the threat of a nuclear holocaust challenges all followers of Jesus Christ to deepen their understanding of faithful discipleship in a nuclear age. Nothing less than renewal of the church is needed. We agree with the bishops that we are at a "new moment"[2] in the nuclear arms race and that the church must energetically speak to this issue.

In addition to the arms control and disarmament proposals described in the previous chapter, which are designed to reduce the risks of war, there are other positive steps Christians can take both as citizens of this nation and as members of the church of Jesus Christ. The absence of war is only a partial goal; building peaceful relations between the superpowers is the additional challenge.

PUBLIC POLICY OPTIONS FOR THE GOVERNMENT

1. We affirm the bishops' proposal that our government encourage the study of nonviolent means of resistance to evil.[3] While we believe that the nation has the right to defend itself, its citizens, and its values, we would advocate federal funding in support of developing nonviolent means of conflict resolution. The following recommendations are examples of practical steps in this direction:

a. we concur with the bishops' observation that nonviolent means of conflict resolution deserve more study than they have received so far, and therefore we support the bishops' proposal that federal funds equivalent to at least 1/10 of 1 percent of our current budgetary allotments for military purposes be used in support of conflict resolution and peace research. Concentrated research on the nature, causes, and risks of war is needed as well as studies on building structures of interdependence and global cooperation. A shift in federal funding priorities is necessary to encourage this research, and the government can assist constructively by such an initiative. Reliance on private sources of funding is not adequate, although continued funding from those sources should be encouraged.

Federal funding of peace research would assist colleges and universities in the development of interdisciplinary research programs designed to train "peacemaking experts." University leadership and governing boards must also be willing to undertake similar programs on their own initiative. It is here that colleges and universities that have a distinctive religious heritage can make a significant contribution. The development of a theology of peace that can serve as a foundation for our peacemaking and reconciliation efforts in a nuclear age is critical. Christ's own teachings and example are the basis on which both Catholic and Protestant colleges and universities can build. These institutions should have equal access to federal funding in this area.

b. We also join the bishops in their support of the proposed United States Academy of Peace. In their report to the President, the Commission that was formed to study the feasibility of such an academy proposed that it be established with three functions:

—education and training on the graduate and postgraduate levels on negotiations, mediation, conciliation, and arbitration in international conflicts;

—interdisciplinary scholarship in the field of peace research; and,

—information service to further the " 'corporate memory'

of the field of peace learning so as to make its literature and knowledge easily retrievable and useful."[4]

We concur with Commissioner John Dellenback's statement that

> I don't think that there is any more important issue that this Nation and the world is facing at this moment, aside from the decisions we make on matters of faith and theology, than the question of world peace; and, if you will, those two link together. ... The United States Academy of Peace will not be a panacea to the conflict problems of the world, but it is highly appropriate that the United States do whatever it can to epitomize our commitment to doing everything we can to reach for peace in the world.[5]

Support for the Academy of Peace would be another example of a practical way in which the study of nonviolent means of resistance to evil could be encouraged.

2. A second major area where governmental initiatives are recommended concerns the need to broaden our understanding of the Soviet Union. This subject deserves more attention than it received in the pastoral letter. While significant amounts of our federal budget are spent annually in an effort to defend ourselves from the threat to our security posed by the Soviet Union, very little is expended to learn more about that nation. A few statistics will quickly highlight the comparative disadvantage we have in this area vis-à-vis the Soviets and the low priority it has received so far in our federal budget:

—there are more English-language teachers in the Soviet Union than there are Russian-language students in the United States;

—while the Soviet Union has approximately 7,500 specialists on the United States and three major research institutions devoted to the study of America's political, military, and economic structures, only about 200 Americans each year complete their doctorates in a Soviet-related field;

—America's annual production of Ph.D.s with advanced training in Soviet foreign policy, for example, rarely exceeds seven or eight, and the number of Soviet specialists who write books on this subject is probably less than thirty; and finally,

—we spend more money building one-fourth of one mile of interstate highway than we do on all of our exchange programs with the Soviet Union and the Warsaw Pact countries.[6]

Concerned citizens need to inform their elected officials that this kind of ordering of budget priorities is both shortsighted and dangerous. Increasingly, high-ranking government officials have warned us that we cannot afford to be so completely ignorant of Soviet society.[7] Funding for Soviet studies has decreased by 70 percent between 1965 and the present and the number of Americans doing research on the Soviet Union is one-half of what it was in the mid-1970s. If the 26 percent drop in the population of 18-year-olds between 1979 and 1994 is proportionately reflected in the loss of faculty positions in Slavic languages and literature, for example, this would mean a decrease of 600 from the previous total of only 2,300 faculty positions. This would follow a decline of one-third in Russian-language enrollments in the colleges and a 70 percent drop at the secondary level during the period 1972-80.[8] This is the making of a national crisis. We would therefore recommend the following:

a. a major funding effort by the government to promote our nation's independent factual knowledge of the Soviet Union and Eastern European countries;[9]

b. increased federal funding for exchange programs between the United States and the Soviet Union, and between the United States and Eastern European countries;[10] and,

c. creation of a U.S.–Soviet Union student exchange program that would provide for an ongoing country-to-country exchange of qualified young people of both high school and college ages.[11]

While in all three recommendations private support would be both welcomed and encouraged, the expenditure of federal monies would be essential. For Christians who see their calling as peacemakers and reconcilers affecting their role as citizens, overcoming our ignorance of Soviet society is critical and deserves our support as a constructive step toward peace.

3. A third arena for creative public policy initiatives involves the building of constructive relationships with the Soviet Union. A narrow focus on military competition between the superpowers blinds us to the urgent need to find ever broadening areas of mutual interest with full recognition of the differences that exist in ideology and perceived security needs. Despite the incompatibility of our two political and economic systems, significant areas still exist where our two nations can take constructive steps toward building working relationships that benefit each country. Although the pastoral letter makes some reference to findings areas of mutual interest, more specificity here would be helpful. The following are just a few examples of initiatives we would recommend:

a. we would support renewed efforts to negotiate a U.S.–Soviet space cooperation agreement that was allowed to expire in 1982. The success of our joint space effort, highlighted by the dramatic linkup of the Apollo and Soyuz spacecraft in 1975, helped to overcome problems of information exchange and verification. This type of cooperative effort will bear more positive results than our current emphasis on a space weapons race with the Soviet Union.[12]

b. we would support efforts to increase U.S.–Soviet trade, which has grown dramatically since 1972 but was restricted in 1979 following the Soviet invasion of Afghanistan.[13] The negotiation of new long-term agricultural and industrial trade agreements, in addition to the recent grain agreement, seem to be judicious steps toward building more constructive relationships between the superpowers.[14]

c. we would also encourage the renewal of the bilateral agreements signed between our two countries during President Richard Nixon's administration. Eleven bilateral agreements on scientific and technical cooperation were negotiated, and are subject to periodic renewal. While the agreements on agriculture, environmental protection, public health, and artificial heart research were renewed recently, others (e.g., space cooperation, energy, and pollution control) were not.[15]

None of these recommendations will in itself or even together bring about a dramatic improvement in U.S.–Soviet relations, but they can serve as building blocks. A realistic view of the differences between our two nations quickly makes evident that there is no easy way to alleviate the animosities and fears that presently exist, but quiet efforts at creating cooperative programs would be a constructive first step.[16]

4. A final public policy concern, in which we would join the bishops, relates to the role of conscience and the right of conscientious objection.[17] On behalf of all conscientious objectors, including a significant part of the evangelical community represented by the "historic peace churches"—the Quakers or Friends, the Mennonites, and the Brethren in Christ, we affirm the bishops' statement that the government has a right in principle to require military service of its citizens, but it does not have the right to demand blind obedience. Individuals must act according to their own conscience on the question of participation in war, and the government must respect and legislatively protect the right of both conscientious objectors and selective conscientious objectors. We would also support alternative community service by such persons, service not related to our military establishment.

These four areas of public policy are examples of the initiatives Christians should be supporting as citizens of our nation. The first three in particular represent constructive steps that can be taken to reduce fears and tensions that add momentum to the nuclear arms race between the United States and the Soviet Union. They are examples of approaches our governmental officials can take to change the direction of our present policy of confrontation and military rivalry. We now need to address the role the church can play as a community of Jesus' disciples.

PRIVATE INITIATIVES FOR THE CHURCH

The message of the kingdom of God that is portrayed in Scripture as both present reality and future hope calls us as followers of Jesus Christ not only to resist evil, but to overcome evil with good.[18] Scripture not only informs us of the rightful responsibility of civil authority, but also instructs us concerning the proper role of the church as a "called out" people. Therefore, we affirm the bishops' observations concerning the particular role the church has to play in our society in creating a "positive conception of peace."[19] While we recognize that the fullness of Christ's kingdom will not be evident until he returns a second time, we also know that we have been empowered by the Holy Spirit to be agents of his kingdom in our present context.

While the government is the primary institution with responsibility for establishing our nation's relationship with the Soviet Union, the church of Jesus Christ has an important role to play as well. Not only do church members have citizenship obligations that, among other things, should encourage them to hold our public officials accountable or even to set limits restricting their freedom of action, as a church the Christian community has an obligation to speak the truth "in love,"[20] in light of the insights given to us by the Word of God. If Scripture is a "lamp to [our] feet" and a "light for [our] path,"[21] its illumination should be shared with the rest of our society. Here is an appropriate area for private initiatives.

While governmental policies are the appropriate vehicles for restraining evil and preventing or limiting the violence of war, the government is not equipped to create a positive vision of peace. Here the church is ideally positioned. Peace is not just the absence of war, but involves a full sense of wholeness, well-being, and health as portrayed in the Hebrew word *shalom* in the Old Testament and the Greek work *eirēnē* in the New Testament. We believe that Evangelicals, along with other Christians, have a major role to play in building this vision of peace. What the government can never do, the church of Jesus Christ has been called to do, and has been especially equipped for the task by the power of the Holy Spirit.[22]

Although we would base our authority solely on Scripture and not equally on the writings of St. Augustine, St. Aquinas, and various papal teachings as the bishops have done, we would affirm the biblical vision of shalom that they describe in the pastoral letter. Our beginning point would be the Lordship of Jesus Christ and its implications for all areas of life, including our politics and our defense programs. We would agree with the bishops that the church should "rethink the meaning of national interest" and not simply accept conventional wisdom that argues for the pursuit of "self-interest," even benevolent self-interest.[23]

If we ground our view of the world in Scripture and are

convinced, like the Apostle Paul, that "all things" were created by and for Jesus Christ and that in him "all things hold together,"[24] then our perspective on foreign policy and defense policy would be different from that of the conservatives or the liberals, the Republicans or the Democrats, the "hawks" or the "doves." The foundation on which we build our view of the world and the rightful role of government in the international arena should not be national self-aggrandizement and increased economic prosperity for our own people. Scripture provides an alternative set of norms that should serve as our foundation. These norms are:

1. Shalom

The biblical view of shalom is a magnificent four-layered tapestry that in itself is a picture of the nature of God's kingdom. The norm of peace, in the biblical view, involves

—peace between God and humanity, between Creator and creature;[25]

—peace within ourselves because we have a right relationship with God the Father;[26]

—peace between individuals within and beyond the church, peace between races, tribes, and nations;[27]

—and, finally, peace with God's created order, which involves a right relationship with our environment.[28]

This is what God desires for us, and this is what we will experience eternally in his kingdom. Part of our present task, aided by the Holy Spirit, is to work toward this kind of peace now through the reconciling blood of Jesus Christ.

2. Justice

The Bible repeatedly informs us that the single most important task of government is to pursue justice. When justice becomes the primary objective of governmental policy, rather than liberty or equality as in Western democracies or preservation of the state or the power of the ruling elite in authoritarian regimes as illustrated by the Soviet Union or numerous governments in Asia and Latin America, a healthy, vibrant society will result.

Justice is also intimately linked to the biblical vision of peace. The prophet Isaiah makes it clear that where there is no justice, there can be no peace.[29] The same theme is evident in the Psalms.[30]

3. Sanctity of Human Life

A related biblical norm is the sanctity of human life created in the image of God. The creation story of Genesis 1 and 2 clearly shows God's obvious pleasure with his own creation of the human family, a creation that he described as "very good";[31] from the original creation of Adam and Eve all humanity has come.

With the bishops we affirm the basic biblical truth of the unity of the human family. We recognize that nation-states are sources of authority and order in the world, but their existence and our obligations to them do not supersede our deeper relationships to other people for whom Christ also died. We share with all other people the image of God himself, and it is men and women who have ultimate worth and who will live eternally, not governments or nation-states.

A biblical view of the sacredness of all human life leads us to join the Catholic Church in an effort to renew everyone's awareness of the worth and dignity of each person. We strongly affirm what appears to us to be a clear biblical imperative, that all human life, born and unborn, needs to be protected. The bishops' plea that "all who work to end the scourge of war . . . begin by defending life at its most defenseless [stage], the life of the unborn,"[32] needs the support of the entire Christian community. This would be a solidly biblical pro-life position.

These biblical foundations, along with other norms such as stewardship, should shape the way we view all of reality. When these norms are viewed as parts of a tightly woven fabric that together give us a glimpse of the full tapestry—the kingdom of God, we can begin to sense what the Apostle Paul means when he describes the kingdom of God as "righteousness, peace and joy in the Holy Spirit."[33]

Our view of the nature of the church as an international body, transcultural and multiracial in scope, leads us to affirm the bishops' emphasis on the theme of interdependence. While we would put less confidence in the United Nations as a vehicle for global cooperation, we would agree that new structures are needed. Here again the church is ideally positioned to be a source of reconciliation. Where governments are afraid to act, the church should be fearless.

What practical steps can the church take to build a creative vision of peace? What specific actions would begin to move the church toward a fulfillment of its peacemaking function? The following list of proposals, some of which overlap with those of the bishops, is not meant to be exhaustive, but only suggestive:

a. prayer—we concur with the bishops in their call for a "continuing prayer for peace."[34] This would be our first priority. Prayer, both personal and communal, not only allows us the necessary solitude to raise our petitions to our Creator God concerning issues of war and peace, but also allows God to speak to our hearts, change our values, and remove our fears.

b. preaching of the Word—we agree that our ministers have a critical role to play in the life of the church through their preaching ministry. One goal of their preaching should be the cultivation of a biblical vision of peace both as a way of life and as a calling for all Christians in whatever career or locality they are in. Biblical instruction concerning a full-orbed vision of peace, not just a peace that refers to a horizontal relationship to God or to an inner "peace of mind," needs to be expounded from our pulpits. Our ministers must legitimize the "peace issue" by instructing the laity in biblical views on this subject. Issues of war and peace must be seen not as "political issues," but as deeply spiritual issues that obviously have some political dimensions to them.

c. education of the laity—we again affirm the bishops' emphasis on educating our church members, not only from the pulpit, but also through our educational efforts such as Sunday School and midweek programs. Insights concerning the biblical vision of peace, peace as a way of life, the significance of reconciliation as a calling for the church, need to be communicated to the laity. Application of these biblical insights to the issues of our day also needs to be addressed with a freedom that allows a diversity of views to be expressed. We need to struggle personally and communally with how our calling as peacemakers should impact the way we, as members of a church and as citizens of the state, act. What would obedient discipleship mean for us? That's an issue that should be a priority for the church of Jesus Christ.

d. outreach programs—there is also a whole range of initiatives that the church should take in an effort to spread the "good news" concerning the Prince of Peace. One outstanding example is "Target Seattle," a nine-day-long program involving more than 25,000 people in the state of Washington. Emerging out of the private initiative of a handful of concerned citizens, over 800 volunteers from Seattle and 5,000 contributors sponsored a series of public forums, symposiums, neighborhood coffee-discussion groups, and localized training seminars for teachers and church leaders. They also drafted a letter to the people of Tashkent, Seattle's sister city in the Soviet Union, urging its citizens to join them in working to prevent nuclear war. 40,000 Seattle residents signed this letter, and a group from Seattle personally delivered copies to officials and residents in Tashkent.[35] A similar program of building linkages between American and Soviet cities is administered by the Ground Zero Pairing Project.[36] Local churches or denominations could take a similar initiative. "Adopt a Soviet city" or "adopt a Russian church"— these are the first steps of a peacemaker.

CONCLUSION: OUR CALLING

The bishops concluded their letter with this question: Why do we address these matters? Their answer: "We are simply trying to live up to the call of Jesus to be peacemakers in our own time and situation." Then they asked: What are we saying? Their response: "Fundamentally, we are saying that the decisions about nuclear weapons are among the most pressing moral questions of our age. . . . In our [nation's] quest for more and more security we fear we are actually becoming less and less secure."[37] To this conclusion, we give a loud "amen."

In the face of increasing secularization in American society, Christians must unite in proclaiming Christ's Lordship over all creation. The biblical vision of peace must be creatively cultivated as a constructive way of bringing about the "moral about-face" for which the bishops plead.

Conclusion: Evangelicals and the Challenge of Peace

DEAN C. CURRY

The Catholic bishops' pastoral—"The Challenge of Peace"—represents the most significant statement on the biblical, moral, and strategic dimensions of war and peace to be written in the nuclear age. The importance of the pastoral has been acknowledged by all the contributors to this volume. There is a consensus that the bishops have identified the central issues of our day in a manner relevant for all who are disciples of Jesus Christ. The bishops' pastoral draws on church tradition, biblical interpretation, and the most contemporary strategic thinking to produce a broad and scholarly response to the realities of a world that, for the first time in history, has the ability to destroy itself. Yet, while the contributors acknowledge the debt all Christians owe to the bishops for their magnificent work, there is little agreement among them concerning the bishops' conclusions.

The response of the authors mirrors the pluralism of viewpoints that has characterized the American public debate over war and peace since Vietnam and has characterized Christian attitudes for centuries. The response of these evangelical scholars reminds us that the church is divided over how Christians should respond to the realities of our nuclear world. Christians, one suspects, have a more difficult time accepting diversity than do nonbelievers. We would like to believe that the Word of God is clear and unambiguous; that there is *one* Christian view or position on all issues. The preceding chapters demonstrate that there are, in fact, many different Christian views on war and peace. In acknowledging this reality we are not suggesting that there is not a Christian view of war and peace that is relevant to the compelling nuclear realities humankind now faces. We are not asserting a Christian relativism. To the contrary, a Christian perspective on war and peace emerges from the diversity of perspectives represented in the contributions found in this book. As John E. Hare reminds us, the church of Jesus Christ is called to prophesy as well as to administer; we are to be kings as well as prophets. These God-ordained roles are not mutually exclusive; rather, these roles, which too frequently appear at odds with each other, reflect the tension and the hope of a people who are, at once, citizens of two kingdoms: the kingdom of God and the kingdom of the earth.

The diversity of views represented in this book, therefore, should not be viewed as a reflection of a fundamental and unbridgeable chasm between two irreconcilable views of Scripture, two irreconcilable sets of social ethics, or two irreconcilable prescriptions for public policy. The contributors certainly differ in their responses to the pastoral; however, these differences—while important—should not obscure the points of affirmation that are common to each of their perspectives. These points of affirmation reflect the common world view each of the authors brings to his analysis. Their differences reflect their different understandings of how to apply that world view to the world in which each of us lives. A systematic examination of the contributors' affirmations and divergencies relative to the bishops' pastoral yields a Christian view of war and peace that is true to God's mandate that his disciples be both prophets and kings.

First, the contributors affirm, in the words of the pastoral, "that the world is at a moment of crisis. . . ." Nuclear weapons give humankind the ability to do that which until forty-five years ago was only within the power of God: to destroy the earth. It is, then, the technology of nuclear weaponry coupled with the proliferation of those weapons in a world of sovereign nation-states, each claiming allegiance only to its own national interests, that brings us to this "supreme crisis." If history has any lesson to teach us, it is that nations know no law but power. Hence John E. Lawyer concludes that the world will probably witness a nuclear war before the end of this century. While our authors would disagree as to the morality and "usefulness" of such a nuclear exchange, Professor Lawyer's grim prediction alerts us to the uncertainties and dangers of living in a world of international anarchy.

The nuclear peril is real. Christians, therefore, have an urgent responsibility, as children of the God of peace, to work at constructing a more peaceful world. As John A. Bernbaum emphasizes, the Christian church is ideally suited to create a "positive vision of peace." The church's responsibility, however, involves more than the articulation of a theology of peace; it involves actively working at building that peace. "Peacemaking," Steven E. Meyer notes, "suggests activity, not passivity." The contributors to this volume endorse the bishops' call that the church of Jesus Christ fulfill its role as peacemaker.

Third, the contributors, as Christians whose faith is rooted in the sole authority of the Word of God, affirm, as John S. Bray states, the central place the bishops give to Scripture in their discussion of war and peace. The Bible alone provides us with a true understanding of the creation order; of our responsibility and of God's plan for his world. It is in the Scriptures that we learn of the nature of God and what it means to be kingdom people. Moreover, it is in God's Word that we learn of true justice and peace. Richard J. Mouw echoes the message of the pastoral letter that only when we understand the biblical vision of peace can we attempt meaningfully to impact a fallen world.

The all-pervasive impact of the fall means, as St. Paul clearly points out (Rom. 8:22ff.), that all of creation groans, waiting for its redemption. This is the Christian hope. Hence the views of the contributors reflect the tension between the "already" of the kingdom in which God now reigns and the "not yet" of living in a world that has yet to be fully reconciled. The authors of this volume would affirm the bishops' statement that "(t)he fulness of eschatological peace remains before us in hope, and yet the gift of peace is already ours in the reconciliation effected in Jesus Christ." Our authors certainly differ in their views of eschatology; some would challenge what John E. Hare has called the bishops' "doctrine of progressive realization." There is, however, a common motif in each of the chapters that as kingdom people Christians participate in the "already" of the kingdom while anticipating the "not yet" of the eschatological vision.

Fifth, and flowing directly out of the previous point, the contributors reflect in their chapters the dual nature of Christian citizenship. In the words of Richard Mouw, we are a "pilgrim people" with a dual citizenship. It is because we live in both "Athens" and "Jerusalem" that we are confronted with the realities of a conflict-ridden world but at the same time have hope. And it is from this hope that our responsibility, as God's co-workers, emerges.

Sixth, while several of our authors are highly critical of the policies various governments have embraced relative to the possession, development, and deployment of nuclear weapons, there is at the same time a common affirmation, rooted in the authority of Scripture, that (1) government is ordained of God; (2) we are to be subject to the governing authorities; and (3) "the nation has the right to defend itself (and) its citizens. . . ." Our authors are not as sanguine as the bishops concerning the ability of the United Nations or other transnational organizations to act, in John Bernbaum's words, "as a vehicle for global cooperation." None of the authors predicts or even advocates the demise of the nation-state. There is, however, an underlying concern that a Christian approach to issues of war and peace must be rooted, as Theodore R. Malloch and James W. Skillen suggest, in a "Christian understanding of the state."

Deriving from the acknowledgment that government has a responsibility to protect its citizens, there is a common affirmation among our authors that the bishops are on solid biblical ground in asserting, in Hubert Morken's words, that it is the "duty of government before God" to defend its people. The nature of this defense against unjust aggression includes, as the pastoral states, "armed force is necessary." With the bishops the contributors endorse the legitimacy and justice of war as long as it meets certain criteria and is conducted according to the specific limitations defined in the traditional just-war doctrine. At the same time and in concert with the bishops, the writers would seem to be in agreement with John A. Bernbaum's statement that while governments act justly in defending themselves against armed aggression, individual Christians "must act according to their own conscience on the question of participation in war (and governments) must . . . respect . . . and protect the right of . . . conscientious objecters."

Conversely, and the eighth point of common affirmation of our authors, is the view that war must always be a last resort. "(W)ars should be avoided whenever possible," Hubert Morken writes, "and fought with reluctance and restraint. . . ." Furthermore, to the extent that a war does not meet the criteria of the just-war doctrine, it is unjust and cannot be supported by Christians.

Finally, each of the contributors to this book acknowledges in one manner or another that nuclear war, to the extent that it maims body, mind, and soul, is horrible and is to be prevented. This is the "moral imperative" of the nuclear age.

The aforementioned represent those points of convergence—of common affirmation—of the contributors to this volume. They reflect the foundational presuppositions each of our authors brings to his discussion of the bishops' pastoral on war and peace. These shared presuppositions are a testimony to the unity of faith and commitment to peace that unite all of the contributors. Yet as was noted in the Introduction, while the contributors are committed to building a more peaceful world, there are clear and certain differences in how they seek to build that peace. Just as their common affirmations reflect their common understanding of God's mandate to build a peaceful world, so their differences provide evidence of their different understanding of what it means to be peacemakers.

The very nature of peace itself elicits the first major area of disagreement among our authors. According to several contributors, Evangelicals can learn much from the bishops' discussion of the essence of peace. Richard J. Mouw suggests that Evangelicals' understanding of peace has for too long been characterized by "distortions and misunderstandings," with biblical peace being understood as an "individualized 'personal peace.' " Similarly John A. Bernbaum argues that biblical peace, properly understood, reflects the "full sense of wholeness, well-being, and health portrayed in the Hebrew word *shalom*. . . ." This viewpoint affirms the bishops' understanding that ". . . peace is already ours in the reconciliation effected in Jesus Christ." It is this peace—corporate as well as individual—which, again in John A. Bernbaum's words, "God desires for us" and toward which we are to work. In other words, the peace God speaks of and promises in both the Old and New Testaments is more than a "spiritualized" personal peace; it is a peace mandated for all corporate, even international, relationships as well.

Not all of our authors, however, agree with the bishops' understanding of the essence of peace. John S. Bray, for example, acknowledges that "(t)he bishops are . . . very insightful in their understanding of . . . peace" but on whole finds "serious problems" with the bishops' discussion. In the New Testament specifically, Bray argues, the bishops are too simplistic in their interpretation of the nature of peace (e.g., the Sermon on the Mount) or ignore certain key passages of the New Testament (e.g., Rom. 13) that are problematical in light of the peace ethic they attempt to develop. In short, the "complexity of the biblical data" is such that one cannot argue that the private ethic that, for example, Jesus advocates in the Sermon on the Mount can be considered as an applicable public ethic governing the relationships among nations. Ronald B. Kirkemo argues the bottom line for those who disagree with the manner in which the bishops (and their evangelical supporters) deal with the nature of peace when he writes that the bishops' belief in the possibility of "genuine peace" defies the evidence of history. In losing sight of the "continuties of history," argues Kirkemo, the bishops "lose perspective on the difference between what is desirable and what is possible."

For our evangelical authors, therefore, peace is a laudable goal that Christians, as kingdom-builders, must help to achieve. Addressing the issues of what kind of peace is possible in this world and how that peace can best be built in this world is where our authors part ways.

To one extent or another, either explicitly or implicitly, each of the contributors to this volume expresses his concern for peace in terms of an acceptance or rejection of the strategy of nuclear deterrence. In a real sense, the morality and utility of deterrence is the focal point of this book; likewise, it is the central concern of the bishops' pastoral. That this is so is not surprising since it is the very nature of nuclear weapons that has spawned the deterrence doctrine—a doctrine wrought with paradox and uncertainty. Apart from the issue of the quality of peace that is possible in this world, is deterrence the way to a more peaceful world? Is the deterrence strategy moral? What conditions are necessary for deterrence to "work"? Does deterrence "work" at all? Does the just-war doctrine provide evaluative criteria that are relevant to judge the morality of nuclear deterrence? These questions, in turn, raise a multitude of related concerns including the question of whether or not nuclear war in any form—limited or unlimited—is thinkable and moral. These are difficult and complex strategic, political, and philosophical questions.

Our authors are in agreement that the immediate threat to world peace is to be found in the hostility that has characterized U.S.–Soviet relations since the Second World War. At the same time, none of the contributors suggests that the root sources of this hostility are amorphous; to the contrary, there appears to be shared understanding that the threat that the Soviet Union poses to world peace, justice, and human dignity is real. Robert DeVries refers to the "onerous, sometimes brutal, side of the Soviet state" while James W. Skillen and Theodore R. Malloch stress that the "United States and the Soviet Union are not moral equals."

Nevertheless, can the nature of the Soviet Union itself justify the possession, intention to use, and even use of weapons that have the potential to reduce the world to ashes? For several of our contributors the answer to this question is a clear no. They echo the thesis of the pastoral that the nature of nuclear weapons and the morality of deterrence are such that Christians can only allow for a "strictly conditioned moral acceptance of nuclear deterrence." As the pastoral letter conditionally approves nuclear deterrence, so several of our contributors seem to suggest that the mere possession of nuclear weapons may be immoral. In all cases the normative base used to condemn deterrence is the just-war doctrine. Richard J. Mouw points out that the pastoral letter "stands firmly in the just-war tradition" and it is in light of the criteria established by that tradition that the "actual use of weapons of mass destruction" must be forbidden. Furthermore, Mouw continues, the just-war criteria "raise serious doubts about the mere possession of such weapons."

In a similar vein, Skillen and Malloch, while uncomfortable with the bishops' qualified acceptance of deterrence, share the bishops' discomfort with deterrence. To them nuclear deterrence is "morally reprehensible at worst, and morally ambiguous at best." Applying the just-war criterion of proportionality, they argue that "no goal could ever legitimate or justify the use of such massive violence. . . ." Ultimately Skillen and Malloch go beyond the conclusions of the Catholic bishops and reject deterrence as inconsistent with a Christian ethic: "deterrence . . . is nothing more than the domination of fear." The pastoral letter's conditional acceptance of nuclear deterrence is rejected as "means-ends rationalizations."

Just as several of this volume's contributors share the reservations of the pastoral letter vis-à-vis the morality of deterrence, so several also reject, with the bishops, the possibility and morality of limited nuclear war. According to this view, to talk of winnable nuclear wars and nuclear war-fighting strategies is ridiculous as well as immoral. The assumption of this perspective is that nuclear war by its very nature means total war, total holocaust: omnicide. To act under the assumption that nuclear war can be controlled is to make a choice that almost certainly will bring humanity face to face with the apocalypse.

The concern here on the part of our contributors is with the movement away from the mutual assured destruction and countercity (countervalue) targeting strategy of the late 1950s and early 1960s and the movement on the part of American strategic planners toward a flexible response and counterforce targeting strategy during the past fifteen years. The shift in this strategy has been made possible by ever more accurate "first-strike" delivery systems (such as the MX and SS-19) and the increasing sophistication of technologies that make possible, at least theoretically, a nuclear defense. This formal shift in strategies on the part of the American government is reflected recently in Carter's Presidential Directive 59 and in Reagan's "star wars" nuclear defense proposal.

For the bishops and their supporters in this volume, the only strategy more morally unconscionable than MAD is a strategy that accepts the utility and morality of limited nuclear war. To quote Skillen and Malloch, the belief that "nuclear weapons can be discriminating on a limited scale is illusory." Limited nuclear war is ruled out on the basis that it does not meet the *jus in bello* criterion of discrimination and because of the skepticism on the part of several of our authors—and the bishops— that limited wars can be kept limited. Even as strong an apologist for deterrence as Mark R. Amstutz rejects the possibility of limited nuclear war. Very simply, writes Amstutz, ". . . nuclear arms do not provide a state with 'usable' force . . . and . . . there is no method of defending against nuclear attack. . . ."

The rallying point for those opposed to the strategy of nuclear war-fighting is moral opposition to the initiation of nuclear war. In the words of the pastoral, "(w)e do not perceive any situation in which the deliberate initiation of nuclear warfare *on however restricted a scale* can be morally justified" (emphasis added). Consequently the bishops' endorsement of a no-first-use policy is rightly seen by Stephen P. Hoffmann as a "challenge to established nuclear weapons policy. . . ." In his discussion of the no-first-use proposal of the bishops as well as the proposal of Bundy, Kennan, McNamara, and Smith (in *Foreign Affairs*), Hoffmann notes that the no-first-use strategy is intended as a direct counter to war-fighting strategies, particularly NATO's nuclear strategy in Europe. For Bundy et al. a no-first-use policy is more politically viable than the current U.S. strategy; but as Hoffmann points out, for the bishops, and for several of our contributors, a no-first-use strategy is a moral imperative. While stressing the limitations of the bishops' position concerning no first-use, Hoffmann nonetheless writes that "(t)he case for no first-use . . . is a strong one. . . . The Catholic bishops are convincing when they argue that no first-use is more consistent with important biblical principles relating to peace and the use of force than is reliance on peace through strength."

Not all of the contributors to this volume, however, are critical of deterrence or of the utility and morality of limited nuclear war. There are differences among this group; some in supporting deterrence reject the move toward nuclear war-fighting strategies while others, in affirming deterrence, advocate a movement away from MAD toward counterforce strategies. Regardless of these different emphases, the authors who share this point of view feel strongly that deterrence provides humanity with the best method for achieving peace. Moreover, deterrence—even nuclear war-fighting for some—is morally justifiable.

Professor Amstutz raises the central issue for several of our authors when he argues that critics of deterrence—bishops or Evangelicals—fail to realize that the just-war doctrine has little, if any, relevance in our nuclear age. Nuclear weapons, writes

Amstutz, "are not easily encompassed in the historic principles of just war." According to this perspective, the very nature of nuclear weapons makes them unusable; hence they can never be used. "There can ... be no 'just' nuclear war," Amstutz writes. "(J)ust war," Amstutz concludes, "concerns the justice of war and deterrence deals with the avoidance of war."

At the same time it is deterrence that guarantees peace. To reject deterrence or to weaken its foundations, as many of our contributors argue the bishops have done, is to make peace less likely. In building his case for a strong American nuclear deterrent, Ronald B. Kirkemo argues that "(a) morality of nuclear weapons must be based not only on the call to peace, but also on the factors that create and maintain peace. . . ." It is unrealistic, Kirkemo stresses, to assume that peace among nations can be built on mutual trust and goodwill; "nations may have a common nightmare," he writes, "but that does not produce common dreams." While admitting the "terrible" paradox of deterrence, Kirkemo nevertheless strongly states that the only way to prevent the unthinkable is to threaten to do the unthinkable. To "renounce the use of nuclear weapons . . . makes war more possible."

These supporters of deterrence acknowledge, however, that it is a morally complicated concept. To put it simply, in Amstutz's words, "(o)ne of the important messages of the pastoral is that not all expressions of deterrence are necessarily moral." What is, for example, the ethical calculus that allows us to accept or reject the morality of the use of nuclear weapons, the intention to use nuclear weapons, the threat to use nuclear weapons, and the possession of nuclear weapons? There is a logic to deterrence that is important if deterrence is to be morally justifiable as well as effective as a strategy of peace. Both Professor Amstutz and Professor Hare raise serious questions relative to the logical consistency of the bishops' discussion of deterrence.

Amstutz points out that the bishops' two major guidelines for accepting the morality of deterrence (i.e., prohibition of countervalue targeting the rejection of nuclear war-fighting strategies) are logically inconsistent. According to Amstutz, the bishops are saying that "deterrence is OK but it cannot be morally supported through policies that are themselves immoral." Hence the very strategies needed to maintain an effective deterrent are denied. In doing this, Amstutz writes, "(the pastoral) weakens the very policy it seeks to promote."

In a similar fashion Professor Hare expresses "logical unease" concerning the bishops' moral judgment of deterrence. Hare argues, among other things, that the intention to use nuclear weapons and the possession of such weapons are not necessarily logically connected. The intention to do that which is immoral is not the same as threatening to do that which one does not in fact intend to carry out. Hare affirms the morality of this "strategy of bluff." He is careful to note that to defend deterrence "is not to say 'yes' to nuclear war . . ."; yet Hare suggests that an ethic of deterrence can be found in the Scriptures. While Hare, like Amstutz, expresses reservations about the usability and morality of all-out nuclear war, both affirm the morality of deterrence itself. Deterrence has been and continues to be effective in maintaining peace. In a world of sovereign nation-states who, in Amstutz's words, "live with the reality of nuclear weapons . . . ," deterrence is the "cornerstone" of peace. Hare goes a step further in also noting that "the shadow of the destruction of civilization is real, but so is the shadow of the suppression of freedoms that are the fruit of that civilization."

Among our authors who endorse the morality and effectiveness of deterrence, at least two go beyond the position of Amstutz and Hare in (1) asserting that limited nuclear war is a realistic and moral strategy and (2) arguing that counterforce targeting is a more moral targeting strategy than the countervalue targeting strategy that has been foundational to the MAD "version" of deterrence.

Professor Lawyer echoes the sentiment of the other contributors in stating that in a nuclear age "all-out war is no longer a viable policy resort. . . ." However, Lawyer is quick to point out that "neither is a diplomatic acceptance of aggression" viable. Lawyer rejects the position of the pastoral letter that a limited nuclear war will inevitably escalate into a general nuclear war. "Escalation to higher levels," Lawyer writes, "is not at all automatic." After discussing the "tactical realities" of NATO's military position in Europe, Lawyer rejects a no-first-use doctrine; he states that ". . . adherence to the principle of not using nuclear weapons in limited ways is likely to bring about the event not desired. . . ." The bishops' rejection of limited nuclear war leaves us "ill-equipped morally" to deal with the problem of avoiding total war and "acquiescence in the face of aggression. . . ." "In practice," Lawyer concludes, "if we ignore limited nuclear war as an important political category we will probably reap the worst of both options. . . ."

Steven E. Meyer also begins his discussion acknowledging that "everyone will lose in a nuclear exchange." Furthermore, Meyer criticizes the pastoral letter for narrowing "deterrence options to such an extent that, if adopted as national policy, . . . they could easily undermine the credibility of nuclear deterrence." He also rejects the bishops' no-first-use proposal as being potentially "dangerous and destabilizing." The bottom line for Meyer is that the pastoral letter develops "no clear policy of deterrence. . . ." For Meyer the bishops talk of peace but suggest no realistic way to build peace. According to Meyer's discussion, deterrence is a necessary requirement in a world that cannot ignore the reality of nuclear weapons and in a world where our values and freedoms are threatened. A credible deterrent, therefore, is one that our adversaries are certain we will employ. It is here that Meyer parts company with Professor Amstutz. For while Amstutz sees counterforce weapons and strategies as being destabilizing to deterrence, Meyer sees the MAD strategy of countervalue targeting as "violating the just-war criteria in extreme." Hence, Meyer concludes, ". . . the uncertainty of counterforce weapons is better than the certainty of countervalue weapons."

In summary, there are three distinct views of deterrence and its relationship to the just-war doctrine that are represented in the contributions to this book. One view argues—and this is the position of the bishops in the pastoral—that the just-war doctrine is still relevant to our nuclear age. Because the very nature of nuclear weapons is such that their use cannot meet the criteria of *jus ad bellum* or *jus in bello,* nuclear war is immoral and deterrence can only be conditionally accepted as a short-term means of ensuring peace. The second view also accepts the continued relevance of the just-war doctrine but it goes on to assert that nuclear war (i.e., limited nuclear war) can meet the just-war criteria as does, by implication, deterrence. The third view argues that the just-war doctrine has been rendered an anachronism by the destructive nature of nuclear weapons. Consequently, a new criterion must be used to judge the morality of deterrence and this criterion is whether or not deterrence succeeds in preventing nuclear war. Accordingly, deterrence is deemed moral.

The aforementioned discussion demonstrates that the differences that exist among the contributors to this volume are real and important. They are rooted in different notions of peace, different perspectives as to what kind of world we can build, different understandings of the causes of the tensions that threaten the peace of the world, and different prescriptions for creating a more peaceful world. It is unfortunate, however, that in discussing the issues of war and peace we, as Evangelicals, tend to spend more time debating our differences than acknowledging our common calling. Our responsibility is nothing less than kingdom-building; we are coworkers with the sovereign God of the universe in seeking to restore all of creation to its righteous, just, and perfect God-created order. As citizens of the earthly kingdom we cannot flee our earthly responsibilities; as citizens of the heavenly kingdom we are called to be faithful to heavenly principles. This is what it means to be both prophets and kings.

While we may never be completely able in our fallen state to reconcile our two callings, we can learn from those whose understanding of these issues is different from our own. It is for this reason that Evangelicals should welcome the Catholic bishops' pastoral letter on war and peace. The bishops have done all Christians—indeed all people—a great service by clearly and incisively raising the important moral and strategic questions of our day. Perhaps most importantly, the bishops have redirected the public debate over war and peace back to its proper theological roots. The dialogue we have begun in this volume demonstrates that not all Christians see these issues in the same light. We recognize our differences and we acknowledge the difficulties we face in building a more peaceful world in our nuclear age. But, above all, we affirm the hope that we have through our commitment to the Lord of history.

ENDNOTES

Introduction: The Origins and Relevance of the Bishops' Pastoral Letter

1. *Washington Post,* 1 May 1983.
2. J. Brian Benestad, *The Pursuit of a Just Social Order* (Washington, D.C.: Ethics and Public Policy Center, 1982), p. 3.
3. Thomas A. Shannon, ed., *War or Peace? The Search for New Answers* (Maryknoll, N.Y.: Orbis Books, 1980), p. x.
4. "The Challenge of Peace: God's Promise and Our Response," Introduction.
5. Ibid., II.
6. Ibid., II.A.
7. David Hollenbach, *Nuclear Ethics: A Christian Moral Argument* (New York: Paulist Press, 1983), p. 2.
8. For an overview of early and recent pacifist movements within the Roman Catholic Church see Tom Cornell, "The Catholic Church and the Witness Against War," in *War or Peace?,* ed. Shannon.
9. Founded in the 1950s by a young French priest—Bernard Lolande—who had spent five years in a Nazi prison camp, Pax Christi was originally conceived of as an organization that had as its goal a Franco-German rapprochement, although technically not a pacifist organization. As the organization grew it evolved into the Catholic Church's first international peace movement under the control of the bishops. In 1983 nearly sixty of America's bishops belonged to the U.S. affiliate. See Joseph Gremillion, ed., *The Gospel of Peace and Justice: Catholic Social Teaching since Pope John* (Maryknoll: Orbis Books, 1976), p. 69.
10. Ibid., p. 68.
11. Edward Laarman has identified five different responses within the American Catholic Church to issues of war and peace since the 1960s—all presumably consistent with the teachings of *Pacem in Terris* and Vatican II. On the one end of the spectrum one finds a traditional kind of pacifism as articulated by J. W. Douglass. At the other end of the spectrum one finds advocates of nuclear war-fighting such as the

late John Courtney Murray. In between these extremes Laarman identifies the nuclear pacifist/unilateralist position (Walter Stein), the bluff position (J. Bryan Hehir), and the supporters of deterrence (Michael Novak). See Edward Laarman, "The American Bishops: Moving to the Forefront of the Peace Movement" (unpublished paper), pp. 5ff. Finally, the fact that the German and other European bishops have taken a much different stand vis-à-vis nuclear weapons than their American counterparts supports the contention that *Pacem in Terris* and Vatican II can be and have been interpreted differently.

    12. *Pacem in Terris,* 112.

    13. Ibid., p. 127.

    14. See Michael Novak, "Arms and the Church," *Commentary* 27 (March 1982), pp. 37-38; and J. Bryan Hehir, "The Just War Ethic and Catholic Theology: Dynamics of Change and Continuity," in *War or Peace?*, ed. Shannon, p. 20.

    15. Hehir, p. 20.

    16. *Gaudium et Spes,* 80.

    17. Ibid.

    18. Ibid., p. 78.

    19. Ibid., p. 79.

    20. Hehir, p. 21.

    21. *Gaudium et Spes,* 79.

    22. Ibid., p. 81.

    23. Some have argued that the nature of the contemporary American Catholic Church is the result of the conscious design of Belgian Archbishop Jean Jadot. Sent to the United States as the special envoy of Pope Paul VI in 1973, Jadot was given the responsibility of making sure Vatican II reforms were carried out in the United States. Jadot was responsible for almost single-handedly transforming the American episcopacy. Jadot's selections for bishops were younger men who did not always hold to traditional views and were open to change in the Church. (See *Washington Post,* 1 May 1983.) In the ten years since Jadot arrived in the United States nearly 60 percent of the U.S.'s 300 bishops have been appointed. It should also be noted that while Jadot has since left the United States for another assignment, he has yet to be appointed a cardinal—a previously assumed certainty in light of the prestige of his American assignment. Some see in this "oversight" the disapproval on the part of Pope John Paul II of Jadot's U.S. episcopal selections.

    24. Among the specific recommendations were, *inter alia,* a call to end peacetime conscription, a rejection of the planned ABM system, and support for the ratification of the UN convention on genocide.

    25. "To Live in Christ Jesus: A Pastoral Reflection on the Moral Life," *Origins* 6 (November 25, 1976), p. 368.

    26. Beginning in the 1960s it became the established view within the U.S. government that the most optimal way to ensure peace and guarantee nuclear stability was through the survivability of both superpowers' nuclear arsenals. Thus developed the strategy of mutual

assured destruction (MAD) whereby both sides had a second strike ability to inflict unacceptable human and material losses on the other in the advent of a nuclear exchange. Such a MAD strategy entails holding civilians hostage to the possibility of annihilation. It should be noted parenthetically that while the Eisenhower nuclear strategy of "massive retaliation" implied countervalue targeting, this strategy did not envision a "balance of terror" that would guarantee nuclear stability and peace. Such is the assumption of the MAD doctrine.

27. See "SALT II, A Statement of Support," *Origins* 9 (September 13, 1979), pp. 195-99.

28. "The Church and Nuclear War," *Origins* 9 (September 27, 1979), p. 236.

29. Quoted in Benestad, p. 49. Hehir went on in his testimony to argue, on behalf of the USCC, against the United States adopting a counterforce targeting strategy. Hehir, who as we have seen above is a proponent of a "bluff" strategy—that is, possession but no use—has argued repeatedly that there is less probability of crossing the line from a conventional war to a nuclear war with a countervalue or countercity targeting strategy. Consequently, Hehir has argued for a countercity strategy. Commenting on a paper Hehir wrote in 1976 in which Hehir challenged the positions of Paul Ramsey and Walter Stein, Benestad writes that Hehir "was able to accept the countercity strategy ... because of his belief that it is morally legitimate to threaten what can never be done without moral guilt. ... Hehir could accept the countercity strategy as long as the United States intended never to fire any nuclear weapons. He would also accept the deception required to convince other nations that we would employ our nuclear arsenal if necessary. ... Hehir also argues that this is the position of the U.S. Bishops" (ibid., p. 51). The impact of Hehir's position is clearly reflected in the final draft of the pastoral letter; see "The Challenge of Peace," II.D.

30. The first draft, entitled "God's Hope in a Time of Fear," has not, as of the summer of 1983, been made publicly available.

31. For a sample of Catholic responses see "The Bishops and the Bomb: Nine Responses to the Pastoral on War and Peace," *Commonweal* (August 13, 1982), pp. 424-40; and "The Bishops Blink," *Christianity and Crisis* (August 9, 1982), pp. 227, 245-46. The Reagan Administration responded to the first draft through letters written to the bishops' committee by National Security Adviser William Clark in July 1982 and Secretary of Defense Caspar Weinberger in September 1982. Both stressed, among other things, the imperative of a first-use declaration in light of NATO's inferiority vis-à-vis the Warsaw Pact in Europe, the necessity of a *credible* deterrent, and the nature of the Soviet threat to peace. This correspondence began a series of direct contacts between the bishops and the Administration that would continue until the approval of the final letter. The complete text of Weinberger's letter is found in "Defense Secretary: The Bishops' War and Peace Pastoral," *Origins* 12 (October 21, 1982), pp. 292-94.

32. Pope John Paul II, "Deterrence is Morally Acceptable," in *The Apocalyptic Premise,* eds. Ernest W. Lefever and E. Stephen Hunt (Washington: Ethics and Public Policy Center, 1982), p. 337.

33. "U.S. Bishops Debate War and Peace Pastoral," *Origins* 12 (December 2, 1982), p. 395.

34. Ibid., p. 396.

35. Ibid.

36. Ibid.

37. See "The Challenge of Peace: God's Promise and Our Response," *Origins* 12 (October 28, 1982).

38. Ibid., p. 317.

39. Ibid.

40. Ibid.

41. Ibid., p. 315.

42. In discussing the issue of use relative to the criteria for justifiable use according to traditional just-war teaching—discrimination and proportionality—the bishops, in their second draft, conclude that there is an "overwhelming probability that a nuclear exchange would have no limits" (ibid., p. 314).

43. Ibid., p. 312.

44. For example, Archbishop Philip Hannan, in his formal presentation before the NCCB, argued that the second draft did not mention the "aggression and repression of the Reds." Seattle's Archbishop Raymond Hauthausen, on the other hand, argued that the draft did not go far enough, that it should "state more clearly that nuclear deterrence is idolatry. . . ." For the full text of these addresses and other responses on the part of members of the NCCB to the second draft see "Presentations of Five Bishops on Proposed War and Peace Pastoral," *Origins* 12 (December 2, 1983), pp. 401-8.

45. For the full text of the Clark letter see ibid., pp. 398-401. Subsequent quotations from the letter are from that text.

46. The summary minutes of the meeting are reprinted in *Origins* 12 (April 7, 1983), pp. 690-96. It should be noted that while the Pope did not attend the January meetings the Vatican's Secretary of State—Agostino Casaroli—and other high-ranking Vatican officials did. After these meetings, Roach, Bernardin, and Hoye met privately with Pope John Paul, although the pastoral was not discussed—at least according to official statements.

47. See ibid. All the following quotations are taken from this text.

48. Ibid., p. 696.

49. *Washington Post,* 25 March 1983.

50. The full text of the final draft is reprinted in *Origins* 13 (May 19, 1983), pp. 1-32.

51. "The Challenge of Peace," I.

52. Ibid.

53. See ibid., I.C.

54. Archbishop Hannan stated after the final vote that "as far as

I'm concerned it's (the pastoral letter) totally nonbinding and that's what I'm going to tell people" (*Washington Post,* 4 May 1983).

55. Thomas Healy, S.J., "The Church Can Hardly Be Silent," *Washington Post,* 11 November 1982.

56. Criticisms of the bishops have been of two kinds. There have been those who have questioned the substantive conclusions of the document itself; see for example Albert Wohlstetter, "Bishops, Statesmen, and Other Strategists," *Commentary* 75 (June 1983), pp. 15-35; and Michael Novak, "Moral Clarity in a Nuclear Age," *Catholicism in Crisis* 1 (March 1983). Others from within the Church have argued that the bishops overstepped their authority in the letter; see for example John C. Haughey, S.J., "Church/Public Policy Linkage Stirs Debate," *Woodstock Report* (April 1983), pp. 1-2.

57. An extensive sample of denominational statements on war and peace is found in John Donaghy, ed., *To Proclaim Peace: Religious Statements on the Arms Race* (Nyack, N.Y.: Fellowship of Reconciliation, 1981).

58. Both the Presbyterian Church (USA) and the United Methodist Church have endorsed the pastoral letter and urged their members to study it.

59. For a useful overview of the growth of a "peace movement" among Evangelicals see John Bernbaum, "Evangelicals and Peace," *The Reformed Journal* 33 (June 1983), pp. 2-4. The issue of whether or not the proliferation of peace statements on the part of Evangelicals reflects a shift in fundamental attitudes on the part of American Evangelicals is a controversial one. The evidence is certainly ambiguous. A 1983 Gallup Poll commissioned by the National Association of Evangelicals would seem to support the contention that evangelical attitudes toward war and peace have not undergone a significant transformation in recent years. For example, while 60 percent of American Evangelicals favor a nuclear freeze (15 percent fewer than the general public), 85 percent agree that "a person can be a good Christian and still support possession of nuclear weapons."

1: Biblical Peace and the Kingdom of God

1. "The Challenge of Peace: God's Promise and Our Response," I.
2. Ibid.
3. Ibid., I.A.
4. Ibid.
5. Ibid.
6. Ibid.
7. Ibid.
8. Ibid.
9. Ibid.
10. Ibid.
11. Ibid.

12. See Peter C. Craigie, *The Problem of War in the Old Testament* (Grand Rapids: Wm. B. Eerdmans Publishing Company, 1978); and Millard C. Lind, *Yahweh is a Warrior: The Theology of Warfare in Ancient Israel* (Scottdale: Herald Press, 1980).

13. Colin Brown, ed., *New International Dictionary of New Testament Theology* (Grand Rapids: Zondervan Publishing House, 1976), II, 776-83.

14. "The Challenge of Peace," I.A.

15. Ibid.

16. G. E. Wright, *The Old Testament and Theology* (New York: Harper & Row, 1969), pp. 121-50.

17. Craigie, p. 38.

18. "The Challenge of Peace," I.A.

19. Ibid.

20. Ibid.

21. Ibid.

22. Ibid.

23. Ibid.

24. A brief summary of interpretation may be found in Robert A. Guelich, *The Sermon on the Mount: A Foundation for Understanding* (Waco: Word Books, 1982), pp. 14-22. For a more comprehensive treatment of the history of interpretation see Warren S. Kissinger, *The Sermon on the Mount: A History of Interpretation and Bibliography* (ATLA 3. Metuchen: Scarecrow, 1975).

25. David Hill, *The Gospel of Matthew* (Grand Rapids: Wm. B. Eerdmans Publishing Company, 1972), p. 129.

26. D. A. Carson, *The Sermon on the Mount: An Evangelical Exposition of Matthew 5-7* (Grand Rapids: Baker Book House, 1978), p. 52. See also Guelich, p. 254.

27. Guelich, p. 107.

28. "The Challenge of Peace," I.A.

29. For a helpful exposition of this tension see John R. W. Stott, *Christian Counter-Culture: The Message of the Sermon on the Mount* (Downers Grove: InterVarsity Press, 1978), pp. 103-24.

30. "The Challenge of Peace," I.

31. Ibid.

2: Biblical Justice and Peace

1. Joseph Gremillion, ed., *The Gospel of Peace and Justice: Catholic Social Teaching Since Pope John* (Maryknoll, N.Y.: Orbis Books, 1976).

2. Ibid., p. 202.

3. Ibid., p. 225.

4. Ibid., p. 8.

5. Ibid., p. 75.

6. "The Challenge of Peace: God's Promise and Our Response," I.A.

7. Ibid., I. Introduction.
8. Ibid.
9. Ibid.
10. Ibid.
11. Ibid.
12. Stephen Charles Mott, *Biblical Ethics and Social Change* (New York: Oxford University Press, 1982), p. 63.
13. "The Challenge of Peace," I.A.
14. Ibid., I.B.
15. Ibid.
16. Ibid., I.C.
17. Ibid.
18. Ibid.
19. John Calvin, *Institutes of the Christian Religion,* ed. J. T. McNeill, trans. F. L. Battles (Philadelphia: Westminster Press, 1960), IV, xx, 12.
20. "The Challenge of Peace," I.C.
21. Ibid.
22. Ibid.
23. Ibid.
24. Ibid., I.B.

3: Jus ad Bellum

1. Press release, Billy Graham Evangelistic Association on the arrival of Billy Graham in the United States, May 9, 1982.
2. Robert Booth Fowler, *A New Engagement: Evangelical Thought, 1966-1976* (Grand Rapids: Eerdmans, 1982).
3. "The Challenge of Peace: God's Promise and Our Response," IV.B.
4. Ibid., IV.A.
5. Ibid., IV.B.
6. Ibid., Conclusion.
7. Ibid, I.
8. Abraham Heschel, *The Prophets,* I (New York: Harper & Row, 1962), 187-94.
9. Hebrews 11:6.
10. Amos 1, 2 (NIV).
11. Jonah 4.
12. Isaiah 42:4.
13. "The Challenge of Peace," Introduction.
14. Ibid., I.C.
15. Ibid., I.C.
16. Ibid., I.C; III.A.
17. Ibid., I.B.
18. Ibid., I.C.
19. Ibid., I, II.
20. The Harvard Nuclear Study Group, *Living with Nuclear Weapons* (New York: Bantam Books, 1983), p. 62.

21. Ibid., pp. 245-48; "The Challenge of Peace," II.B.
22. Jacques Ellul, *The Betrayal of the West* (New York: The Seabury Press, 1978), p. 19.
23. Michael Pillsbury, "Strategic Acupuncture," *Foreign Policy* 41 (Winter 1980-81), pp. 44-61.
24. Andrei Sakharov, "The Danger of Thermonuclear War," *Foreign Affairs* 61:5 (Summer 1983), pp. 1001-16.
25. Ronald Sider and Richard Taylor, *Nuclear Holocaust* (Downers Grove: InterVarsity Press, 1982).
26. National Association of Evangelicals news release, July 5, 1983. Gallup Poll (June 1983) on Evangelical Views about the Nuclear Arms Race.
27. Romans 13.
28. John Lawyer, Jr., "The Politics of Nuclear Disarmament," *Christian Scholars Review* 12:3 (1983), pp. 195-209.
29. Harold Brown, "The Crusade or Preventive War," *War: Four Christian Views,* ed. Robert Clouse (Downers Grove: InterVarsity Press, 1981), pp. 166-67.
30. Michael Novak, "Moral Clarity in the Nuclear Age," *National Review* 35:6 (April 1983).
31. Genesis 18:23-25.
32. Arthur Holmes, "The Just War," *War,* p. 135.
33. For recent World Council of Churches perspectives see Ecumenical Press Service, 83 vol. 64, and *The United Methodist Newscope* 11:33 (August 19, 1983).

4: Jus in Bello

1. See Roland H. Bainton, *Christian Attitudes Toward War and Peace* (Nashville: Abingdon Press, 1960); and Robert Heyer, ed., *Nuclear Disarmament: Key Statements* (Ramsay, NJ: Paulist Press, 1982).
2. "The Challenge of Peace: God's Promise and Our Response," Summary. Helmut Gollwitzer made these points years ago, saying, "These new weapons sound the death knell of all military ethics, destroying all connections between war and justice. The modern just war theory recognized the enemy's right to live and exist in a sovereign state—these are now abolished." From *Therefore Choose Life: Essays on the Nuclear Crisis* (Alkmaar, The Netherlands: International Fellowship of Reconciliation, 1961), p. 3.
3. Ibid.; see especially II.D.
4. Ibid., II.D.
5. Ibid., II.C, D.
6. Ibid.
7. See, among others, the Boston Study Group's *Winding Down: The Price of Defense* (San Francisco: Freeman and Company, 1979).
8. "The Challenge of Peace," I.C.
9. Harold Ford and Francis X. Winters, eds., *Ethics and Nuclear Strategy* (New York: Orbis Books, 1972), p. 145.

10. ACDA, "Worldwide Effects of Nuclear War" (1978).

11. See Sam Goldbloom, *The Arms Race: Inflation, Unemployment and Nuclear Oblivion* (Melbourne, Australia: Congress for International Cooperation and Disarmament, 1978). Contrary to what Colin Gray has argued, third-generation nuclear weapons are not just bullets. There are no totally clean counterforce weapons. And to dream up a decapitation exercise of the Soviet military is to commit, by way of collateral damage, genocide on the very population he wants to save from communism.

12. As quoted in *Time* (December 27, 1982), p. 75.

13. "The Challenge of Peace," I.C. See also James Fallows, *National Defense* (New York: Vintage Books, 1981), chap. 6.

14. Remarks in a conference lecture at the Center for Philosophy and Public Policy, University of Maryland, March 4, 1983.

15. See Bruce Russett, *The Prisoners of Insecurity: Nuclear Deterrence, The Arms Race, and Arms Control* (San Francisco: Freeman and Company, 1983), pp. 137ff.

He postulates: $x = Ky - ax + g(1)$
$y = 1x - by + h(2)$,

or, a two-nation arms race is influenced by (1) military expenditures of the other; (2) economic burdens of paying for defense; and (3) the underlying grievances held against each other.

16. Philip Green, *Deadly Logic: The Theory of Nuclear Deterrence* (Columbus: Ohio State University Press, 1966), pp. 230ff.

17. "The Effects of Nuclear War," *U.S. Defense Department Annual Report* (1979).

18. Quoted in William Lavoette, "Changing Targets," *National Journal* (September 6, 1980), p. 42.

19. Ibid., pp. 42-43.

20. Colin Gray and Keith Payne, "Victory is Possible," *Foreign Policy* 39 (Summer 1980), p. 17.

21. "The Challenge of Peace," II.A.

5: Nuclear Targeting

1. "The Challenge of Peace: God's Promise and Our Response," III.B.

2. "The Challenge of Peace," III.B.

3. Quoting W. H. Kincade and J. D. Porro, *Negotiating Security: An Arms Control Reader* (Washington: 1979). The bishops define deterrence as "dissuasion of a potential adversary from initiating an attack or conflict, often by the threat of unacceptable retaliatory damage" (II.D).

4. Ibid., II.D.

5. Ibid., II.D.

6. Quoting from a letter to the bishops by William Clark, national security advisor, dated January 15, 1983 (footnote 81 in the bishops' letter).

7. Unfortunately, at the present time, even if we and our allies were attacked solely with conventional weapons in Western Europe (an unlikely scenario because of Soviet military doctrine), we could, in the words of General Bernard W. Rogers, Supreme Allied Commander, Europe, "only sustain ourselves conventionally for a relatively short time." See the interview with General Rogers in *Armed Forces Journal* (September 1983), pp. 72-84.

8. Donald R. Cotter, James H. Hansen, and Kirk McConnell, *The Nuclear "Balance" in Europe: Status, Trends, Implications* (United States Strategic Institute, Washington, D.C., USSI Report 83-1, 1983), pp. 6-7.

9. "The Challenge of Peace," II.D.

10. Hardness is measured by the pressure per square inch (PSI) of overpressure (i.e., pressure in excess of normal atmospheric pressure) a target can sustain. Soviet ICBM silos, which are priority U.S. targets, can measure more than 2,000 PSIs. By comparison, a typical house might have a PSI of 3 or 5.

11. CEP is a statistical expression designating the radius of a circle within which 50 percent of the warheads fired at a target are expected to fall.

12. James Fallows, *National Defense* (New York: Vintage Books, Random House, 1981), p. 150.

13. Ibid., p. 152.

14. David Halloway, *The Soviet Union and the Arms Race* (New Haven: Yale University Press, 1983), p. 50.

6. Limited Nuclear War

1. "The Challenge of Peace: God's Promise and Our Response," II.C.

2. Ibid., I.C.

3. Ibid., II.A.

4. Ibid., II.C.

5. Ibid., II.D.

6. Ibid.

7. Ibid., III.A.

8. Ibid., III.B.

9. Ibid., II.C.

10. Ibid., III.A.

7. No First-Use of Nuclear Weapons

1. McGeorge Bundy, George F. Kennan, Robert S. McNamara, and Gerard Smith, "Nuclear Weapons and the Atlantic Alliance," *Foreign Affairs* 60 (Spring 1982), pp. 753-68. Kennan advocated a no-first-use policy nearly thirty years ago in *Realities of American Foreign Policy* (Princeton: Princeton University Press, 1954), pp. 84-85. Messrs. Bundy

et al. drew attention to their article by announcing its conclusions at a well-publicized press conference on April 7, 1982 (*The New York Times*, 8 April 1982). The most concentrated discussion of the question is to be found in the following articles and comments that appeared in the next issue of the same journal: General Bernard W. Rogers, "The Atlantic Alliance: Prescriptions for a Difficult Decade"; Karl Kaiser, Georg Leber, Alois Mertes, and Franz-Josef Schulze, "Nuclear Weapons and the Preservation of Peace: A German Response"; and "The Debate over No First Use" (letters); all *Foreign Affairs* 60 (Summer 1982), pp. 1145-80. The matter was also the subject of articles in a variety of other journals (some of which are cited below) and of guest editorials such as that by General Maxwell Taylor in the *Washington Post*, 18 April 1982.

2. All quotations in this paragraph and the next are from "The Challenge of Peace: God's Promise and Our Response," II.B.

3. Bundy et al., p. 762.

4. Ibid., p. 754.

5. See, for example, "A Christian's View of the Arms Race," in *The Nuclear Delusion* (New York: Pantheon Books, 1983), pp. 201-7.

6. Bundy et al., p. 764.

7. These are drawn from a number of different articles. Only those points identified with a particular one are cited.

8. See especially Jonathan Dean, "Beyond No First Use," *Foreign Policy* 48 (1982), pp. 43-47.

9. Bundy et al., p. 757; see also Robert S. McNamara, "The Military Role of Nuclear Weapons: Perceptions and Misperceptions," *Foreign Affairs* 62 (Fall 1983), pp. 70-71.

10. Louis René Beres, "Tilting Toward Thanatos: America's 'Countervailing' Nuclear Strategy," *World Politics* 34 (October 1981), pp. 28-29.

11. *The Nuclear Delusion*, p. 245.

12. Rogers, p. 1155; and Dean, p. 47.

13. Earl C. Ravenal, "No First Use: A View from the United States," *Bulletin of the Atomic Scientists* (April 1983), pp. 11-16.

14. Francois de Rose, "Inflexible Response," *Foreign Affairs* 61 (Fall 1982), pp. 139-40.

15. Christine Zauzich, "Bishops' Messages for Peace Deserve More Than a Hasty Reading," *The German Tribune* (21 August 1983), p. 4.

16. "The Challenge of Peace," I.

17. Cited in *Time*, 26 September 1983.

18. "Moral Clarity in the Nuclear Age," *National Review* (April 1, 1983), pp. 364, 382-86.

19. Zauzich.

20. "The Challenge of Peace," I. and Conclusion.

21. Bundy et al., p. 763.

8. Renouncing the Use of Nuclear Weapons

1. "The Challenge of Peace: God's Promise and Our Response," II.D, III.B.

2. Jonathan Schell, *The Fate of the Earth* (New York: Knopf, 1982), p. 226.

3. "The Challenge of Peace," III.B.

4. Quoted in Samuel P. Huntington, *Political Order in Changing Societies* (New Haven, Conn.: Yale University Press, 1968), p. 196.

5. Donald M. Joy, "Response," *Perfect Love and War,* ed. Paul Hostetler (Nappanee, Ind.: Evangel Press, 1974), p. 54.

6. The list is taken from William Faulkner, "Man will Prevail," *Pulitzer Prize Reader,* eds. Leo Hamalian and Edmond L. Volpe (New York: Popular Library, 1961), pp. 502-3.

7. See George H. Quester, *Offense and Defense in the International System* (New York: John Wiley & Sons, 1977).

8. See Bernard Brodie, *Strategy in the Missile Age* (Princeton: Princeton Univeristy Press, 1959), pp. 71-106; and Michael Howard, *Studies in War and Peace* (New York: Viking Press, 1959), pp. 141-53.

9. Brodie, pp. 107-46; and Lawrence Martin, *Arms and Strategy* (New York: David McKay Company, Inc., 1973), p. 88.

10. Paul Warnke, "Statement," United States Congress, Senate, Committee on Foreign Relations, *Nuclear Weapons and Foreign Policy,* 93rd Congress, 2nd Session (Washington, D.C.: Government Printing Office, 1974), p. 51.

11. Stanley Hoffmann, *The State of War* (New York: Frederick A. Praeger, 1966), p. 40.

12. In 1919 the submarine was seen as an inhuman instrument of war because it attacked without warning, killed innocent civilians, and was unable to take responsibility for survivors, but the attempt to abolish it at the peace conference after World War I proved to be impossible. For an analysis of that effort that reveals the problems of such weapon abolition proposals see Warner R. Schilling, "Weapons, Doctrine, and Arms Control: A Case from the Good Old Days," *The Use of Force,* eds. Robert J. Art and Kenneth N. Waltz (Boston: Little, Brown and Company, 1971), pp. 448-78.

13. Faulkner.

14. This is called a "counter-factual" argument, that is, one that cannot be proven true or false, by E. P. Thompson, "Deterrence and 'Addiction,' " *The Yale Review* 72:1 (October 1982), pp. 8-10. For an argument that nuclear weapons have kept the peace in Europe, see Karl Kaiser et al., "Nuclear Weapons and the Preservation of Peace: A German Response," *Foreign Affairs* 60:2 (Summer 1982), pp. 1157-70.

15. B. H. Liddell Hart, *Strategy* (New York: Frederick A. Praeger, 1964), p. 335.

16. Warner Schilling, "U.S. Strategic Nuclear Concepts in the 1970's," *International Security* 6:2 (Fall 1981), p. 60.

17. Caspar W. Weinberger, "Statement," United States Congress,

Senate, Committee on Armed Services, *Department of Defense Author-
ization for Appropriation for Fiscal Year 1984,* 98th Congress, 1st Session
(Washington, D.C.: Government Printing Office, 1983), pp. 49, 56,
469; and Gene R. La Rocque, "Statement," United States Congress,
Senate, Committee on Armed Services, *Strategic Force Modernization
Programs,* 97th Congress, 1st Session (Washington, D.C.: Government
Printing Office, 1981), pp. 404-5.

18. James Dunnigan, *How To Make War* (New York: Quill Pub-
lishers, 1983), p. 119.

19. Ray Bonds, *The U.S. War Machine* (New York: Crown Pub-
lishers, Inc., 1978), pp. 162, 174, 202.

20. Publicly estimated in 1976 at 80 percent of ICBM forces by
Sidney D. Drell, "Statement," United States Congress, Senate, Committee on Foreign Relations, *Effects of Limited Nuclear Warfare,* 94th
Congress, 1st Session (Washington, D.C.: Government Printing Office,
1976), pp. 21, 31.

21. The Harvard Study Group, *Living With Nuclear Weapons* (New
York: Bantam Books, 1983), p. 118.

22. James R. Schlesinger, "Statement," United States Congress,
Senate, Committee on Foreign Relations, *Briefings on Counterforce At-
tacks,* 93rd Congress, 2nd Session (Washington, D.C.: Government
Printing Office, 1975), p. 6.

23. See Committee on Foreign Relations, *Effects of Limited Nuclear
Warfare,* pp. 7-40, 45, 58; and Spurgeon M. Keeny, Jr., and Wolfgang
K. H. Panofsky, "MAD Versus NUTS: The Mutual Hostage Relationship of the Superpowers," *Foreign Affairs* 60:2 (Winter 1981/82),
pp. 287-304.

24. "The Challenge of Peace," II.D.

25. Ibid.

26. Walter Slocomb, "The Countervailing Strategy," *International
Security* 5:4 (Spring 1981), p. 23.

27. Edmund O. Stillman, "Civilian Sanctuary and Target Avoidance Policy in Thermonuclear War," The American Academy of Political and Social Science, *The Annals* 392 (November 1970), pp. 123-32.

28. There are many sources in government documents and professional journals. For a source in the public market see Winston Chur-
chill II, *Defending the West* (Westport, Conn.: Arlington House Pub-
lishers, 1981), pp. 87-101.

29. For a statement to this effect by the French Ambassador to
NATO, see Francois de Rose, "Inflexible Response," *Foreign Affairs*
61:1 (Fall 1982), p. 149.

30. Uri Ra'anan, "Statement," United States Congress, Senate,
Committee on Armed Services, *Department of Defense Authorization for
Appropriations for Fiscal Year 1983,* Part 7, 97th Congress, 2nd Session
(Washington, D.C.: Government Printing Office, 1982), p. 4119.

31. George Liska, *Beyond Kissinger: Ways of Conservative Statecraft*
(Baltimore: Johns Hopkins University Press, 1975), p. 12.

32. See the discussion of the French nuclear force in Raymond

Aron, *The Great Debate: Theories of Nuclear Strategy* (Garden City: Doubleday & Co., Inc., 1963), pp. 100-43.
33. Morton Halperin, "Statement," *Nuclear Weapons and Foreign Policy,* pp. 16, 27.
34. For an early analysis of these three choices, and one that remains valid today, see William Y. Elliott, "Time for Peace?", *Virginia Quarterly Review* 22:2 (April 1946), pp. 161-78.
35. Robert J. Art, "To What Ends Military Power?", *International Security* 4:4 (Spring 1980), p. 22.
36. See, for one example of concern about the public's impact on foreign policy, George Kennan, *American Diplomacy* (New York: New American Library, 1951), pp. 58-59, 64-65.
37. For an excellent short autobiographical intellectual journey of a "moral primitive," one who loses sight of connections and comparisons, operates with abstract and absolute qualities, and disregards the marginal character of particular factors, see Morton Kaplan, "The Education of a Moral Primitive," *Strategic Thinking and Its Moral Implications,* ed. Morton A. Kaplan (Chicago: The University of Chicago Press, 1973), pp. 149-54.

9. The Intention to Use Nuclear Weapons

1. The argument in the three middle propositions is supposed to go like this: Moral wrongness descends from actions to intentions because to condemn an agent is (at least) to condemn his intention; it descends from intention to preparations because it would be inconsistent to condemn an intention, but not the preparations to carry it out; it descends from preparations to possession either because acquisition and hence possession is the most obvious way to prepare to implement the intention, or because possession would be wrong (because ineffective) without the relevant preparations having been made. But the view of the present writer is that this argument contains what can be called a pragmatic equivocation. The wrongness of the (conditional) intention to use the weapons implies the wrongness of the preparations only if the preparations are seen as accompanied by the (conditional) intention. But if so, the wrongness of the preparations does not imply the wrongness of the possession (which may not be accompanied by the intention). The possibility of making preparations for use without having formed the (conditional) intention to use means that the third proposition has to be rejected.
2. Michael Walzer, *Just and Unjust Wars* (New York: Basic Books, 1977), p. 272.
3. See Paul Ramsey, "A Political Ethics Context for Strategic Thinking," in Morton A. Kaplan, ed., *Strategic Thinking and Its Moral Implications* (Chicago: University of Chicago Press, 1973), pp. 134-35.
4. For example, I Thessalonians 2:4-6, where Paul is asking the Thessalonians to judge the heart, as God does.

5. William Frankena, *Ethics* (Englewood Cliffs, NJ: Prentice-Hall, 1963), pp. 9-11. This distinction might have helped George Mavrodes, "The Morality of Nuclear Threats," *The Reformed Journal* 32 (September 1982), pp. 8, 31-32.

6. Putting the nuclear forces on a higher stage of alert (as in the Middle East crisis in 1973) is itself a signal to an opponent that his actions are being taken more seriously. The stakes are being raised.

7. See J. E. Hare and Carey B. Joynt, *Ethics and International Affairs* (London: Macmillan, 1982), pp. 118-20.

8. This view was presented to the bishops, but not endorsed.

9. Edward Laarman discusses this view in *The Reformed Journal* 32:6 (June 1982), and George Mavrodes replies.

10. See J. E. Hare and Carey B. Joynt, pp. 102-9.

11. There is probably a continuum of threat-effectiveness from threats accompanied by the fully formed intention to carry them out, through bluff, to threats accompanied by the fully formed intention not to carry them out. But the effectiveness will also depend on the visibility of the intentions or of their absence, as well as the availability of the threatened punishment and the perceived size of the stake to the threatener.

12. Technically, these two variables should be multiplied together.

13. To say this is not to deny that the presence or absence of the intention is important to the moral evaluation of deterrence.

14. Eisenhower, for example, though pressed to make this decision, firmly resisted it several times.

15. Carter was presented by his National Security Adviser with a number of scenarios, but is reported not to have come to a decision.

16. See J. E. Hare and Carey B. Joynt, pp. 110-12.

17. Michael Walzer, p. 272.

18. It may also be argued that the American armed forces, like the West German but unlike the British, have manuals that include an explicit instruction that all commands are to be evaluated morally before they are carried out. But in practice this will not often be done; and the system of military training and discipline is designed to encourage it not to be done. It is probably unrealistic to expect that there could be widespread independence in the matter of obedience in an effective military force. What is in question here, however, is not a general independence of mind, but the suspension of judgment by those involved about what they would do if they both knew that the step they were ordered to take was the last and irreversible one, and they did not know the reasons for the order.

19. It is not just their moral anguish that is relevant here. If the President has hired pathological killers for the job, they might still have been wronged by having been ordered to do it.

20. For example, John C. Bennett and Harvey Seifert, *U.S. Foreign Policy and Christian Ethics* (Philadelphia: Westminster Press, 1977), pp. 105-19, or Hedley Bull, *The Anarchical Society* (New York: Columbia University Press, 1977), pp. 124-26.

21. Dwight D. Eisenhower said to the American Society of Newspaper Editors in 1953: "Every gun that is made, every warship launched, every rocket fired signifies, in the final sense, a theft from those who hunger and are not fed, those who are cold and are not clothed."

22. There are many different accounts of what kinds of weapons "destabilize" deterrence. As that word was used in the freeze resolution that passed the House of Representatives in 1983, it was intended by those who introduced the word to refer to weapons that would give either side the capacity to destroy the retaliatory capacity of the other side.

23. Arms control has been an unusually live issue recently in Congress. If there had been as much popular support in 1978-79 as in 1982-83, SALT II might have been ratified.

24. Francis Schaeffer says that failure to sustain deterrence would mean "more of the world living in the horrible conditions of our brothers and sisters under the Soviet Union, with their not only lack of general freedom, but lack of freedom to teach their own children about truth and about Christ," in "The Secular Humanistic World View versus The Christian World View and The Biblical Perspectives on Military Preparedness" (speech at the Mayflower Hotel, Washington, D.C., 22 June 1982).

25. At the end of 1982 the North Atlantic Assembly passed two resolutions, one calling for more emphasis on conventional weapons, the other declaring that such an emphasis could not be afforded at present. For a more optimistic view of the costs, see the report of the European Security Study, *Strengthening Conventional Deterrence in Europe* (New York: St. Martin's Press, 1983), esp. pp. 236-50.

26. Soviet Diplomacy and Negotiating Behavior, prepared by Joseph G. Whelan for the Committee on Foreign Affairs, 1979, gives an exhaustive examination of the historical record, which ends with this conclusion.

27. There is also the danger that the threat of certain new deployments may convince the Soviets that the United States is not negotiating in good faith.

28. For the earlier teaching, see Luke 10:4.

29. See Isaac's refusal to bless Esau, "you will live by the sword" (Gen. 27:40), and the refusal to allow David to build the temple because he was "a man of blood" (I Chron. 28:3).

30. In Congress, no serious political voice is advocating either unilateral disarmament or the "winnability" of nuclear war. The debate lies between these extremes, and concerns the question of which weapons systems and which arms control proposals will contribute to keeping deterrence stable and persuading both sides to agree to substantial reductions.

31. The conditions about being a step toward disarmament, and about no direct targeting of civilians are put forward with full authority; the other four identified in this chapter are less certain.

32. Thomas Aquinas, *Summa Theologica,* II-III, Q. 64, art. 7, "moral

acts take their species according to what is intended, and not according to what is beside the intention."

33. John C. Ford, "The Morality of Obliteration Bombing," reprinted in Richard Wasserstrom, *War and Morality* (Belmont: Wadsworth, 1970).

34. John C. Ford, pp. 22-23.

35. For some of the legal difficulties, see H. L. A. Hart and A. M. Honore, *Causation in the Law* (Oxford: Clarendon Press, 1959), esp. pp. 59-78. For some of the philosophical difficulties, see Donald Davidson, "Agency," in *Agent, Action and Reason,* ed. Robert Binkley et al. (Toronto: University of Toronto, 1971), pp. 3 25.

36. In the Second World War the destruction of civilian morale was cited as a reason for strategic bombing. It might be argued that placing civilian populations under threat puts effective pressure on their governments; see Sir Solly Zuckerman, *From Apes to Warlords* (New York: Harper and Row, 1978), esp. p. 405.

37. This "issuing forth" will not include literal war, according to the letter, since war in the book of Revelation is an "image" ("The Challenge of Peace: God's Promise and Our Response," I.A.) of the eschatological struggle between God and Satan.

38. Consistent with this, the letter talks of the gradual transformation of the Israelite understanding of God (ibid., I.A).

39. Ibid., II.C.

40. The letter is curious here. For flexible response does not work because of the recognition that large-scale conventional war could escalate to the nuclear level *through accident or miscalculation* (as the letter says), but through deliberate choice.

41. Ibid., I.C.

42. Ibid., I.C. See n. 1.

43. Ibid., II.D.

44. Ibid., II.D, quoting W. H. Kincade and J. D. Porro, *Negotiating Security: An Arms Control Reader* (Washington: 1979).

45. Ibid., IV.C.

46. Ibid., II.D.

47. The letter claims awareness of the argument that war-fighting capabilities enhance the credibility of the deterrent. This argument is not, however, discussed.

48. This is the Administration's justification for accepting both the arms control framework of the Scowcroft Report and the recommendation in favor of 100 MX missiles.

49. The letter makes a strictly conditional judgment that is said to yield criteria for moral assessment. The letter then makes specific evaluations on the basis of these criteria, and some judgments and recommendations about present U.S. policy. But neither the conditions nor the criteria are systematically laid out.

50. For one account of the balance see Lee H. Hamilton, "The Military Balance: Questions and Answers," *Congressional Record,* December 29, 1982, Extension of Remarks.

51. *The Defense Guidance Paper for Fiscal Years 1984-88* is reported to have said that the armed forces must have enough offensive nuclear ability "so that the U.S. would never emerge from a nuclear war without nuclear weapons while still threatened by enemy nuclear weapons" (*New York Times,* 4 June 1982).

52. Caspar Weinberger, speech to Army War College at Carlisle Barracks, 3 June 1982, or letter to *Los Angeles Times,* 25 August 1982. But the distinction is not yet clear.

53. It has always been recognized as desirable policy to avoid putting the opponent's retaliatory forces at such risk that he is tempted to use them preemptively. But it is not clear to what extent the Soviets accept this rationale.

10: Deterrence: An Assessment of the Bishops' Nuclear Morality

1. For an excellent short analysis of the elements of strategic stability see Jerome H. Kahan, *Security in the Nuclear Age* (Washington, D.C.: The Brookings Institution, 1975), pp. 272-82 and 330-37.

2. Charles Krauthammer, "How to Prevent Nuclear War," *The New Republic* (April 28, 1982), p. 15.

3. Jonathan Schell, *The Fate of the Earth* (New York: Avon Books, 1982), pp. 201-5.

4. Secretary of Defense, *Annual Report to the Congress, 1983* (Washington, D.C.: Government Printing Office, 1982), p. I-18.

5. "The Challenge of Peace: God's Promise and Our Response," II.D.

6. Schell, p. 217.

7. It is significant that the second draft of the bishops' letter refers to deterrence as a "sinful situation" and briefly lists some of the major moral shortcomings of deterrence. The final edition omits these negative references to deterrence and portrays this policy in a more positive perspective than the first two drafts.

8. R. A. Markus, "Conscience and Deterrence," in G. E. M. Anscombe et al., *Nuclear Weapons—A Catholic Response* (New York: Sheed and Ward, 1961), p. 71.

9. See, for example, J. E. Hare and Carey B. Joynt, *Ethics and International Affairs* (New York: St. Martin's Press, 1982), pp. 101-12; George Mavrodes, "The Morality of Nuclear Threats," *The Reformed Journal* 32 (September 1982), pp. 8 and 31-32; and Michael Novak, "Moral Clarity in the Nuclear Age," *National Review* (April 1983), pp. 383-86.

10. Arthur Hockaday, "In Defense of Deterrence," in Geoffrey Goodwin, ed., *Ethics and Nuclear Deterrence* (New York: St. Martin's Press, 1982), pp. 82-85.

11. Michael Walzer, *Just and Unjust Wars* (New York: The Free Press, 1977), p. 382.

12. "The Challenge of Peace," II.D.

13. Ibid., II.A.

14. George F. Kennan, *The Nuclear Delusion* (New York: Pantheon Books, 1982), p. 202.

15. Bernard Brodie, *The Absolute Weapon* (New York: Harcourt, Brace, 1946), p. 76.

16. Robert S. McNamara, "The Military Role of Nuclear Weapons: Perceptions and Misperceptions," *Foreign Affairs* (Fall 1983), p. 79.

17. The relevant passage from the Vatican II's pastoral constitution *Gaudium et Spes* is Article 81, which reads in part: "Scientific weapons, to be sure, are not amassed solely for use in war. The defensive strength of any nation is considered to be dependent upon its capacity for immediate retaliation against an adversary. . . . Many regard this state of affairs as the most effective way by which peace of a sort can be maintained between nations at the present time."

18. "The Challenge of Peace," II.D.

19. McNamara, p. 75.

20. The most influential and provocative article to suggest this view is McGeorge Bundy, George F. Kennan, Robert McNamara, and Gerard Smith, "Nuclear Weapons and the Atlantic Alliance," *Foreign Affairs* (Spring 1982), pp. 753-68. See also the response to this article published in *Foreign Affairs* (Fall 1982), pp. 1157-80.

21. "The Challenge of Peace," II.C.

22. Ibid., III.A. The bishops say: "It may well be that some strengthening of conventional defense would be a proportionate price to pay, if this will reduce the possibility of a nuclear war. We acknowledge this reluctantly. . . ."

23. Ibid., II.C.

24. Ibid., II.D.

25. The bulk of Paul Ramsey's articles, papers, and pamphlets on nuclear and conventional war are collected in his book *The Just War: Force and Political Responsibility* (New York: Charles Scribner's, 1968). See also his "A Political Ethics Context for Strategic Thinking," in *Strategic Thinking and Its Moral Implications,* ed. Morton A. Kaplan (Chicago: University of Chicago Center for Policy Study, 1973) and "The MAD Nuclear Policy," *Worldview* (November 1972).

26. McGeorge Bundy, "The Bishops and the Bomb," *The New York Review of Books* (July 21, 1983), p. 3.

27. The just-war doctrine has historically been divided into those principles by which the commencement of hostilities is justified *(jus ad bellum)* and the principles governing the justice of combat *(jus in bello).*

28. Walzer.

11: Arms Controlled or Uncontrolled

1. "The Challenge of Peace: God's Promise and Our Response," III.A.

2. Ibid., II.D.

3. Ibid.
4. Ibid.
5. Ibid.
6. See George Kennan, *The Nuclear Delusion* (New York: Pantheon Books, 1982), p. 159. A tightly reasoned, interesting case for unilateral nuclear disarmament is given by Barry Paskins, "Deep Cuts Are Morally Imperative," *Ethics and Nuclear Deterrence,* ed. Geoffrey Goodwin (New York: St. Martin's Press, 1982), pp. 94-116.
7. The achievement of the ABM Treaty is sometimes cited as an exception to this pattern by proponents of an arms buildup. The late Senator Henry Jackson, for one, argued that the Soviet Union was unwilling to negotiate a limitation on ABM systems until the United States had begun to deploy its own ABM system (*The New York Times,* 4 June 1983, p. 4). Whether the record shows this causal connection is debatable. What does seem clear from Congressional hearings, however, is that doubts about technical feasibility were a telling factor in U.S. willingness to limit its own ABM deployment in the ABM Treaty.
8. U.S. Arms Control and Disarmament Agency, *Arms Control Report* (July 1976), p. 3.
9. The texts and narrative explanations of these and other treaties discussed in this chapter, to which the United States has either become a signatory or a party, can be found in U.S. Arms Control and Disarmament Agency, *Arms Control and Disarmament Agreements* (Washington: U.S. Government Printing Office, 1982).
10. For a list of states who have ratified or acceded to the Treaty by 1982 see ibid., pp. 96-98.
11. *The Christian Science Monitor,* 22 August 1983, p. A22.
12. The United States displayed a regrettable lack of support when it temporarily withdrew from the IAEA. This was in response to the exclusion of the Israeli delegation from the 1982 annual general conference of the IAEA in retaliation for the Israeli bombing of the Iraqi nuclear reactor.
13. "The Challenge of Peace," III.A.
14. For a discussion of these weapons see Clarence A. Robinson, Jr., "Beams Weapons Technology, Expanding," *Aviation Week and Space Technology* (May 25, 1981), pp. 46ff.; and Donald Snow, "Over the Strategic Horizon: Directed Energy Transfer Weapons and Arms Control," *Arms Control Today* 9:10 (November 1979), pp. 8-9. For excerpts of statements of various proponents and opponents of space defense see "Onward and Upward with Space Defense," *Bulletin of the Atomic Scientists* 39:6 (June/July 1983), pp. 4-8.
15. See, for example, the authoritative study of arms control by John Barton and Lawrence Weiler, *International Arms Control* (Stanford: Stanford University Press, 1976).
16. See, for example, Snow, p. 8.
17. *Fiscal Year 1981 Arms Control Impact Statements; Statements Submitted to the Congress by the President,* 96th Congress, 2nd Session, May 1980, pp. 228ff.

18. Andropov's proposal was made at a meeting with nine Democratic members of the U.S. Senate on August 18. See *The New York Times,* 19 August 1983, p. A3. Andropov also pledged that the Soviet Union would not deploy anti-satellite weapons so long as others did not do so. Some observers believe that Andropov made his proposal at this time to head off American testing of an anti-satellite missile that would be launched from an F-15 aircraft. The Soviets, however, had previously tabled a draft treaty banning orbiting ASATs at the United Nations. The Soviet Union's ASAT system is thought to be nearly operational, but most military experts consider the American ASAT system, scheduled for testing this fall, to be far superior. See *The Christian Science Monitor,* 25 August 1983, p. A24, and Robinson.

19. The bishops also discussed civil defense programs as a possible measure to provide protection against nuclear attack. Civil defense is not evaluated here because it does not fit under the arms control typology used in this chapter and is also a very complex issue. The bishops contend that the public is confused over the intentions and value of civil defense programs and therefore call for an "independent commission of experts" to study the matter. ("The Challenge of Peace," III.A). Many experts have already challenged the effectiveness of civil defense shelter and relocation plans. See, for example, Fred M. Kaplan, "The Soviet Civil Defense Myth: Parts I and II," *The Bulletin of the Atomic Scientists* 34:3, 4 (March and April 1978), pp. 14-20 and pp. 41-46. A standard source on this issue should also be consulted: U.S. Congress, Office of Technology Assessment, *The Effects of Nuclear War* (Washington: U.S. Government Printing Office, 1979).

20. Sykes and Evernden, "The Verification of a Comprehensive Nuclear Test Ban," *Scientific American* 247:4 (October 1982), pp. 47-55.

21. "The Challenge of Peace," II.D.

22. The bishops recommend the ratification of both the Threshold and the PNE treaties (ibid., III.A).

23. Ibid., II.D.

24. For a thoughtful critique of the freeze proposal see Charles Krauthammer, "How to Prevent Nuclear War," *The New Republic* 189:17 (April 28, 1982), pp. 15-20.

25. Besides these measures and proposals to prohibit nuclear weapons tests, steps have also been taken to prohibit biological and chemical weapons, which the international community has considered to be especially odious in their effects. The two treaties are the Geneva Protocol (1925), which prohibits the *use* of asphyxiating gases; and the Biological Weapons Convention (1972), which prohibits the development and stockpile as well as use of biological weapons. The bishops simply urge that these treaties be "affirmed and observed" ("The Challenge of Peace," III A)

26. Both proposals are discussed in Nye, "A New Start for Strategic Arms Control," *International Portfolio* 1:1 (Spring 1983), pp. 8-9.

27. On NATO weapons see *The Christian Science Monitor,* 23 March

1983, p. 1. On the Congressional decision see *The Christian Science Monitor,* 25 August 1983, p. 1.

28. "The Challenge of Peace," II.D.

29. See, for example, the Congressional Testimony of NATO commander, General Bernard R. Rogers, Jr., *The Christian Science Monitor,* 3 March 1983, p. 1.

30. Kennan's position is set forth with that of three other eminent former officials, Robert McNamara, McGeorge Bundy, and Gerard Smith, "Nuclear Weapons and the Atlantic Alliance," *Foreign Affairs* 60:4 (Spring 1982), pp. 753-68. General Rogers' position and a similar one issued in a report by a group of Western military and civilian experts is cited in *The Christian Science Monitor,* 7 April 1983, p. 8 and 21 July 1983, p. A1; and *The New York Times,* 15 May 1983, p. L15.

31. "The Challenge of Peace," III.A.

32. Former U.S. Ambassador to the Mutual and Balanced Force Reduction Talks, Jonathan Dean, for example, argues that NATO has some important advantages in specific areas: air force effectiveness; precision guided munitions, which may give defense an edge over offense; and especially reliability of allies, which, among other problems, might make it hard for the Soviets to secure their lines of communication through Eastern Europe. See Dean, "Beyond First Use," *Foreign Policy,* No. 48 (Fall 1982), pp. 43ff. Similar points by other experts and reports are cited in *The Christian Science Monitor,* 30 June 1983, p. 3.

33. *The Christian Science Monitor,* 30 June 1983, p. 3.

34. "The Challenge of Peace," III.A.

35. *The Christian Science Monitor,* 6 June 1983, p. 28 and 21 June 1983, p. 3.

36. *The New York Times,* 18 July 1983.

37. The Scowcroft Commission, which President Reagan set up to study the issue of MX deployment, did recognize the superiority of a small single warhead missile compared to the MX missile for promoting strategic stability but nonetheless recommended the deployment of MX missiles for largely "political" reasons.

38. Nye, p. 9.

39. The idea of "graduated reciprocity" was first proposed by Charles Osgood, *An Alternative to War* (Champaign: University of Illinois Press, 1962). Though the idea has been around for a long time it has not been attempted in any concerted fashion on weapons of any great significance, hence the idea is brought up again.

40. This initiative is proposed by Thomas Hirschfeld in *The Christian Science Monitor,* 26 July 1983, p. 23.

41. "The Challenge of Peace," III.A.

12: Shaping a Peaceful World

1. "The Challenge of Peace: God's Promise and Our Response," Conclusion.

2. Ibid., II.A.

3. Ibid., III.A.

4. Commission on Proposals for the National Academy of Peace and Conflict Resolution, *To Establish the United States Academy of Peace* (Washington, D.C.: Government Printing Office, 1981), pp. 180-83.

5. Ibid., p. 172. Dr. John Dellenback, President of the Christian College Coalition, was one of the nine members of the Commission. Legislation was introduced in the Senate (S. 564 by Spark M. Matsunaga) and the House of Representatives (H. R. 1249 by Dan Glickman) in February 1983 to establish such an Academy. Most supportive legislative activity has occurred in the Senate where the bill was favorably reported by the Committee on Labor and Human Resources. Legislative activity in the House will not occur until the bill is passed by the Senate, according to Senate Committee staff. Senators and Representatives should be encouraged to support this bill.

6. John Stremlau (Associate Director of the Rockefeller Foundation), "What We Don't Know About the Soviets," *Washington Post,* 14 August 1983; "Wanted: Soviet Scholars," *Newsweek* (October 25, 1982), p. 129; Representative Paul Simon, "United States–Soviet Relations," *Congressional Record* (6 January 1983), pp. H 62-63.

7. Former Secretary of State Cyrus Vance was "appalled" when he joined the government and looked for Soviet experts. "Not only was there a paucity of people within the government itself but as I looked around at the academic world, what Soviet research that did exist had fallen on hard times" (*Newsweek* [October 25, 1982], p. 129).

8. "Dear Colleague" letter from John Glad, Secretary of the Kennan Institute for Advanced Russian Studies, Woodrow Wilson International Center for Scholars, Washington, D.C., 20 June 1983.

9. Legislation was introduced in the 98th Congress to support a national program for advanced research and training to enhance our knowledge of the Soviet Union and Eastern European countries. The Senate bill (S. 873 by Richard Lugar) and the House bill (H. R. 601 by Lee Hamilton), both titled the "Soviet-Eastern European Research and Training Act of 1983," propose the development of a research agenda, establishment of a fellowship program, support of the Woodrow Wilson Center for advanced research, and funding for the International Research and Exchange Board to conduct reciprocal programs with these nations that facilitate access for American specialists to research resources overseas. Congressional committee staff members are "cautiously optimistic" about the prospects for this legislation.

10. Legislation was introduced in the 98th Congress by Representatives Paul Simon and Lee Hamilton (H. R. 1220) to provide further funding for exchange programs between the United States and the Warsaw Pact countries. The future of this legislation is presently unknown, but deserves to be supported.

11. A joint resolution was introduced in the House of Representatives on April 28, 1983, by Morris Udall (H. J. Res. 254) that requested that the President negotiate with the Soviet Union for the

creation of a U.S.–Soviet student exchange for peace a program that would involve at least 2,000 youth from each country. This is one example of an initiative that deserves support by the churches.

12. Spark Matsunaga submitted a concurrent resolution (S. Con. Res. 16) in the Senate on March 10, 1983, relating to cooperative East-West ventures in space, along with letters by scientific experts in support of this proposal. For the text of this resolution and the supporting letters, see the *Congressional Record* (10 March 1983), pp. S 2603-8.

13. U.S. exports to the Soviet Union grew from $542 million in 1972 to $3.6 billion in 1979; the Department of Commerce predicted an increase to $4.8 billion by 1980, but the Afghan invasion and resulting U.S. restrictions on trade dropped actual exports to $1.5 billion (Friends Committee on National Legislation [FCNL], "Deterrence by Fear or by Friendship?" Staff Study G-14, April 1982, pp. 10-13).

14. The recent five-year grain agreement signed in Moscow on August 25, 1983, is a constructive step by the Reagan Administration. This agreement, which commits the Soviet Union to purchase a minimum of 9 million tons of grain a year (up to 12 million tons without additional negotiation), an increase of 50 percent over previous single-year agreements, will be worth $7-8 billion in sales to American farmers over the next five years. The estimated U.S. share of the Soviet import market for grain will be 40 percent. Similar agreements for other agricultural and industrial commodities should also be a priority.

15. For further information on these bilateral agreements, see FCNL's Staff Study G-14, pp. 18-28.

16. The two superpowers have exercised real and effective cooperation for years through nine UN agencies (for example, the World Health Organization, the Universal Postal Union, the International Civil Aviation Organization), and these efforts have not been adversely affected by political tensions. Two multilateral treaties (Antarctic Treaty and the Law of the Seas Treaty) have also generated U.S.–Soviet cooperation (FCNL, "Washington Newsletter" [March 1982], p. 2).

17. "The Challenge of Peace," III.A.

18. Romans 12:21.

19. "The Challenge of Peace," III.B.

20. Ephesians 4:15.

21. Psalm 119:105.

22. As Jesus predicted (Acts 1:8), the church has been empowered by the Holy Spirit beginning at Pentecost (Acts 2). Particular gifts have been given to members of the Body of Christ (Rom. 8:22-23; I Cor. 12) that promote human health and wholeness in the world (Gal. 5:22; I John 4:12-15).

23. "The Challenge of Peace," III.B.

24. Colossians 1:16-17.

25. This facet of peace is discussed, for example, in Ephesians 2:14-17.

26. This aspect of peace, which the Apostle Paul often addresses, is evident in Philippians 4:7 and Romans 14:17.

27. Scripture also tells us that peace should be our norm for relationships with all people (Ps. 34:14; Eph. 5:13-15 and 22-26), even our enemies (Prov. 16:7).

28. This dimension of peace is especially pronounced in the prophetic writings; see, for example, Isaiah's vision recorded in Isaiah 32:17-20.

29. Isaiah 59:8.

30. Psalm 85:8-13.

31. Genesis 1:31.

32. "The Challenge of Peace," IV.B.

33. Romans 14:17.

34. "The Challenge of Peace," IV.B.

35. For more information on "Target Seattle," write to the following address: Target Seattle, 909 4th Avenue, Seattle, WA 98104; a feature-length video-film documentary is also available through the Planet Earth Foundation, 5204 37th Avenue NE, Seattle, WA 98105.

36. For information on the pairing of cities, contact the Ground Zero Pairing Project, P.O. Box 19049, Portland, OR 97219.

37. "The Challenge of Peace," Conclusion.

Summary of the Bishops' Pastoral Letter

The Second Vatican Council opened its evaluation of modern warfare with the statement: "The whole human race faces a moment of supreme crisis in its advance toward maturity." We agree with the council's assessment; the crisis of the moment is embodied in the threat which nuclear weapons pose for the world and much that we hold dear in the world. We have seen and felt the effects of the crisis of the nuclear age in the lives of people we serve. Nuclear weaponry has drastically changed the nature of warfare, and the arms race poses a threat to human life and human civilization which is without precedent.

We write this letter from the perspective of Catholic faith. Faith does not insulate us from the daily challenges of life but intensifies our desire to address them precisely in light of the gospel which has come to us in the person of the risen Christ. Through the resources of faith and reason we desire in this letter to provide hope for people in our day and direction toward a world freed of the nuclear threat.

As Catholic bishops we write this letter as an exercise of our teaching ministry. The Catholic tradition on war and peace is a long and complex one; it stretches from the Sermon on the Mount to the statements of Pope John Paul II. We wish to explore and explain the resources of the moral-religious teaching and to apply it to specific questions of our day. In doing this we realize, and we want readers of this letter to recognize, that not all statements in this letter have the same moral authority. At times we state universally binding moral principles found in the teaching of the Church; at other times the pastoral letter makes specific applications, observations and recommendations which allow for diversity of opinion on the part of those who assess the factual data of situations differently. However, we expect

247

Catholics to give our moral judgments serious consideration when they are forming their own views on specific problems.

The experience of preparing this letter has manifested to us the range of strongly held opinion in the Catholic community on questions of fact and judgment concerning issues of war and peace. We urge mutual respect among individuals and groups in the Church as this letter is analyzed and discussed. Obviously, as bishops, we believe that such differences should be expressed within the framework of Catholic moral teaching. We need in the Church not only conviction and commitment but also civility and charity.

While this letter is addressed principally to the Catholic community, we want it to make a contribution to the wider public debate in our country on the dangers and dilemmas of the nuclear age. Our contribution will not be primarily technical or political, but we are convinced that there is no satisfactory answer to the human problems of the nuclear age which fails to consider the moral and religious dimensions of the questions we face.

Although we speak in our own name, as Catholic bishops of the Church in the United States, we have been conscious in the preparation of this letter of the consequences our teaching will have not only for the United States but for other nations as well. One important expression of this awareness has been the consultation we have had, by correspondence and in an important meeting held at the Vatican (January 18-19, 1983), with representatives of European bishops' conferences. This consultation with bishops of other countries, and, of course, with the Holy See, has been very helpful to us.

Catholic teaching has always understood peace in positive terms. In the words of Pope John Paul II: "Peace is not just the absence of war. . . . Like a cathedral, peace must be constructed patiently and with unshakable faith." (Coventry, England, 1982) Peace is the fruit of order. Order in human society must be shaped on the basis of respect for the transcendence of God and the unique dignity of each person, understood in terms of freedom, justice, truth and love. To avoid war in our day we must be intent on building peace in an increasingly interdependent world. In Part III of this letter we set forth a positive vision of peace and the demands such a vision makes on diplomacy, national policy, and personal choices.

While pursuing peace incessantly, it is also necessary to limit the use of force in a world comprised of nation states, faced with common problems but devoid of an adequate international political authority. Keeping the peace in the nuclear age is a moral and political imperative. In Parts I and II of this letter we set forth both the principles of Catholic teaching on war and a series of judgments, based on these principles, about concrete policies. In making these judgments we speak as moral teachers, not as technical experts.

I. Some Principles, Norms and Premises of Catholic Teaching

A. On War

1. Catholic teaching begins in every case with a presumption against war and for peaceful settlement of disputes. In exceptional cases, determined by the moral principles of the just-war tradition, some uses of force are permitted.

2. Every nation has a right and duty to defend itself against unjust aggression.

3. Offensive war of any kind is not morally justifiable.

4. It is never permitted to direct nuclear or conventional weapons to "the indiscriminate destruction of whole cities or vast areas with their populations. . . ." (*Pastoral Constitution,* #80.) The intentional killing of innocent civilians or non-combatants is always wrong.

5. Even defensive response to unjust attack can cause destruction which violates the principle of proportionality, going far beyond the limits of legitimate defense. Thus judgment is particularly important when assessing planned use of nuclear weapons. No defensive strategy, nuclear or conventional, which exceeds the limits of proportionality is morally permissible.

B. On Deterrence

1. "In current conditions 'deterrence' based on balance, certainly not as an end in itself but as a step on the way toward a progressive disarmament, may still be judged morally acceptable. Nonetheless, in order to ensure peace, it is indispensable not to be satisfied with this minimum which is always susceptible to the real danger of explosion." (Pope John Paul II, "Message to U.N. Special Session on Disarmament," #8, June 1982.)

2. No *use* of nuclear weapons which would violate the principles of discrimination or proportionality may be *intended* in a
strategy of deterrence. The moral demands of Catholic teaching
require resolute willingness not to intend or to do moral evil
even to save our own lives or the lives of those we love.
3. Deterrence is not an adequate strategy as a long-term
basis for peace; it is a transitional strategy justifiable only in
conjunction with resolute determination to pursue arms control
and disarmament. We are convinced that "the fundamental principle on which our present peace depends must be replaced by
another, which declares that the true and solid peace of nations
consists not in equality of arms but in mutual trust alone." (Pope
John XXIII, *Peace on Earth*, #113.)

C. The Arms Race and Disarmament

1. The arms race is one of the greatest curses on the human
race; it is to be condemned as a danger, an act of aggression
against the poor, and a folly which does not provide the security
it promises. (Cf. *Pastoral Constitution*, #81, *Statement of the Holy
See to the United Nations*, 1976.)
2. Negotiations must be pursued in every reasonable form
possible; they should be governed by the "demand that the arms
race should cease; that the stockpiles which exist in various
countries should be reduced equally and simultaneously by the
parties concerned; that nuclear weapons should be banned; and
that a general agreement should eventually be reached about
progressive disarmament and an effective method of control."
(Pope John XXIII, *Peace on Earth*, #112.)

D. On Personal Conscience

1. *Military Service:* "All those who enter the military service in loyalty to their country should look upon themselves as
the custodians of the security and freedom of their fellow coun-
trymen; and when they carry out their duty properly, they are
contributing to the maintenance of peace." (*Pastoral Constitution*,
#79.)
2. *Conscientious Objection:* "Moreover, it seems just that
laws should make humane provision for the case of conscientious objectors who refuse to carry arms, provided they accept

some other form of community service." (*Pastoral Constitution,* #79.)

3. *Non-violence:* "In this same spirit we cannot but express our admiration for all who forego the use of violence to vindicate their rights and resort to other means of defense which are available to weaker parties, provided it can be done without harm to the rights and duties of others and of the community." (*Pastoral Constitution,* #78.)

4. *Citizens and Conscience:* "Once again we deem it opportune to remind our children of their duty to take an active part in public life, and to contribute towards the attainment of the common good of the entire human family as well as to that of their own political community. . . . In other words, it is necessary that human beings, in the intimacy of their own consciences, should so live and act in their temporal lives as to create a synthesis between scientific, technical and professional elements on the one hand, and spiritual values on the other." (Pope John XXIII, *Peace on Earth,* #146, 150.)

II. Moral Principles and Policy Choices

As bishops in the United States, assessing the concrete circumstances of our society, we have made a number of observations and recommendations in the process of applying moral principles to specific policy choices.

A. On the Use of Nuclear Weapons

1. *Counter Population Use:* Under no circumstances may nuclear weapons or other instruments of mass slaughter be used for the purpose of destroying population centers or other predominantly civilian targets. Retaliatory action which would indiscriminately and disproportionately take many wholly innocent lives, lives of people who are in no way responsible for reckless actions of their government, must also be condemned.

2. *The Initiation of Nuclear War:* We do not perceive any situation in which the deliberate initiation of nuclear war, on however restricted a scale, can be morally justified. Non-nuclear attacks by another state must be resisted by other than nuclear means. Therefore, a serious moral obligation exists to develop non-nuclear defensive strategies as rapidly as possible. In this letter we urge NATO to move rapidly toward the adoption of

a "no first use" policy, but we recognize this will take time to implement and will require the development of an adequate alternative defense posture.

3. *Limited Nuclear War:* Our examination of the various arguments on this question makes us highly skeptical about the real meaning of "limited." One of the criteria of the just-war teaching is that there must be a reasonable hope of success in bringing about justice and peace. We must ask whether such a reasonable hope can exist once nuclear weapons have been exchanged. The burden of proof remains on those who assert that meaningful limitation is possible. In our view the first imperative is to prevent any use of nuclear weapons and we hope that leaders will resist the notion that nuclear conflict can be limited, contained or won in any traditional sense.

B. On Deterrence

In concert with the evaluation provided by Pope John Paul II, we have arrived at a strictly conditional moral acceptance of deterrence. In this letter we have outlined criteria and recommendations which indicate the meaning of conditional acceptance of deterrence policy. We cannot consider such a policy adequate as a long-term basis for peace.

C. On Promoting Peace

1. We support immediate, bilateral verifiable agreements to halt the testing, production and deployment of new nuclear weapons systems. This recommendation is not to be identified with any specific political initiative.

2. We support efforts to achieve deep cuts in the arsenals of both superpowers; efforts should concentrate first on systems which threaten the retaliatory forces of either major power.

3. We support early and successful conclusion of negotiations of a comprehensive test ban treaty.

4. We urge new efforts to prevent the spread of nuclear weapons in the world, and to control the conventional arms race, particularly the conventional arms trade.

5. We support, in an increasingly interdependent world, political and economic policies designed to protect human dignity and to promote the human rights of every person, especially the least among us. In this regard, we call for the establishment

of some form of global authority adequate to the needs of the international common good.

This letter includes many judgments from the perspective of ethics, politics and strategy needed to speak concretely and correctly to the "moment of supreme crisis" identified by Vatican II. We stress again that readers should be aware, as we have been, of the distinction between our statement of moral principles and of official Church teaching and our application of these to concrete issues. We urge that special care be taken not to use passages out of context; neither should brief portions of this document be cited to support positions it does not intend to convey or which are not truly in accord with the spirit of its teaching.

In concluding this summary we respond to two key questions often asked about this pastoral letter:

Why do we address these matters fraught with such complexity, controversy and passion? We speak as pastors, not politicians. We are teachers, not technicians. We cannot avoid our responsibility to lift up the moral dimensions of the choices before our world and nation. The nuclear age is an era of moral as well as physical danger. We are the first generation since Genesis with the power to threaten the created order. We cannot remain silent in the face of such danger. Why do we address these issues? We are simply trying to live up to the call of Jesus to be peacemakers in our own time and situation.

What are we saying? Fundamentally, we are saying that the decisions about nuclear weapons are among the most pressing moral questions of our age. While these decisions have obvious military and political aspects, they involve fundamental moral choices. In simple terms, we are saying that good ends (defending one's country, protecting freedom, etc.) cannot justify immoral means (the use of weapons which kill indiscriminately and threaten whole societies). We fear that our world and nation are headed in the wrong direction. More weapons with greater destructive potential are produced every day. More and more nations are seeking to become nuclear powers. In our quest for more and more security we fear we are actually becoming less and less secure.

In the words of our Holy Father, we need a "moral about-face." The whole world must summon the moral courage and technical means to say no to nuclear conflict; no to weapons of mass destruction; no to an arms race which robs the poor and the vulnerable; and no to the moral danger of a nuclear age which places before humankind indefensible choices of constant terror or surrender. Peacemaking is not an optional commitment. It is a requirement of our faith. We are called to be peacemakers, not by some movement of the moment, but by our Lord Jesus. The content and context of our peacemaking is set not by some political agenda or ideological program, but by the teaching of his Church.

Ultimately, this letter is intended as an expression of Christian faith, affirming the confidence we have that the risen Lord remains with us precisely in moments of crisis. It is our belief in his presence and power among us which sustains us in confronting the awesome challenge of the nuclear age. We speak from faith to provide hope for all who recognize the challenge and are working to confront it with the resources of faith and reason.

To approach the nuclear issue in faith is to recognize our absolute need for prayer: we urge and invite all to unceasing prayer for peace with justice for all people. In a spirit of prayerful hope we present this message of peace.